**Literary Research: Strategies and Sources**
**Series Editors: Peggy Keeran & Jennifer Bowers**

Every literary age presents scholars with both predictable and unique research challenges. This series fills a gap in the field of reference literature by featuring research strategies and by recommending the best tools for conducting specialized period and national literary research. Emphasizing research methodology, each series volume takes into account the unique challenges inherent in conducting research of that specific literary period and outlines the best practices for researching within it. Volumes place the research process within the period's historical context and use a narrative structure to analyze and compare print and electronic reference sources. Following an introduction to online searching, chapters will typically cover these types of resources: general literary reference materials; library catalogs; print and online bibliographies, indexes, and annual reviews; scholarly journals; contemporary reviews; period journals and newspapers; microform and digital collections; manuscripts and archives; and Web resources. Additional or alternative chapters might be included to highlight a particular research problem or to examine other pertinent period or national literary resources.

1. *Literary Research and the British Romantic Era* by Peggy Keeran and Jennifer Bowers, 2005.
2. *Literary Research and the Era of American Nationalism and Romanticism* by Angela Courtney, 2008.
3. *Literary Research and American Modernism Era* by Robert N. Matuozzi and Elizabeth B. Lindsay, 2008.
4. *Literary Research and the American Realism and Naturalism Period* by Linda L. Stein and Peter J. Lehu, 2009.
5. *Literary Research and Irish Literature* by J. Greg Matthews, 2009.
6. *Literary Research and the Literatures of Australia and New Zealand* by H. Faye Christenberry and Angela Courtney, 2011.
7. *Literary Research and British Modernism* by Alison M. Lewis, 2010.
8. *Literary Research and the British Renaissance and Early Modern Period* by Jennifer Bowers and Peggy Keeran, 2010.
9. *Literary Research and the Victorian and Edwardian Ages, 1830–1910* by Melissa S. Van Vuuren, 2011.
10. *Literary Research and Canadian Literature* by Gabriella Natasha Reznowski, 2011.

# Literary Research and Canadian Literature

## Strategies and Sources

Gabriella Natasha Reznowski

*Literary Research: Strategies and Sources, No. 10*

THE SCARECROW PRESS, INC.
*Lanham • Toronto • Plymouth, UK*

Published by Scarecrow Press, Inc.
A wholly owned subsidiary of The Rowman & Littlefield Publishing Group, Inc.
4501 Forbes Boulevard, Suite 200, Lanham, Maryland 20706
http://www.scarecrowpress.com

Estover Road, Plymouth PL6 7PY, United Kingdom



British Library Cataloguing in Publication Information Available

**Library of Congress Cataloging-in-Publication Data**

Reznowski, Gabriella Natasha, 1974–
Literary research and Canadian literature : strategies and sources / Gabriella Natasha Reznowski.
p. cm. — (Literary research: strategies and sources ; no. 10)
Includes bibliographical references and indexes.
ISBN 978-0-8108-7768-9 (pbk. : alk. paper) — ISBN 978-0-8108-7769-6 (eBook)
1. Canadian literature—Research—Methodology. 2. Canadian literature—Information resources. I. Title.
PR9184.3.R49 2011
810.9'971072—dc22 2010037406

# Contents

# Acknowledgments

A great many people are responsible for assisting me in bringing this volume to completion. First, I would like to thank series editors Peggy Keeran and Jenny Bowers for their unwavering patience, guidance, and support. I am also indebted to Loriene Roy for generously sharing her knowledge and expertise of Native authors with me.

I work with an amazing team of librarians at Washington State University and would like to acknowledge Greg Matthews, Beth Lindsay, and, in particular, Bob Matuozzi, for leading the way, as well as for their encouragement. Dave Smestad and the staff of the WSU Libraries Access Services Department processed innumerable interlibrary loans, and their conversation and camaraderie offered cheerful respite.

To my children, Avila, Xavier, Sasha, Inez, and Anissa, who each took turns keeping me company into the wee hours of the night while preparing this manuscript. Also, to Dave, for being a perfect foil to my idiosyncrasies. Likewise, to my siblings, Tony, Tanya, Ted, and Daniella, for staying in touch and for their gentle reminders of my place within the pecking order.

I could not write a book on literary research without acknowledging Earle Ferguson and Bill Wsiaki, my former supervisors at Saint Paul's College, for giving me my first "big break" in the library world. Additionally, to the many English professors at the University of Manitoba, including George Amabile, John Butler, and Steve Snyder, all of whom instilled a love of literature and continue to inspire. Certainly, one of my fondest memories is of Vick Cowie, a one-man theatrical production, who brought Shakespeare to life in a University College classroom.

I would like to recognize the generosity of Frank Davey and David Staines for graciously answering the e-mails of an inquisitive librarian. I am grateful to both Candice Bjur and Erwin Wodarczak of the University of British

Columbia Archives for their patient assistance. Also, to my dear friends Viva and Mike Schurch of Langley, for their warmth and hospitality while I was conducting research for this project in Vancouver. To Laura Tombari of Fossano, Italy, an unforgettable friend whose companionship I will forever treasure.

Above all, to my mother and father, Joan and Lorne Reznowski, for giving me the best childhood a kid could dream of—stories and adventures to last a lifetime.

# Introduction

> The past two decades have witnessed the evolution of Canadian literature from a struggling curiosity into a global cultural presence. Our national voice is now heard as separate and distinct from that of our American neighbours, with a tone and a timbre quite different from those of our literary ancestors.
>
> —*Who's Who in the Writers' Union of Canada*: *A Directory of Members*, 4th ed. (Toronto: The Writers' Union of Canada, 1993), back cover

The above quote, found in the twentieth-anniversary issue of *Who's Who in the Writers' Union of Canada* (1993), was written when Canadian literature was truly coming of age. Margaret Atwood was now an internationally recognized author, Michael Ondaatje had been awarded the Booker Prize for *The English Patient*, and Carol Shields was soon to be recognized with a Pulitzer Prize for *The Stone Diaries*. Canadian writers continue to produce a wide range of works, exhibiting an eclectic mix of talent and satisfying a variety of literary interests and tastes. As a scholarly discipline, Canadian literature has grown and developed in tandem with a body of reference material to address its study. In common with other titles in the Literary Research: Strategies and Sources series, this volume aims to equip the literary researcher with tools and tactics for exploring Canadian authors and their works.

In today's rapidly changing research environment, Canada's national literature presents a complex set of issues for the researcher embarking on a study of Canadian writers and themes. As the discipline evolves, scholars struggle with the criteria for determining an author's "Canadianness," while the literature itself eludes simple classification. As M. G. Vassanji eloquently cautions, "To define this country or its literature seems like putting a finger on Zeno's arrow: no sooner do you think you have done it than it has moved on."[1] Although literary critics have attempted to establish the boundaries of nationality and citizenship, in a country that promotes immigration and multiculturalism, it would seem presumptuous for a writer to disclaim another's right to identify as "Canadian." In fact, Northrop Frye's famous quote still resonates, stating that the Canadian sensibility "is less perplexed by the question 'Who am I?' than by some such riddle as 'Where is here?'"[2] For literary scholars operating in a global society, the questions "What is Canada," "Who is Canada," and "Where is Canada" become even more complex. Not only did Canada's earliest published writers originate from outside the country, but contemporary Canadian literature continues to be informed by an immigrant perspective. Robert Hayman, credited as Newfoundland's first poet, was not born, nor did he die, in Canada. Likewise, Robert Service, a giant of Canadian poetry, was born in England and remained a British subject until his death in Brittany. Contemporary Canadian writers, such as Rohinton Mistry, M. NourbeSe Philip, and Yann Martel, further extend the boundaries of citizenship, diaspora, hybridity, and nationality. It would not be unusual for a second country to claim a Canadian author as its own, either because they were born outside of Canada, or due to the characteristic transience of some writers. Curiosities include whether a writer, such as Malcolm Lowry, would himself want to be identified as Canadian, and how to classify Bharati Mukherjee, who iconoclastically challenged traditional stereotypes of Canada, leaving an indelible mark on the country.

The continued diversity of Canada's literary experience can be attributed in part to the Canadian government's vigorous funding of writer's grants, resulting in increased opportunities for up-and-coming authors to develop and distribute their works. The literary community has likewise been receptive to showcasing new voices, creating a mosaic of established and emerging First Nations, English, francophone, Quebec, foreign-born, ethnic, and diasporic writers. In fact, the "mosaic versus melting pot" position may be what attracts some authors, such as Carol Shields, to identify Canada as their literary homeland. Canada's policy of official bilingualism, coupled with its multicultural demographic, produces a literature as diverse as the nation it represents.

Over the past fifty years, Canadian literature has expanded, both as a genre and as a field of study. Today's Canadian literary researcher is fortunate to have an abundance of resources at his or her disposal, including extensive and freely accessible digital content. Programs such as the Department of Canadian Heritage's Canadian Culture Online continue to speak to Canada's commitment to promoting and preserving its literary and cultural history. This volume therefore addresses the complex and varied discipline of Canadian literary research. In a rapidly changing scholarly environment, strategies for locating established and innovative, academic and popular, as well as historical and contemporary sources, are explored. While the computer age has blurred the boundaries between print and electronic resources, this work considers approaches for conducting research using a variety of tools, such as online library catalogs, databases, and the Web, in addition to traditional materials published in paper format. A survey of the best print indexes, annual reviews, and general and specialized reference works will serve the researcher in identifying tools for satisfying his or her own scholarly needs, and for facilitating new insight and knowledge. Additional chapters address special topics and research areas, such as archival and microform collections and the wealth of digital material available for the study of Canadian literature. Although literary research is the main focus of this work, today's interdisciplinary scholarly environments naturally encompass a larger variety of resources, such as those that inform historical, cultural, and political inquiry. Scholarly journals useful for the study of Canadian literary studies and its broader disciplinary ties to Canadian studies in general are reviewed, providing insight into noteworthy publications from both Canada and abroad. Recognizing that the items explored throughout this guide cannot anticipate every research scenario, a concluding chapter works through a sample topic to model the application of the resources, tools, and methods toward the scholarly process. As a whole, this work will facilitate an informed perspective on Canadian literary research. Conversely, scholars interested in a particular type of resource, such as journals or digital collections, may target their reading to an individual chapter.

In keeping with the tradition of other reference works for Canadian literature, this volume examines both preconfederation and postconfederation writers who have either been associated with Canada or, through their ability to represent the Canadian experience, have been adopted into the Canadian literary scene. Recognizing that, as a bilingual country, Canadian literary research is not limited to English-language material, this guide seeks to be inclusive of journals, reference works, periodicals, and online sources published in either of Canada's official languages. Material to address special research areas, such as First Nations, francophone, Quebec, and multicultural literature are incorporated throughout. Although an in-depth survey of any one of these unique areas would require a separate study, it is hoped that the researcher will find adequate treatment herein.

The bounty of resources available to today's literary scholar testifies to the ongoing development of a Canadian literary consciousness. In the past, Canadians have struggled with a certain degree of insecurity regarding the quality of their literary output, including the attitude that Canadian literature is pedestrian, limited in scope, plagued by an incestuous literary community, and lacking in universal themes. Today, such judgments seem incongruous in characterizing a literature that exerts innovation, creativity, and consistent recognition on the international scene. The chapters that follow are written to guide and inspire further research into Canada's rich literary culture.

## NOTES

1. M. G. Vassanji, "Am I a Canadian Writer?" *Canadian Literature* 190 (Autumn 2006): 7–13.
2. Northrop Frye in his conclusion to Carl Frederick Klinck's *A Literary History of Canada* (Toronto: University of Toronto Press, 1965), 826.

# *Chapter One*

# Basics of Online Searching

> The point is that the electronic situation we have today is all grounded in a physical reality.
>
> —Suzanne S. Bell, *Librarian's Guide to Online Searching* (Westport, CT: Libraries Unlimited, 2006), 3

The electronic age has both complicated and facilitated the process of locating relevant material for research. While online environments provide access to millions of electronic records, the results of an information-seeking session can potentially be overwhelming. Although we may view online searching as a haphazard exercise, it is in fact a process by which language can be manipulated and strategies employed to modify the outcome. By planning online inquiry in terms of a search strategy, one that is responsive and flexible, your results are more likely to drive your research and inform new directions. As you develop and execute an online query, pay attention to the conversation that develops between yourself and the electronic resource; when the process returns unexpected outcomes, evaluate these and modify your search accordingly. The tips discussed below will help you in planning searches, understanding the language of online searches, and modifying those searches.

## STEP 1: DEVELOPING THE RESEARCH QUESTION

In order to frame your research problem as an adequate and manageable topic, it is important to put your idea into words. For your inquiry to be meaningful, your focus should neither be too broad nor too narrow. If you are having a hard time choosing a topic, you may want to skim the subjects of a specialized encyclopedia, such as the *Encyclopedia of Literature in Canada*, for inspiration. Such resources illustrate the range and diversity of subjects related to literary studies. As you develop your thesis statement, focus on what you would like to gain from the project that you are about to begin. If, for example, you have been interested in the influence of early Canadian author Susanna Moodie on Margaret Atwood, you might say, "I want to learn about the influence of Susanna Moodie on the works of Margaret Atwood." The main concepts of this statement are *Susanna Moodie*, *influence*, and *Margaret Atwood*. These will inform and assist you in the development of keywords for searching, which we will discuss in the next section. Using another example, you may be interested in examining how nature influences identity in Canadian literature. In this case, you might state your topic as follows: "I want to explore the relationship between nature and identity in Canadian literature." Here the concepts would be fourfold: *relationship*, *nature*, *identity*, and *Canadian literature*.

## STEP 2: BRAINSTORMING KEYWORDS

The term "keyword" is self-descriptive in that keywords have the potential to unlock records from within a catalog or database that may inform your research. Using the concepts that you have already identified, the goal here is to imagine other aspects of these concepts and to anticipate words that might be used to approach them. Let's use our final example above, exploring the relationship between nature and identity in Canadian literature. In fact, we might want to expand the scope of our investigation by also considering the *influence* of nature on identity. The term *nature* could likewise be expanded to include *landscape*, *environment*, *ecologies*, and *wilderness*, while *identity* could also entail exploring *self-perception*, *self*, and *Canadianness*. Carefully selecting and manipulating your keywords can mean the difference between finding the perfect book for your project, or missing an item because your search did not interface well with the language of the database. As you expand your concept into a list of keywords, it may be useful to keep track of them in a table, both to assist you in conceptualizing your search, and to help you trace the history of your search (see table 1.1).

## STEP 3: LOOKING UNDER THE HOOD: UNDERSTANDING ELECTRONIC RECORDS

In some respects, performing an online search can be compared to driving a car. As drivers, we are often not aware of the mechanics of the vehicle; how-

**Table 1.1. Possible keywords for searching the topic of "the relationship between nature and identity in Canadian Literature"**

| *Concept #1* | *Concept #2* | *Concept #3* |
|---|---|---|
| relationship | nature | identity |
| influence | landscape | self-perception |
| | environment | self |
| | ecologies | Canadianness |
| | wilderness | |

ever, the engineering and care that goes into the production of the car will reflect on the automobile's performance, dependability, and the driving experience itself. Likewise, the attention that goes into developing an electronic record affects how the record will interface with a user attempting to retrieve relevant items. When we click a search button, a series of processes occur as the fields of records are searched to match the keywords selected in building the query. Whether you are searching a library catalog, an online database, or the Internet through a Web browser, fields, records, and indexes make up the nuts and bolts of automated searching.

In order to look under the hood at the process of a search, we will examine the standard method for structuring library catalogs, the Machine Readable Cataloging (MARC) record. MARC records are an industry standard for most libraries in Canada and the United States. When a book is published, catalogers take the item in hand and attempt to provide a brief, yet adequate, description of the work. Libraries use MARC records to organize these descriptions, which often include the book's title, author, and subject. A MARC record can contain a variety of information, from a book's physical details, such as the dimensions of the item, to notes that might illuminate a particular feature of the work itself. Individual libraries select which MARC fields (generally author, title, subject, and notes) to include in the catalog's index. When you perform a catalog keyword search, the database will search for any occurrence of your keywords within these indexed fields. For this discussion, we will look at the MARC fields that are commonly indexed and are therefore most applicable to keyword searching. In MARC records, each field is assigned a number, so, for example, the title field carries the number 245, as illustrated in figure 1.1 for the title *Ethnic and Native Canadian Literature: A Bibliography*.

The author, John Miska, is listed in the 100 field, along with his biographical dates. The place of publication and publisher, Toronto, University of Toronto Press, as well as the year of publication, 1990, are all listed in field 260. Field 500 contains a general note about the work itself, in this case provided by the author to indicate that the bibliography is a derivative work. The 500 field can contain a variety of general information supplied by the author,

```
001     21448823
005     19950727074820.4
008     900302s1990    onc      b    001 0 eng d
010       |acn 90093936
015     C90-93936-2
020     0802058523 :|c$135.00
035     WSU000749587
040     CaOTU|beng|cCaOTU|dCaOONL|dWaOLN
055 00  Z1376 E87|bM57 1990 fol.
055 02  Z1376*
082 00  016.8088/9971|220
100 1   Miska, John P.,|d1932-
245 10  Ethnic and native Canadian literature :|ba bibliography /
        |cJohn Miska.
260     Toronto :|bUniversity of Toronto Press,|c1990.
300     xv, 445 p. ;|c29 cm.
500     Includes index.
500     "Part of the material is derived from my preliminary
        bibliography entitled Ethnic and native Canadian
        literature 1850-1979, published in microform in 1979"--P.
        vii.
650  0  Canadian literature|xMinority authors|vBibliography.
650  0  Canadian literature|xHistory and criticism|vBibliography.
```

**Figure 1.1. Modified MARC record for *Ethnic and Native Canadian Literature: A Bibliography*, with tags 100, 245, 260, and 650 highlighted. Source: Washington State University Libraries, Griffin Catalog.**

cataloger, or publisher regarding the material in hand. A 500 field note is generally incorporated at the discretion of the cataloger and may not necessarily be included in a MARC record.

The 650 field can be very helpful, as it lists the subject headings assigned by the cataloger to describe the topic of the book itself. In this case, the cataloger has assigned *Canadian literature—Minority authors—Bibliography*, as well as *Canadian literature—History and criticism—Bibliography*, to the item. In selecting these subject headings, the cataloger likely consulted a prescribed list of terms published as the *Library of Congress Subject Headings*, or *LCSH*. Subject headings therefore are not arbitrarily contrived by the cataloger but rather represent a list of controlled vocabulary developed to describe the possible subjects of an item. Increasingly, many MARC records also include 505 fields, which give the table of contents for a work. The 505 field can be particularly useful in helping the researcher uncover content that may not be readily apparent in the item's title or through the assigned subject headings. For example, in figure 1.2, the title of the book (listed in MARC field 245) may not obviously indicate to the reader that the work encompasses treatment of Canadian literature. Information in the table of contents, or 505 field, therefore offers the researcher a richer view of the scope of the work.

```
245 00 Native North America :|bcritical and cultural perspectives
       : essays /|cby Patricia Monture Angus ... [et al.] ;
       edited by Renée Hulan.
260    Toronto :|bECW Press ;|aChicago, Ill. :|bdistributed in
       the United States by LPC Group,|cc1999.
300    274 p. ;|c22 cm.
504    Includes bibliographical references.
505 0  Introduction / Renée Hulan -- Native America and the
       literary tradition / Patricia Monture Angus -- Native
       American Indian literatures : narratives of survivance /
       Gerald Vizenor -- Spirit and law in native American
       narratives / Clifford E. Trafzer -- Nations within as seen
       from without : ten theses on German perspectives on the
       literature of Canada's first nations / Hartmut Lutz -- Why
       native literature? / Armand Garnet Ruffo -- "Great stories
       are told" : Canadian native novelists / Agnes Grant --
       Aboriginal writing in Canada and the anthology as
       commodity / Margery Fee -- "There is nothing but white
       between the lines" : parallel colonial experiences of the
       Irish and aboriginal Canadians / Ron Marken -- "That
       murderin' half-breed" : the abjectification of the
       mixedblood in Mark Twain's Adventures of Tom Sawyer /
       Patricia Riley -- Savage erotica exotica : media imagery
       of native women in North America / Marianette Jaimes-
       Guerrero -- When the good guys don't wear white :
       narration, characterization, and ideology in Leslie Marmon
       Silko's Almanac of the dead / Jo-Ann Thom -- Beginner's
       mind : learning to read the Ghost dance songs / Charlotte
       Hussey -- Memory alive : an inquiry into the uses of
       memory in Marilyn Dumont, Jeannette Armstrong, Louise
       Halfe, and Joy Harjo / Jeanne Perreault.
650  0 Canadian literature|xIndian authors|xHistory and
       criticism.
650  0 American literature|xIndian authors|xHistory and
       criticism.
650  0 Indian literature|zCanada|xHistory and criticism.
650  0 Indian literature|zUnited States|xHistory and criticism.
650  0 Indians in literature.
650  0 Indians of North America.
700 1  Monture-Angus, Patricia.
700 1  Hulan, Renée.
```

**Figure 1.2. Modified MARC record for *Native North America: Critical and Cultural Perspectives*, with 505 and selected 650 tags highlighted. Source: Washington State University Libraries, Griffin Catalog.**

Likewise, while the vocabulary used is controlled, two subject headings in the 650 field, *Indian literature—Canada—History and criticism* and *Canadian literature—Indian authors—History and criticism*, both indicate that the work examines Canadian First Nations authors.

In examining these MARC records, you are beginning to see how important it is that the vocabulary you choose to describe your topic matches the language used by libraries and database vendors. After some experience searching a library catalog or database, you will begin to familiarize yourself with the language of the online system, and this will in fact help you develop more focused searches. We will discuss these implications further in the next section.

## STEP 4: THE SEARCH STRATEGY

While some searches are straightforward (such as instances in which you are searching for a specific title, a given author, or a predefined subject), most online research involves converging concepts and ideas. In the case of more complex searches, however, we began to see how controlled vocabulary can constrict the results of a search. Since Library of Congress subject headings are in fact driven by language used in the United States, terms commonly used in Canada may not be reflected. For example, if you were to do a subject search for one of the preferred terms for describing the Native peoples of Canada, such as *First Nations* or *aboriginal*, you would find that these terms are not consistently incorporated into the controlled vocabulary of the Library of Congress. In fact, the term *First Nations* is not used as a subject heading, and the term *aboriginal* is more often associated with the indigenous peoples of Australia in *LCSH*. In order to beat the system, so to speak, we must therefore develop a search strategy that will maximize the possibility that the results returned relate to our research problem, and that relevant records are not accidentally excluded. To assist us in this, the keyword search is the most adaptable; it does not limit the search to one field in the record, as say a title or subject search would. Keywords on their own, however, can be problematic, as they can sometimes be misinterpreted or produce a search that returns too many irrelevant results. The keyword search can be optimized by the application of Boolean logic through the Boolean operators *and*, *or*, and *not*. Boolean logic continues to be relevant in building an online search, even as database systems are improved to incorporate natural language.

### The *And* Operator

Using the *and* operator between keywords indicates that each of the keywords selected must appear in the search results. So, taking our nature and Canadian identity example, the *and* search would link the three concepts identified as follows:

*Nature* ***and*** *Canadian literature* ***and*** *identity*

Venn diagrams are used to illustrate how Boolean operators limit the results of an *and* search, as seen in figure 1.3. This search retrieved twelve results of varying relevancy in the *MLA International Bibliography*, or *MLAIB*. Published by the Modern Language Association as a standard database for indexing books and journals to inform literary, linguistics, and folklore studies, the *MLAIB* is also useful for identifying material relevant to Canadian literary studies. One example is provided in figure 1.4.

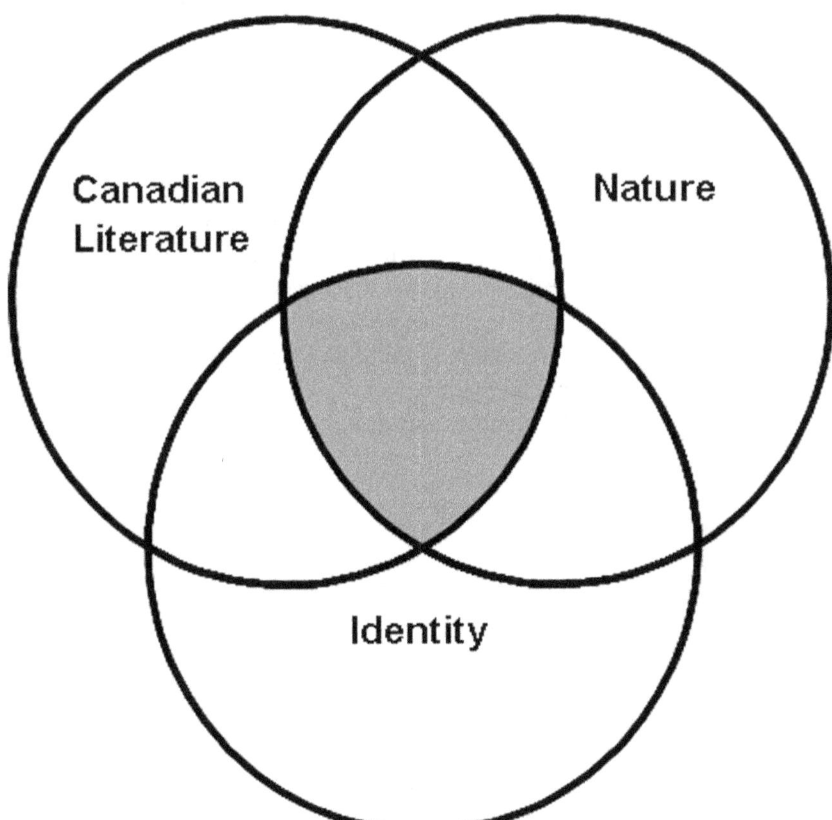


**Figure 1.3. Venn diagram for *Nature* and *Canadian literature* and *identity*.**

Title: 'Death by Landscape': Race, ***Nature***, and Gender in ***Canadian*** Nationalist Mythology

Author(s): Mackey, Eva

Source: ***Canadian*** *Woman Studies/Les Cahiers de la Femme* 2000 Summer; 20 (2): 125-30.

General Subject Areas:
*Subject Literature:* ***Canadian literature***;
*Period:* 1900-1999;
*Primary Subject Author:* Atwood, Margaret (1939- );
*Primary Subject Work:* Survival (1972);
*Genre:* criticism;

Subject Terms:
on race; gender; ***nature***; relationship to cultural politics; national ***identity***; compared to Frye, Northrop (1912-1991): The Bush Garden (1971); Canada First movement; painting; by Group of Seven

**Figure 1.4. A Boolean search for *Nature* and *Canadian literature* and *identity*. Source: MLA *International Bibliography* via EBSCO.**

## The *Or* Operator

This operator will broaden the search, increasing the number of search results retrieved. The *or* operator is particularly useful in instances where you would like to incorporate synonyms, variant spelling, or closely related concepts, or where you simply want to increase the scope of your search. When searching a database that includes records in multiple languages, an *or* search may be employed to incorporate equivalent words. A useful application of an *or* search is illustrated in incorporating various terms used for the native people of Canada:

*First Nations* ***or*** *native* ***or*** *aboriginal* ***or*** *indigenous*

The *or* search will capture all of the records which include one of the above terms, as illustrated in the Venn diagram in figure 1.5. A standard online database for Canadian journals and magazines is the *Canadian Periodical Index*, or *CPI.Q*. A search for *"Canadian Literature"* ***and*** *(First Nations* ***or*** *aboriginal* or *indigenous* ***or*** *native)* in the *Canadian Periodical Index* returned 105 results from academic journals. This search uses parentheses to indicate "nesting," a search technique used to incorporate related terms and to force the order in which the search is processed. Nesting will be further discussed later in this chapter. One of the results of this search is illustrated in figure 1.6.

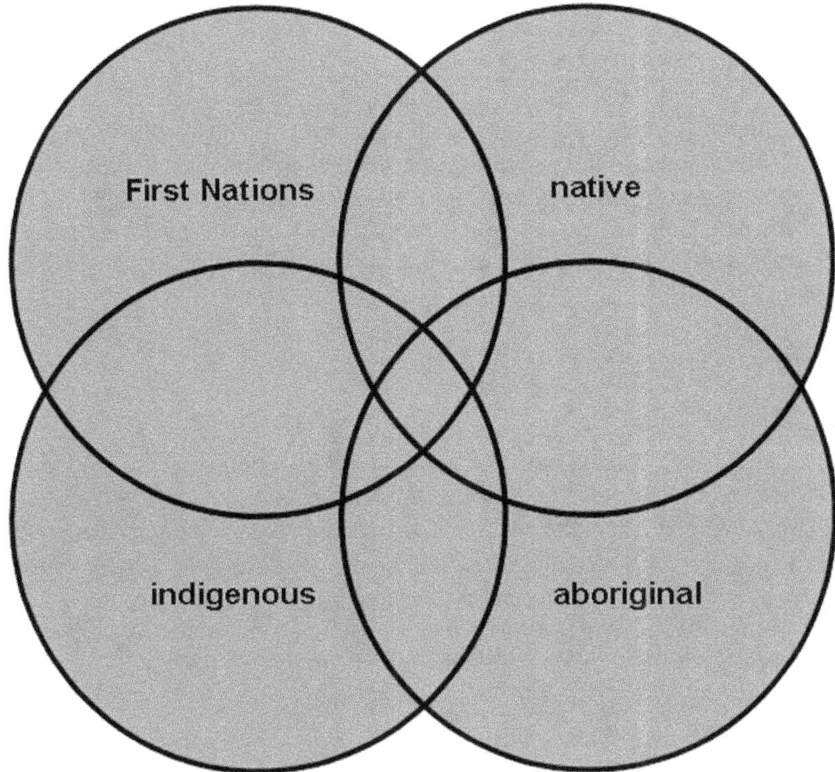


**Figure 1.5. Venn diagram for *First Nations* or *native* or *aboriginal* or *indigenous.***

"Cultural literacy, **First Nations** and the future of Canadian literary studies."

Journal of Canadian Studies 34.3 (Fall 1999): p59(28).
Author(s): Renee Hulan and Linda Warley
Document Type: Magazine/Journal

Abstract:
**First Nations** literature presents a variety of challenges to scholars and teachers of **Canadian literature** to which we have a responsibility to respond. Studying **First Nations** literature is one means by which we can increase our understanding of and respect for First Peoples and create the political will to involve ourselves in the social justice issues that concern them. In this paper, we discuss the reasons for promoting greater cultural literacy (by which we mean the mainstream becoming acculturated by **aboriginal** cultures) in Canadian students, and we offer pragmatic suggestions as to how it might be achieved.

**Figure 1.6. Modified CPI.Q record retrieved from a search for *"Canadian Literature"* and (*First nations* or *aboriginal* or *indigenous* or *native*). Source: CPI.Q via Gale.**

## The *Not* Operator

This operator excludes results containing the terms or words that have been identified as somehow disruptive to your search. This can be very useful if, for example, you notice that the search is returning results that contain your search terms, but not in the context that you had anticipated. If you were to do a search for the terms *nature* and *Canadian literature*, you might notice that the results also include several records that focus on *human nature*. In this case, you might use the *not* operator as follows in order to exclude these results:

*nature* ***not*** *human*

The *not* operator should be used cautiously, however, as the word *human* could appear in a context other than *human nature* within a record, and these results would likewise be excluded in this search.

An example of where the *not* operator might be used can be seen in a previous search, this time from the search for *First Nations* ***or*** *native* ***or*** *aboriginal* ***or*** *indigenous*. You may notice in performing this search for aboriginal literature that records referring to Australian Aboriginal communities are returned. In this case, you could incorporate the *not* operator as follows:

*aboriginal* ***not*** *Australia*

Another use of the *not* operator is illustrated when you are looking for information on an author but find that a particular canonical work by the author appears repeatedly in the results. For instance, if you were researching Michael Ondaatje but wanted to exclude results referring to *The English Patient*, your Boolean search could be as follows:

*Ondaatje* ***not*** *English Patient*

## Full-Text Searches

Options for full-text searches will vary from database to database. Many databases offer the option to search not only the journal article records, but also within the full text of the articles themselves. For example, EBSCO Publishing's *Academic Search Complete*, a general interdisciplinary database, has an option directing the search engine to "also search within the full text of the articles." Conversely, the *Annual Bibliography of English Language and Literature*, or *ABELL*, a well-regarded literary database, presents full-text searching as the default search. Full-text searches are powerful; however, since they direct the search engine to search the entire text of the item, they can also increase the likelihood that irrelevant results will be retrieved.

## Truncation and Wildcard Searches

Truncation is used for substituting one or more letters at the end of a word. As you begin searching, you will likely run into instances where you will want to search for variations of a word. The asterisk (*) is a common truncation symbol used in online systems allowing you to indicate the root of a word and pick up variations of the word beyond this root. A search using the root *Canad**, where * truncates the word, will pick up the following variations: *Canada*, *Canadian*, *Canadien*, *Canadienne*, and *Canadianness*. Use truncation wisely, as to overly truncate a word would likely result in too many irrelevant hits. For example, truncating to *Can** so as to also retrieve the popularized term "Canuck," could result in the retrieval of a multitude of words irrelevant to your search that also begin with *Can*, such as *Canterbury*, *can*, *canning*, *cannot*, and so on.

Wildcard symbols are similar to truncation, except that the wildcard can be embedded in a word. For example, *colo?*r will retrieve searches with both *color* and *colour* in the results. Another example of a common wildcard search would be *wom?n*, to pick up *woman*, *women*, and *womyn*.

In some online search programs, one truncation symbol * will only pick up a specified number of nonspace characters and must therefore be duplicated ** in order to pick up a greater number of nonspace characters. Truncation and wildcard symbols can vary between library catalogs and databases, and in some cases are interchangeable. Besides the asterisk, some common truncation and wildcard symbols are the question mark (?) and the exclamation point (!). Be certain to consult the help or search tips files of the catalog or database in order to ensure that you are using truncation and wildcards correctly.

## Proximity Operators: *Within* and *Near*

Proximity operators can be used when you expect to find two or more search terms in close proximity of each other. The *within* operator, often represented by *w*, tells the search engine to locate words a certain distance from one another, performing the search in the order in which you type them. For example, *Catherine w2 Traill* will retrieve search terms that appear within two words of each other, such as *Catherine Parr Traill*, and even *Catherine Traill*. The *near* operator offers a little more flexibility in that it directs the search engine to locate the search terms within a certain distance of each other, but in any order. For example, *Catherine n2 Traill* will return not only *Catherine Parr Traill* and *Catherine Traill*, but also *Traill, Catherine Parr* and *Traill, Catherine.*

## Phrase Searches

Phrase searches maintain the exact order of a string of words in a search. Some online databases, such as EBSCO, automatically assume phrase searching. Otherwise, phrase searching is generally indicated by enclosing a string of words in quotation marks. Phrase searching can be a powerful tool when used wisely; remember that you are directing the search engine to find instances of a string of words in the exact order in which they have been typed. A phrase search for *"theater history in Canada"* may not therefore return results where the wording is reversed, such as *Canadian theater history*.

## Nesting

Nesting is useful when you want to control the order in which your search is conducted. Many online systems use a default order, prioritizing which Boolean operators it handles first. In many systems, *and* searches are processed first, followed by *or* searches. The order in which the search terms are processed can have a dramatic effect on your search results. In a manner similar to how algebraic expressions are prioritized, nested searches employ the use of parentheses to control the order in which search terms are processed by the online system. Nesting can be particularly useful in an elaborate search, such as the following search for the theme of loneliness as it relates to the female characters in the writing of Margaret Laurence: *(feminist** ***or*** *wom*n* ***or*** *female)* ***and*** *(literature* ***or*** *writing* ***or*** *writers)* ***and*** *Margaret Laurence* ***and*** *(lonel** ***or*** *isolation)*.

## Subject vs. Keyword Searches

A subject search is most useful when you "speak the language" of the database or catalog system. Remember that subject searches are based on controlled vocabulary and employ standardized language to describe a given topic. Subject searches are field searches, meaning that only the words in the subject field of the catalog or database record are being searched. Depending on the context of your search, there are both upsides and downsides to subject searching. Remember that subject searching can be very limiting; however, when you are familiar with the subject terms used within the search system, a subject search can also be a powerful way to focus a search and ensure relevant results.

Keyword searches offer more flexibility and also allow for the searching of new terms and jargon that may not ever become incorporated into the standardized vocabulary of a subject index. An advantage of the keyword search is that it directs the online system to retrieve records that contain your search terms anywhere in the text of the record, versus within a specified field. A drawback of keyword searching is that the search results are likely to include "false drops," or hits that are not necessarily relevant to your search.

### Relevancy Searches

Each catalog or database uses its own set of variables to prioritize relevancy within search results. For example, even in conducting a keyword search, a database might determine that records containing your term within the subject field are the most relevant, followed by the title field, and then in the full text of the record. Some databases offer options for how the search results are displayed. Many will default to display the most relevant results first; however, some sort the results according to the date of publication. Consult the help files to determine how results are ordered, and check the catalog or database interface for further options. Relevancy, date, author, and source are among the sorting options that may be available.

### Using Search Limiters

Many catalogs and databases allow you to limit your search based on the year of publication, language, author, and so on. Likewise, you may be able to limit by format (book, article, media, microfilm, etc.). Another useful limiter when searching article databases can be options that allow you to specify that you would like your results to display scholarly or peer-reviewed articles only.

## STEP 5: USING THE DATABASE

The features described throughout this chapter provide the researcher with the ability to conduct online searches using tools that are recognized by the databases to manipulate your selected keywords in order to develop a search that will connect you with the material you seek. Searching is a process, and your searches should be modified according to the new information you receive while searching. An online search is usually not a one-shot exercise;

if irrelevant results are returned, respond to this information by adapting the search accordingly. Now that we have discussed some of the tools of searching, remember that these tools are sometimes applied and interpreted differently within each database. Many databases have a help or frequently-asked-questions link to assist you in learning how the database will interpret a more advanced search. When using a database for the first time, it is important to consult these help links, as they should clarify the following issues:

- Does the search engine support Boolean searching, and if so, should the operators be capitalized when used?
- Can truncation be used in searching? If so, what is the truncation symbol?
- Are wildcards recognized? If so, what is the wildcard symbol?
- Does the search engine support phrase searches? Are quotations required in phrase searching? Is phrase searching automatically assumed?
- Which limiters are available through the search interface? Can you limit by date, language, peer-reviewed materials, and the like?
- Are proximity searches supported? If so, what is the recognized format?

## STEP 6: INTERPRETING AND MANIPULATING THE RESULTS

Being responsive and applying the appropriate strategy in reexecuting a search are skills that you will develop with practice. In some ways, online searching is a game of strategy and adaptability. Assuming that items relevant to your topic exist, the search terms you select and the search strategy you employ are instrumental in discovering them. Be wary of choosing a topic for which there may not be published research materials, as a lack of scholarship related to your topic will limit your ability to interact with, react to, and incorporate research that relates to your interests. Likewise, if your topic is so narrow that you quickly exhaust your research options, consider broadening your focus.

## STEP 7: THE WORLD WIDE WEB FOR SCHOLARLY RESEARCH

It can sometimes be difficult to make the distinction between a database that contains scholarly information and websites that are posted for public purposes. The Web can sometimes be useful for discerning the extent to which a topic is treated. The biggest downside of the Web for scholarly research is that an Internet search, in and of itself, does not produce scholarly results. If you are curious as to the scope and depth of treatment on your topic within the scholarly universe alone, you may want to try performing a search in Google Scholar. Since Google Scholar does not examine the records of one particular database, a Google Scholar search can also be useful for illuminating relevant materials, including articles, books, conference papers, theses, preprints, and working papers. The strength of Google Scholar currently varies from discipline to discipline, and you may find that its application to humanities research pales in comparison to subject databases such as the *MLAIB* and *ABELL*. As Google continually adds content to this resource, its usefulness can be expected to increase. Interpreting the results of a Google Scholar search can at times be difficult, so tread carefully and seek the assistance of your librarian if you find it difficult to locate or classify the material identified through your search.

## CONCLUSION

Online searching is a process, and your skill in performing searches is likely to improve as you become more familiar with searching techniques in general, and with the intricacies of a given database in particular. Remember to remain responsive to the results returned in a search and to modify your keywords and apply new strategies accordingly. In some ways, searching is a conversation between you and the database, a conversation that is mediated by the search interface. Pay attention to the new information that you receive as a result of your search. Did the database misinterpret your query? If so, why? Are there alternate spellings for the keywords used? Are there additional aspects of the topic apparent in the results that you had not anticipated? Is the scope of the database appropriate for your topic? Did you find additional terms within the results that speak to your topic and could likewise be incorporated into a new search? These are just a few of the questions that will arise as you conduct online research.

# *Chapter Two*

# General Literary Reference Sources

Canadian literature has achieved international renown and therefore receives increased treatment in notable literary reference works. Some of the resources discussed in this chapter may initially seem too general for serious inquiry; however, many recently published literary reference works include a section devoted to Canadian authors and themes. In some general literary sources, Canadian authors may be incorporated within broader headings such as "Commonwealth literature" or "world literature." Since reference collections are usually restricted for in-library use, you will likely have to consult many of these materials within the walls of your library. Even so, you will find that it will be time well spent, as reference materials are an excellent way to whet your appetite for the topic, while providing you with some general background information that can be useful in focusing your research. The books listed below are invaluable for identifying materials for further reading, and in that sense reference books can have a catalytic effect on the research process.

## RESEARCH GUIDES AND REFERENCE SOURCES

Bond, Mary E. *Canadian Reference Sources: An Annotated Bibliography*. Vancouver: University of British Columbia Press, 1996.

Harner, James L. *Literary Research Guide: An Annotated Listing of Reference Sources in English Literary Studies*. 5th ed. New York: Modern Language Association, 2008. Also available in online format.

Jones, Joseph. *Reference Sources for Canadian Literary Studies*. Toronto: University of Toronto Press, 2005.

Marcuse, Michael J. *A Reference Guide for English Studies*. Berkeley: University of California Press, 1990.

In its fifth edition, Harner's ***Literary Research Guide: An Annotated Listing of Reference Sources in English Literary Studies*** continues to be an authoritative source. The work of Texas A&M University professor James L. Harner, the guide provides annotated information on reference sources, including bibliographies, databases, encyclopedias, histories, literary guides, dictionaries, and handbooks. Harner's strategy in compiling the guide was to be selective versus exhaustive, and this works to the reader's advantage. Sifting through mountains of literary materials with evaluative comments, Harner offers a great deal of guidance for navigating a subject area. This monumental work has become so comprehensive that updating must be a daunting task. For those curious as to the genesis of previous editions, Harner gives a breakdown of each update under "Prefaces." The time-constrained researcher is fortunate to profit from Harner's advice, as he assists the seasoned scholar while scaffolding the uninitiated. Although the guide contains chapters devoted to American, Irish, and Welsh literature, the bulk of Canadian treatment comes under the chapter entitled "Other Literatures in English," which also considers Australia, the Caribbean, and New Zealand. Harner highlights many notable reference sources on Canadian literature, with adequate evaluative information to guide the researcher toward useful materials and away from the obsolete, irrelevant, poorly organized, and outdated. With statements such as "an important desktop companion to the literary culture of the country" (547) or "too incomplete to be of much use" (563), Harner's guide at times reads like a New York food critic column, to the delight and benefit of the reader. Found within the section entitled "Canadian Literature" is a selection of guides to primary works, information on databases, and indexes and bibliographies for print and online resources, with a focus on Canadian writing, authors, and scholarship. Also highlighted are dictionaries and bibliographies for Canadian English. Works are organized according to genre, covering fiction, drama, poetry, and prose. For the researcher seeking a quick and painless introduction to Canadian literary research, Harner's work is truly the Michelin Guide of literary sources. The fifth edition is now also available in an online electronic format.

While not as comprehensive, and unrevised since publication in 1990, Marcuse's ***A Reference Guide for English Studies*** is a manageable and user-friendly resource containing a very nice section on Canada. While many of the titles listed could be updated today (for example, the 1983 *Oxford Companion to Canadian Literature* entered its second edition in 1997), the work is still relevant in researching past authors and their works.

Marcuse's treatment of Canadian literature comes under section M, "English Literature," subsection 12, "Canada," which encompasses entries M-130 to M-149. "Some Frequently Recommended Works on Canadian Literature in English" (M-149) contains an interesting and well-thought-out list of notable works on Canadian literature, from Margaret Atwood's *Survival: A Thematic Guide to Canadian Literature* (1972) to Camille Roy's *Histoire de la littérature canadienne-française* (1940). French Canadian literature receives brief treatment within section L, "Literature," subsection 6, "French Language and Literature," where Marcuse refers to Gerard Tougas's *Checklist of Printed Materials Relating to French-Canadian Literature 1763–1968/ Liste de référence d'imprimes relatifs à la littérature canadienne-française.* Marcuse also provides a heading for French Canada under "Some Frequently Recommended Works on French Language and Literature" (L-79). Not a single Canadian author is represented within Marcuse's "Guides to Individual Authors" (M-60), which does however highlight notable Irish, English, and American writers.

University of British Columbia librarian Joseph Jones offers an unprecedented contribution to Canadian literary scholarship in ***Reference Sources for Canadian Literary Studies***. Though focusing on literature in English, selected reference sources for French Canadian, First Nations, Inuit, and multicultural literatures also receive treatment. As the title implies, Jones examines reference works, such as guides, dictionaries, handbooks, bibliographies, catalogs, special collections, databases, and websites. Organized mainly by reference genre, Jones also offers sections on specific formats and categories, including "Periodicals," "Dissertations and Theses," "Children's Literature," and "Biographies." Although not a guide to conducting literary research, Jones aims toward inclusiveness as he exhaustively seeks out and annotates all known titles for Canadian literary research published through 2002. Thoroughly covering the depth and breadth of available reference materials for Canadian literary research, Jones's effort has sometimes been criticized for being too comprehensive. Nevertheless, the serious Canadian literary researcher is likely to appreciate the comprehensive treatment of resources and may find it particularly useful when used in tandem with the present volume. This work earned an "Outstanding Title" designation in the Association of College and Research Libraries publication *Choice: Current Reviews for Academic Libraries*, a premier reviewing resource consulted by libraries to identify noteworthy publications.

Drawing on and expanding Dorothy Ryder's *Canadian Reference Sources: A Selective Guide* (1981), Mary E. Bond's ***Canadian Reference Sources: An Annotated Bibliography*** examines over four thousand reference works. The section entitled "Literature" (pp. 669–761) is divided into eight distinct genres, including "Diaries and Autobiographies," "Drama," "Fiction," and "Poetry," which are further broken down by type of document and/or geographic region. Reference sources for Canadian literature are covered in over close to one hundred pages of descriptive, bilingual annotations. Hailing from the National Library of Canada, Bond has developed an exquisitely organized resource. A 1996 review in *Choice: Current Reviews for Academic Libraries* appropriately categorizes this work as an "Outstanding Title."

## GENERAL ENCYCLOPEDIAS, COMPANIONS, AND GUIDES FOR CANADIAN LITERATURE

Benson, Eugene, and L. W. Conolly, eds. *Encyclopedia of Post-Colonial Literatures in English*. 2nd ed. New York: Routledge, 2005.

Benson, Eugene, and William Toye, eds. *The Oxford Companion to Canadian Literature*. New York: Oxford University Press, 1997. Also available through Oxford Reference Online, www.oxfordreference.com.

Colombo, John Robert. *Canadian Literary Landmarks*. Willowdale, Ontario: Hounslow Press, 1984.

Kröller, Eva-Marie, ed. *The Cambridge Companion to Canadian Literature*. New York: Cambridge University Press, 2004.

Moritz, Albert, and Theresa Moritz. *The Oxford Illustrated Literary Guide to Canada*. New York: Oxford University Press, 1987.

New, William H., ed. *Encyclopedia of Literature in Canada*. Toronto: University of Toronto Press, 2002.

Toye, William, ed. *The Concise Oxford Companion to Canadian Literature*. New York: Oxford University Press, 2001.

Edited by William H. New, a highly recognizable name in Canadian literary research, the ***Encyclopedia of Literature in Canada*** is a selective resource for information on Canadian authors, works, cultural institutions, and themes. In the preface, New deals with the complex and difficult task of defining Canadian authors for this volume, explaining,

> There are some writers who were temporary residents, some who immigrated, some who consider themselves exiles in Canada, some who are expatriates, some who have actively striven to separate from Canada, and some who have relinquished their Canadian citizenship, only to seek later to take it up again. (viii)

In justifying the inclusion or exclusion of a given author, New explains that in the tradition of encyclopedic works, the volume is meant to be "instructional" versus "inclusive." Individually authored entries are arranged alphabetically, with "see also" references to additional articles that complement or shed further light on the topic. Though the entries are fairly brief, many conclude with a list of further reading to assist the researcher in extending his or her inquiry. Three practical indexes are also provided, including an "Index by Contributor." The "Index of Authors" conveniently lists the pages where an author is mentioned, with the author's main entry indicated in boldface. "The Supplementary Index" is useful for identifying the titles of essays that treat a given author, institution, theme, or literary term. A lengthy and detailed section entitled "Awards and Literary Prizes" offers a wonderful primer to the many accolades available and awarded to Canada's literary talent. This is a marvelous and monumental resource edited by a giant of Canadian literary history and research.

The second edition of ***The Oxford Companion to Canadian Literature*** grew substantially in both size and works covered since the publication of the first edition in 1983. As emphasized by the editors in their introduction, the purpose of the title is not to outline a canon of Canadian works, but rather to serve as a companion for readers of Canadian literature. Dedicating the work in memory of a short list of four canonical Canadian authors—Robertson Davies, Margaret Laurence, Hugh MacLennan, and Gabrielle Roy—the editors also stress that their endeavor is designed for both the ordinary reader as well as the specialist. The *Companion* includes 1,112 entries by 325 contributors, primarily with affiliations to Canadian universities, libraries, newspapers, publications, and organizations. The reader would be hard-pressed not to find coverage of a given genre, significant author, work, survey, or phenomenon in Canadian literature. While the *Companion* provides treatment of major Canadian works, it also incorporates essays on Canada's ethnic literatures, such as Ukrainian Canadian, Italian Canadian, Caribbean Canadian, and Yiddish, among others. Organized alphabetically, individually authored essays are not indexed; however, "see also" references should assist the reader in ensuring that material relevant to their study is not overlooked. A novice Canadian literary researcher would be wise to review this resource before proceeding with his or her work. An electronic version of this title is now available through Oxford Reference Online.

Based on the aforementioned *Oxford Companion to Canadian Literature*, ***The Concise Oxford Companion to Canadian Literature*** offers sixty-one entries that were not included in the larger work, covering new authors, such as Peter Oliva and Kenneth Oppel, who have "made a mark" (iii) on the Canadian literary scene. Although the number of entries was noticeably reduced from the larger volume, essays on significant authors remain mainly untouched. In devising this work, the editor hoped to further incorporate Canada's growing body of authors, works, and literary achievements.

Sharing ties to the University of Guelph, editors Eugene Benson and L. W. Conolly ensure that Canadian authors, works, and themes are not lost in the mix of subjects considered in the ***Encyclopedia of Post-Colonial Literatures in English***. The entry “Criticism (Canada),” by Margery Fee, presents an interesting and succinct overview of the Canadian scene, successfully drawing upon critical works, movements, conflicts, and developments. Over two hundred entries were added since the first edition in 1994, incorporating new writers and expanding this previously two-volume work into three. The essay on Carol Shields, for example, has been updated to reflect the publication of *Larry's Party* (1997) and *Unless* (2002), as well as the writer's death in 2003. Author entries highlight biographical information and give a brief critical overview of important works. The reader will find that some more-contemporary Canadian authors, such as Camilla Gibb, have been overlooked. Although mentioned within topic essays, 2001 Man Booker Prize winner Yann Martel likewise does not receive his own biographical entry. Given the international scope of the work, it can be expected that space might not allow for more recently established authors. The work nonetheless offers a variety of entry points for the study of Canadian authors and themes. Unique essays include “Canadian Connections with Caribbean Literature” and “South Asia in Canadian Literature.” Essays covering significant authors are relatively short compared to the information contained in the 1997 *Oxford Companion to Canadian Literature*; however, the entries are nonetheless adequate in providing informative overviews to engage scholarly interests. Essays are individually authored, and many conclude with suggestions for further reading. A unique strength of the work is the potential it allows for side-by-side comparison of postcolonial genres and themes. For example, the entry “Literary Magazines” incorporates separate treatment of Australia, Bangladesh, Canada, Caribbean, Hong Kong, India, New Zealand, Philippines, South Africa, South Pacific, Sri Lanka, and West Africa.

While many of the sources discussed up until now have been designed in a more encyclopedic style, ***The Cambridge Companion to Canadian Literature*** is organized into thirteen individually authored chapters on broad genres and concepts. Edited by renowned Canadian literary researcher Eva-Marie Kröller, this title incorporates essays such as “Aboriginal Writing,” “Writing by Women,” “Regionalism and Urbanism,” “Nature-Writing,” and “Exploration and Travel.” As a collection of essays, this work provides a unique narrative introduction to Canadian literature, successfully covering the past as well as present developments. Kröller is commended for assembling a list of notable scholars from both Canada and abroad who collectively deliver a unique sampling of perspectives. Governor General's Award–winning poet E. D. Blodgett offers the chapter “Francophone Writing,” while playwright Ric Knowles authors the essay “Drama.” Marta Dvorak has been praised by reviewers for a stunning essay entitled "Fiction," while Magdalene Redekop contributes an overview of the Canadian question in her essay "Canadian Literary Criticism and the Idea of a National Literature." Other chapters include "Poetry," "Short Fiction," and "Life Writing." A nice selection of further reading concludes this work.

Though written on a completely different level than other works in this section, ***The Oxford Illustrated Literary Guide to Canada*** provides a wonderful snapshot of the literary character of a given Canadian region. A travelogue of Canadian literary settings, birthplaces, and events, the volume is organized by provinces and territories, from east to west, taking the reader on a cross-country literary tour. Over 950 authors are incorporated within the work's 246 pages; the information found therein is therefore brief. However, as a survey of an area's literary output, or for anecdotal stories regarding an author's connection to a particular village, town, or park, this is still an interesting and unique resource. The index is convenient, as many writers, for example, Louis Riel, are associated with several Canadian locations. Information on foreign authors who visited Canada is also incorporated, such as Charles Dickens, who brands Cobourg, Ontario, "a cheerful, thriving little town." Rare photos and illustrations accompany the text, and interesting anecdotes are included throughout.

Although a *Quill and Quire* reviewer characterized the title as "a browser's delight, not a researcher's refuge,"[1] ***Canadian Literary Landmarks*** nonetheless delivers a unique view of Canada's literary geography. Also a published poet, author John Robert Colombo has contributed numerous works to Canadian studies, including editing *The Penguin Dictionary of Popular Canadian Quotations* (2006). Arranged alphabetically according to province or territory, *Literary Landmarks* incorporates over twelve hundred references associated with more than five hundred authors. Although the entries are brief, in some cases amounting to mere tidbits, *Literary Landmarks* does offer the weary researcher food for inspiration. In this regard, the work may be more useful as a guide for those who are inspired to actually visit the locales discussed. Illustrative of the range of interesting details found within this work is the entry "Flin Flon, Manitoba," where Colombo explains that the town was named for Josiah Flintabbatey Flonatin, the hero of a British dime novel entitled *The Sunless City*.

## GENRE, CULTURAL, AND REGIONAL CANADIAN LITERATURE ENCYCLOPEDIAS AND COMPANIONS

Balay, Robert, and Mel Bohn. *Prairies and Plains: The Reference Literature of a Region*. Chicago: KWS Publishers, 2009.

Benson, Eugene, and L. W. Conolly, eds. *The Oxford Companion to Canadian Theatre*. Toronto: Oxford University Press, 1989.

Jones, Raymond, and Jon C. Scott. *Canadian Children's Books: A Critical Guide to Authors and Illustrators*. Don Mills, Ontario: Oxford University Press, 2000.

Lemire, Maurice, Aurelien Boivin, and Gilles Dorion, eds. *Dictionnaire des oeuvres littéraires du Québec*. 2nd ed. Montréal: Fides, 1980.

Nadel, Ira Bruce. *Jewish Writers of North America: A Guide to Information Sources*. Detroit, MI: Gale Research, 1981.

Unwin, Timothy, ed. *The Cambridge Companion to the French Novel: From 1800 to Present*. New York: Cambridge University Press, 1997.

Witalec, Janet, ed. *Native North American Literature*. New York: Gale Research, 1994.

The ***Dictionnaire des oeuvres littéraires du Québec*** is a large, seven-volume set that seeks to exhaustively reflect the literary activity of Quebec writers during a given period. Volume 1, *Des origines à 1900*, treats not only creative literature, such as novels, poetry, and drama, but also recognizes travel writing, parish histories, collections of speeches, and biographies, as well as historical and geographic works. This first volume acknowledges the role that early works played in laying a foundation for Quebec literary society. Other eras covered include 1900–1939 (vol. 2), 1940–1959 (vol. 3), 1960–1969 (vol. 4), 1970–1975 (vol. 5), 1976–1980 (vol. 6), and 1980–1985 (vol. 7). Work on an eighth volume addressing 1986–1990 began in 2004 and when completed will represent the efforts of over three hundred researchers from both Quebec and around the globe. Depending on the importance of a work to the cultural life of a given period, essays vary in length from 250 to 3,000 words. Brief biographical information, such as date and place of birth, significant events, and date and place of death, precede entries for an author's first work. Entries are accompanied by a bibliographic annotation listing all editions of a work, both those published in French and in translation. Recommendations for further reading follow each discussion and, in the case of early works, often refer the reader to obscure articles published in nascent Canadian periodicals, such as *La Revue Canadienne* and *Le Journal de Québec*. A project which debuted in 1971, much of the material was painstakingly compiled under the direction of a team of literary scholars from Laval University.

Although it would benefit from an update, ***The Oxford Companion to Canadian Theatre*** was identified as an "Outstanding Title" by *Choice Reviews* in 1990. With contributions from 158 scholars, the work offers 703 entries related to Canadian theater and drama. Areas covered include genres, theaters, biographies, criticism, plays, and theater-related subjects. Both

French and English works, playwrights, topics, and actors are incorporated, offering a rich and varied view of the Canadian theatrical scene. Some of the individually authored essays conclude with a list of references to inform further research. Given their brevity, shorter entries are nonetheless incredibly detailed. For example, the essay on Winnipeg's historic Walker Theater provides stage dimensions, seating capacity, and a litany of past performers and performances, as well as the disturbing details of how motion-picture companies systematically eradicated live shows. This essay is also illustrative of the fact that the work could benefit from an update, as the piece concludes with a description of the theater's evolution to an Odeon cinema, installing a false ceiling to close off the gallery. The Odeon was in fact closed one year after the *Companion* was published; the theater has since been restored and was renamed The Burton Cummings Theatre for the Performing Arts in 2002.

***Canadian Children's Books: A Critical Guide to Authors and Illustrators*** is a unique and interesting source. In their introduction, the authors deliver a narrative history of notable publications for children, beginning with the appearance of Mrs. H. Bayley's didactic *Improvement; or, A Visit to Grandmama* in 1832. The guide incorporates 133 entries, mainly on English Canadian authors. French-language authors are only selected if their works have also been published in English translation and if they have achieved notoriety within Anglophone Canada. Author entries provide information on the works, characters, themes, and techniques of a given writer. Also highlighted is basic biographical information for the author, such as place of birth, residence, education, career, and major awards. A bibliography of the writer's works is also presented, identifying selected book reviews where available. Many of the entries are based in part on author interviews from selected literary magazines, such as *Quill and Quire* and *Canadian Children's Literature*, as referenced under the heading "Selected Discussions." Where available, entries conclude with a list of relevant reference titles.

Volume 8 in the American Studies Information Guide series, Ira Nadel's ***Jewish Writers of North America: A Guide to Information Sources***, gives equal time to both Canadian and American authors of Jewish origin. A professor of English at the University of British Columbia, Nadel has authored and edited many studies examining Canadian, American, and Victorian literature. Though it could benefit from an update, the guide offers coverage of Jewish Canadian poets, writers of fiction, and dramatists. Yiddish literature is also addressed in one of two appendixes. Highly recognizable names, such as Leonard Cohen, Irving Layton, Phyllis Gotlieb, and Mordecai Richler stand among the less familiar, including Lionel S. B. Shapiro and David Lewis Stein. In his introduction, Nadel discusses the dual identities of the authors examined, originating "in their quest for a Jewish identity modeled on a

European past but molded by a North American present" (xv). Nadel also provides interesting insight into Canada's mosaic versus melting pot orientation, stating, "The combination of the smaller number of Canadian Jews who have lived more closely together in Canada and the national encouragement of ethnic identities, has resulted in a prolongation of past values and standards" (xvii). Preceding each entry is a brief author biography, followed by a bibliography of works both by and about the writer.

Although perhaps not readily apparent in the title, ***Native North American Literature*** affords excellent coverage of Canadian First Nations authors, both contemporary and historical. Possibly more so than other Canadian authors, First Nations writers often subvert the boundaries defined by the Canada/U.S. border, crossing over, both physically and metaphorically speaking, with regard to literary themes and perspectives. Fittingly, therefore, dual-nationality authors are discussed, such as Cherokee writer Thomas King, who, though born in the United States, holds dual citizenship and is considered an author of Canadian fiction. Entries offer introductory notes which include biographical material as well as background details for the author's more notable works. The information also lists the author's address, when available, and awards earned. An inventory of major works is provided, followed by a useful section on criticism. Reprints of reviews and critical essays are incorporated from popular magazines such as *Maclean's*, and from books and scholarly journals such as *Canadian Literature*. The section "Sources for Further Study" illuminates avenues for additional research. Other authors highlighted are Quebec-born writer and artist Peter Blue Cloud, Mohawk writer and poet Beth Brant, Métis author Maria Campbell, Métis author Beatrice Culleton Mosionier, Cree playwright and novelist Tomson Highway, early female Canadian poet and performer E. Pauline Johnson, Ojibwa author Basil H. Johnston, Ojibwa orator Peter Jones, Inuit novelist Markoosie, Vancouver-born writer Lee Maracle, and the prolific author and editor Daniel David Moses. Interestingly, a similarly titled work, Kathy J. Whitson's *Native American Literatures: An Encyclopedia of Works, Characters, Authors and Themes* (1999) concentrates exclusively on topics that relate to the United States.

Edited by Robert Balay, author of the classic *Guide to Reference Books* (1996), ***Prairies and Plains: The Reference Literature of a Region*** centers on resources for the study of the prairies and plains region of the United States and Canada. Annotations explore encyclopedias, bibliographies, dictionaries, websites, indexes, theses, and government publications. Although interdisciplinary in focus, the literature of the Canadian prairies receives adequate coverage under section BC, "Regional Literature: Canada." Other broad categories of interest include "General Works," "Humanities," "Economics and Business," "Political Science," "History," "Social Sciences," and "Agriculture."

Though only one brief chapter covers Canadian fiction, Denis Boak's "The French-Canadian Novel" finds itself among a series of essays on French literary eras and traditions within ***The Cambridge Companion to the French Novel: From 1800 to Present***. Boak provides an overview of French Canadian literary movements, notable works, and their themes in this succinct synopsis of francophone literature.

## BIOGRAPHICAL SOURCES

Brown, George W., ed. *Dictionary of Canadian Biography/Dictionnaire biographique du Canada*. Toronto: University of Toronto Press, 1966–. Also available online at www.biographi.ca/index-e.html (accessed 12 July 2010).

*Dictionary of Literary Biography*. Detroit, MI: Gale Research, 1978. www.gale.cengage.com.

Hamel, Reginald, John Hare, and Paul Wyczynski. *Dictionnaire des auteurs de langue française en Amérique du Nord*. Montréal: editions Fides, 1989.

Matthew, H. C. G., and Brian Howard Harrison. *Oxford Dictionary of National Biography*. Oxford: Oxford University Press, 2004. www.oxforddnb.com.

Morcos, Gamila. *Dictionnaire des artistes et des auteurs francophones de l'Ouest canadien*. With the collaboration of Gilles Cadrin, Paul Dubé, and Laurent Godbout. Québec: Presses de l'Université Laval, 1998.

Sylvestre, Guy, Brandon Conron, and Carl F. Klinck, eds. *Canadian Writers/Écrivains canadiens: A Biographical Dictionary*. Toronto: Ryerson Press, 1966.

Initiated in 1959, the ***Dictionary of Canadian Biography/Dictionnaire biographique du Canada*** (***DCB/DBC***) represents a joint project between the University of Toronto and Université Laval. As George W. Brown relates in the general introduction to the series, this monumental work was made possible through a bequest by Canadian businessman James Nicholson to the University of Toronto. An avid reader, the British-born Nicholson had a penchant for Canadian and English history and was struck by the fact that businessmen had been instrumental in financing similar projects in both the United States and England. The volumes currently in publication focus on people who died between the years 1000 and 1930, with Icelandic explorer Thorfinnr representing one of the earliest subjects treated. The *DCB/DBC* is also freely available via the Web in both French and English and is fully searchable by keyword. Online functionality has inspired continued enhancements to the work, and portraits from Library and Archives Canada are but one feature soon to be added. Advanced searches can also be performed, and biographies can be limited by profession. Currently, over one thousand authors who lived up until 1930 are included in the dictionary. Therefore, the *DCB/DBC* offers an entry for author Bliss Carman (1861–1929); however, the resource has not yet been expanded to incorporate more contemporary figures.

A search of the online *DCB/DBC* for author Susanna Moodie produced no results; however, a search of the print index provided a "see" reference to her maiden name, Strickland. In the online version, therefore, Susanna Moodie can currently only be found through a search of her maiden name, "Strickland, Susanna." These anomalies are likely to be corrected as enhancements, such as "see" references, continue to be added to the online version. Each entry begins with general biographical information, including place of birth, occupation, marital information, offspring, and place and date of death, when known. Informative, well-researched essays offer information that is relevant both on a scholarly level and as a means to satisfy curious inquiry. Reviewers of the work often make reference to the fact that the *DCB/DBC* makes incredible nightstand reading; if one were to read an entire volume, he or she would likely acquire formidable knowledge of both significant and lesser-known personages in Canadian history. Entries are heavily researched and therefore conclude with detailed bibliographies of references. One interesting aspect of this work is that many of the individually authored essays attribute the information to personal interviews with the relatives of the subjects, who often also afforded access to family documents and letters. Since the work examines many obscure figures, some of the essays constitute the best published biographical information on a given subject. Although the *DCB/DBC* is not yet useful for contemporary authors, its in-depth coverage of early Canadian authors is astonishing.

The ***Oxford Dictionary of National Biography*** (***ODNB***) is another biographical resource that affords a fair amount of content on Canadian subjects. Although the title primarily addresses figures from British history, the dictionary also encompasses personages who influenced British history or played a role in the history of the British Isles. What essentially began in 1882 as the *Dictionary of National Biography* (*DNB*) has developed into a sixty-volume work which is now also available in an online format. The current *ODNB* incorporates the *DNB* (1885–1900) and its supplements (1901–1996), with new or revised entries for the subjects addressed in the original version. The print edition is an attractively published set complemented by over ten thousand illustrations from the National Portrait Gallery, which are likewise incorporated into the online format. Searches can be performed using the name of the subject, and a full-text search option is also available. Certainly British-born authors can be found within the *ODNB*, and contributors sometimes hail from Canada, with Canadian librarian Carl Spadoni, for example, writing the essay on Stephen Leacock. Canadian-born writer Robertson Davies enjoys a lengthy entry, citing his "loyalty to the culture of the Commonwealth" and his reception of an honorary doctorate from Oxford University. Entries offer sources for further reading and also provide notes on related archival collections.

Gale's indispensable ***Dictionary of Literary Biography*** (***DLB***) series first began in 1978. Initially focusing on British and American authors, world writers have received treatment in more recent volumes. Canadian volumes cover both English-language authors as well as those whose works are primarily published in French. Notable Canadian literary critic William H. New edits several volumes in the series, including the following: *Canadian Writers before 1890* (vol. 99); *Canadian Writers, 1890–1920* (vol. 92); *Canadian Writers, 1920–1959, First Series* (vol. 68); *Canadian Writers, 1920–1959, Second Series* (vol. 88); *Writers since 1960, First Series* (vol. 53); and *Writers since 1960, Second Series* (vol. 60). Douglas Ivison's 2002 *Canadian Fantasy and Science-Fiction Writers* (vol. 251) was the first Canadian title in the series to stray from New's editorship. The most recent volume on Canadian writers, *Twenty-first-century Canadian Writers* (vol. 334), edited by Christian Riegel, was added to the series in 2007. This volume examines authors who received some level of literary renown between 1989, when the last general volume on Canadian writing in the series was published, and 2007. Authors in volume 334, such as Joy Kogawa, M. NourbeSe Philip, and Rohinton Mistry, testify to the burgeoning multicultural flavor of Canadian literature during this period. The *Dictionary of Literary Biography* includes not only authors of fiction, poetry, and plays, but also historians, journalists, publishers, and screenwriters. In the foreword of each individual volume, the editors allow a good overview of the era to be studied, highlighting historical developments and the literary trends that would influence the authors of the period. Author entries begin with a list of publications followed by a critical essay on the author's life and works. A list of references is also typically provided, however not consistently. Some essays also conclude with information on where an author's papers are housed, as, for example, in the case of folklorist and ethnologist Marius Barbeau (volume 92). Where available, significant bibliographies and biographies of a given author are listed, as well as published collections of their letters. An illustrative feature of the titles in this series is the incorporation of photos of dust jackets from the first editions of an author's work. Other illustrations include photos, paintings, facsimiles, author portraits, title pages, and copies of pages from author manuscripts and notebooks. The *Dictionary of Literary Biography* delivers an engaging and accessible introduction for novice researchers while reinforcing the work of the seasoned literary scholar. Each volume concludes with a supplementary reading list for the period considered, as well as a cumulative index for the series. Since the series currently boasts over 350 volumes, Gale maintains the Literary Index (galenet.com/servlet/LitIndex), a free online tool for author and title searches to identify relevant Gale sources. As with many reference works formerly available only in print, Gale now offers an online version of the *DLB* with full-text searching of the multivolume series.

Covering over 350 authors, ***Canadian Writers/Écrivains canadiens: A Biographical Dictionary*** remains true to Dr. Lorne Pierce's mandate to examine English and French Canadian authors in juxtaposition, recognizing that both play an equal role in the development of Canada's national spirit. The authors go so far as to write a bilingual "Introduction/Avant Propos," which seamlessly shifts from English to French and back again. Preceding the author entries, a "Chronological Table/Tableau chronologique" traces the development of literary journals, the establishment of literary prizes, the publication of notable titles and critical works, and cultural milestones in Canadian literature between 1606 and 1965. Brief author biographies comprise the bulk of the work and are formatted to include place of birth, educational information, notable works and critical reception, and relevant awards. Entries conclude with a list of selected reviews, where applicable. Biographical essays are written in either English or French, according to an author's primary language of publication. Due to the brevity of the entries, this work may have limited applications and is best used in conjunction with other biographical sources.

Updating the *Dictionnaire pratique des auteurs québécois* (1976), Hamel, Hare, and Wyczynski extend the scope of their study in the ***Dictionnaire des auteurs de langue française en Amérique du Nord***. The expanded work addresses over 1,600 authors from the United States and Canada and examines literature through 1986. This volume is unique in its attempt to cover French authors of the Americas, including Acadian, Franco-Manitoban, Franco-Ontarian, Louisianan, and French-American writers. Subscribing to a broad definition of the term "author," the editors examine those writers whose works contribute to the enrichment of the culture and civilization of the French-speaking Americas. Included therefore are not only novelists, poets, playwrights, journalists, and essayists, but also storytellers, songwriters, historians, bibliographers, literary scholars, biographers, and many other brands of literary craftspeople who have published at least one written work. Essays offer detailed biographical information based on input, wherever possible, from the authors themselves. Each entry concludes both with a list of works by, and studies about, the author. Hamel, Hare, and Wyczynski's resulting effort is a singular work, culling otherwise disparate information into a fine literary reference source.

Gamila Morcos's ***Dictionnaire des artistes et des auteurs francophones de l'Ouest canadien*** is a collection of four hundred bio-bibliographic entries examining French authors, scholars, and artists of the Canadian West. This resource is not limited to authors of creative works but also encompasses writers publishing in a variety of disciplines. Seven years in the making, Morcos enlisted the assistance of several collaborators in the production of this reference source, including members of the University of Alberta's Faculté Saint-Jean. This title represents an impressive study of an otherwise neglected area.

## HISTORIES AND CHRONOLOGIES

Blodgett, E. D. *Five Part Invention: A History of Literary History in Canada*. Toronto: University of Toronto Press, 2003.

Edwards, Gail, and Judith Saltman. *Picturing Canada: A History of Canadian Children's Illustrated Books and Publishing*. Toronto: University of Toronto Press, 2010. See www.canadianchildlit.ca (accessed 12 July 2010).

Fleming, Patricia Lockhart, and Yvan LaMonde, general eds. *History of the Book in Canada/Histoire du livre et de l'imprime au Canada*. 3 vols. Toronto: University of Toronto Press, 2004. See www.hbic.library.utoronto.ca/ (accessed 25 June 2010).

Howells, Coral Ann, and Eva-Marie Kröller. *The Cambridge History of Canadian Literature*. New York: Cambridge University Press, 2009.

New, W. H., ed. *A History of Canadian Literature*. 2nd ed. Toronto: McGill-Queen's University Press, 2003.

Nischik, Reingard M., ed. *History of Literature in Canada: English-Canadian and French-Canadian*. Rochester, NY: Camden House, 2008.

In ***Five Part Invention: A History of Literary History in Canada***, E. D. Blodgett does a marvelous job of attending to Canadian literary history from its various contexts, including francophone, First Nations, Inuit, and ethnic literatures. A chronological list of Canada's published literary histories, beginning with Edward Hartley Dewart's *Selections from Canadian Poets* (1864) and Edmond Lareau's *Histoire de la littérature canadienne* (1874), complements Blodgett's laudable contribution.

While there have been several notable histories published, the most detailed addition to the bibliography of Canadian literary history is the three-volume ***History of the Book in Canada/Histoire du livre et de l'imprime au Canada***. A truly collaborative project involving several Canadian universities, as well as funding from the Social Sciences and Humanities Research Council of Canada, this work is published and available in both French and English. Each volume begins with a chronology of the period covered, and each individually authored essay is heavily researched. Volume 1, *Beginnings to 1840*, considers the genesis of literary culture in Canada initiated by Native oral traditions and inscriptions. Volume 2 examines the period between 1840 and 1918, with essays tracing the development of Canadian publishing, authorship, libraries, book distribution, and print communities, as well as readers and reading. Essays cover a seemingly infinitesimal range of topics relating to the history of the book, as volume 2 includes such chapters as "Print and Black Canadian Culture," "The Mounted Police in Print," and "Reading Practices in Quebec," among others. The development of Canadian periodical literature during this period is well examined within chapter 9, "Serials," with essays such as "The Illustrated Satiric Press," "Yiddish Dailies," and "Popular Magazines in French." The further emergence and development of the Canadian book industry is examined in volume 3, covering the period from 1918 to 1980. As the editors explain, sections in this volume incorporate an article on the Canadian government's impact on the country's print culture. Each volume begins with the editors' introduction, highlighting major historical, political, and cultural developments affecting the literary culture of the period. Contributions are drawn from seasoned researchers (such as William H. New, who pens the article "Read Canadian"), as well as up-and-coming literary scholars from institutions across Canada. As with the *Dictionary of Canadian Biography*, large-scale projects such as this have benefited from funding by the Canadian government toward the development of online content. Dalhousie University currently hosts the site providing access to no fewer than five databases associated with this project. The series truly contains something for everyone, such as coverage of children's book publishing and authorship, the cultural press and books in native languages, as well as newspaper and magazine publishing. A work of astonishing scope, detail, and depth, it is accessible for both book history aficionados and researchers seeking a richer view of Canadian literary history.

Nischik's ***History of Literature in Canada: English-Canadian and French-Canadian*** is a well-devised work. Though self-proclaimed as "the second literary history of Canada by an American publisher" (7), contributors hail from Canada, Australia, France, and Germany. Two of the essays appearing in the work were originally written in French by Quebec scholars and were then subsequently translated for the publication. Nischik's stated aim of the work is to offer researchers a treatment of both English- and French-language titles from an international perspective in order to facilitate comparison while comprehensively covering Canada's literatures. Nischik provides a well-thought-out history of Canadian literature in the introduction, examining significant movements, writers, and events, while weaving both English- and French-language authors into his essay. The work is divided into six sections, entitled "Beginnings"; "The Literature of New France, 1604–1760"; "The Literature of British Canada, 1763–1867"; "From Dominion to the Territorial Completion of the Nation, 1867–1918"; "The Modern Period, 1918–1967"; and "Literature from 1967 to the Present." Among the contributed chapters are "Aboriginal Oral Traditions" by Eva Gruber, "Canons of Diversity in Contemporary English-Canadian Literature," by Georgina Banita, "Orality and the French-Canadian Chanson," by Ursula Mathis-Moser, and "Transculturalism and *écritures migrantes*" by Gilles Dupuis. Through thirty-five essays each focusing on a particular genre, period, or theme, this title delivers a well-rounded and up-to-date perspective on the interplay of English and French Canadian literary history.

William H. New's second edition of ***A History of Canadian Literature*** picks up where the 1989 edition left off, with the addition of the chapter "Reconstructors: Literature into the Twenty-first Century." Although New's histories have been criticized for being overly inclusive of lesser-known authors, with limited attention to more canonical figures, the author's impartial clarity provides the reader with an informed view of Canadian literary development. Organized by period into six chapters, each section begins with information on historical, political, and cultural developments of the era. Although the work is sometimes short on details, through his intimate familiarity with the Canadian literary scene, New succeeds in delivering Canada's literary history in a manner that no other person could likely replicate.

***The Cambridge History of Canadian Literature*** represents the first Cambridge volume exclusively dedicated to the literary production of Canada. Thirty-one information-rich contributions trace Canadian literary history from its origins to contemporary genres and concerns. Part 1, "Old and New World, La Nouvelle-France, the Canadas, Dominion of Canada," guides the reader through the complexities of discovery and the colonial period, examining settler narratives, explorer accounts, the Jesuit *Relations*, and the early contributions of Thomas Chandler Haliburton, Julia Catherine Beckwith Hart, and Frances Brooke. Other sections include "The Post-Confederation Period" (part 2); "Models of Modernity, Post–First World War" (part 3); and "Aesthetic Experiments, 1960 and After" (part 4). French Canadian literature is discussed in part five, "Writing in French," with three essays separately focusing on poetry, fiction, and drama. The editors have assembled a dream team of Canadian literary scholars, such as Réjean Beaudoin, Janice

Fiamengo, Gerald Lynch, E. D. Blodgett, Adrian Fowler, W. H. New, Carole Gerson, Marta Dvorak, and more. As the editors explain in their introduction, Canadian literature's first treatment within a Cambridge *History* was in 1917, when "a modest twenty-page chapter entitled 'English-Canadian Literature'" (1) was incorporated into *The Cambridge History of English Literature*. Additional essays include "Comic Art," "Ghost Stories," "Indigenous Writing," "Contemporary Aboriginal Theater," "Transcultural Life-Writing," and "Multiculturalism and Globalization" to round out a literary history that is logically arranged and accessible to all.

Gail Edwards and Judith Saltman's ***Picturing Canada: A History of Canadian Children's Illustrated Books and Publishing*** marks a fine addition to scholarship on the topic. Commencing with a chronology for 1846 to 2009, individual chapters examine the children's book industry by period, with a final chapter entitled "Canadian Cultural Identity, Canadian Cultural Identities." Exhaustively researched, the work incorporates extensive notes and is enhanced by a thorough bibliography. In their acknowledgments, Edwards and Saltman allude to having conducted 136 interviews during the course of their research, resulting in a singular work crafted through primary research. With the help of graduate research assistants at the University of British Columbia, the authors have developed a website for their project which features a database of short-listed and award-winning illustrated titles.

## INDIVIDUAL AUTHOR SOURCES

Cooke, Nathalie. *Margaret Atwood: A Critical Companion*. Westport, CT: Greenwood Press, 2004.

Hengen, Shannon, and Ashley Thomson. *Margaret Atwood: A Reference Guide, 1988–2005*. Lanham, MD: Scarecrow Press, 2007.

Howells, Coral Ann, ed. *The Cambridge Companion to Margaret Atwood*. New York: Cambridge University Press, 2006. Also available through Cambridge Collections Online, www.cco.cambridge.org.

Magill, Frank N., ed. *Masterpieces of Women's Literature*. New York: HarperCollins, 1996.

New, William H. *Malcolm Lowry: A Reference Guide*. Boston: G. K. Hall, 1978.

A useful volume for researchers embarking on an in-depth study of Margaret Atwood can be found in ***The Cambridge Companion to Margaret Atwood***, edited by Coral Ann Howells. Twelve individually authored essays, including one by Howells, examine the range of Atwood's literary register and celebrity in this, the only title in the Cambridge Companion series dedicated to a Canadian author. An international body of contributors, hailing from France, Germany, England, Italy, India, the United States, and Canada, offer the reader a global perspective on Atwood studies. Introductory material features a chronology of the prolific writer's life and works. This title offers the reader a rich view of Atwood's literary flexibility: as a canonical writer, journalist, literary critic, entertainer, and satirist.

Part of the Critical Companions to Popular Contemporary Writers series, Nathalie Cooke's ***Margaret Atwood: A Critical Companion*** is written for a broad range of Atwood aficionados, addressing both scholars and fans. Although perhaps more elementary in appeal than the above-mentioned Cambridge Companion, Cooke does incorporate six chapters that deal directly with Atwood's fiction, including *The Edible Woman*, *Surfacing*, *Lady Oracle*, *Cat's Eye*, *The Handmaid's Tale*, and *The Blind Assassin*. Cooke offers an extensive bibliography of published criticism and interviews pertaining to the works covered in this volume.

Organized chronologically by year, Hengen and Thomson's ***Margaret Atwood: A Reference Guide, 1988–2005*** is a thorough resource on the writer and her efforts, as the authors scour the unimaginable nooks and crannies of Atwood's output and treatment. Atwood's works, adaptations of her publications, quotations, interviews, scholarly resources, and reviews are annotated where applicable for a given year. Useful supplemental material includes an Atwood chronology and both an author and a subject index. The chapter entitled "Margaret Atwood on the Web" by Alain Lamothe offers detailed description and analysis of Internet content related to the celebrated author. This section should provide researchers with an interesting retrospective assessment of Atwood's Web coverage in the years to come.

A companion volume to *Masterpieces of World Literature* and other Masterpieces titles edited by the prolific Frank Magill, ***Masterpieces of Women's Literature*** contains 175 articles on the canonical works of female writers. Margaret Atwood is the only Canadian author found within this volume; however, three of her novels, *A Handmaid's Tale* (1986), *The Edible Woman* (1969), and *Surfacing* (1972), are among the fictional works covered. Each individually authored essay for these novels includes a list of principal characters and examines the works in the following sections: "Form and Content," "Analysis," "Context," and "Sources for Further Study." Atwood receives adequate treatment, as the essays raise critical issues while positioning her works within their social, historical, and political contexts. The annotated list of "Sources for Further Study" guides the researcher toward books and articles that directly complement the specific works discussed, versus more general author sources.

While it may be controversial to categorize Malcolm Lowry as a Canadian author, William H. New's ***Malcolm Lowry: A Reference Guide*** should be mentioned. The fact that a prominent Canadian literary researcher such as New took to the painstaking task of compiling this work testifies to Lowry's intimate ties with Canada. It is not surprising that a figure as complex as Lowry is difficult to define, and in his introduction, New details the many and mutable literary allegiances that Lowry made to Canada, the United States, and Britain throughout the course of his career.[2] As New explains, Lowry's most noted works, for example, *Under the Volcano*, were written while he lived in a small cabin at Dollarton, British Columbia. True to his usual clarity and authenticity, New provides a well-written survey of Lowry and his works as he attempts to explain some of the ambiguities behind the writer's reception. While the bulk of the materials fall under "Writings about Malcolm Lowry, 1927–1976," other sections include "Manuscript Collections," "Major Writings by Malcolm Lowry," and "Translations of Lowry's Major Writings." Under "Writings about Malcolm Lowry, 1927–1976," New lists Anthony Robertson's review of New's own *Malcolm Lowry*, which raises the controversy of applying and asserting assumptions of Canadianness to authors with dubious affiliations to Canada. New annotates Robertson's review as follows: "A critique of the book, claiming that Lowry is not a Canadian writer" (100). An examination of Robertson's review reveals that Canada's claims to Lowry are met with vehement opposition by some literary researchers. Robertson, for example, categorizes such claims as "cultural headhunting"[3] and concludes with the following statement: "Lowry's writing is not the stuff of which Canadian Writers series are made."[4] While Robertson's statements open wide the debate on Canadian identity, New's work is nonetheless a striking guide to an author who undoubtedly had intimate ties to Canada.

## CONCLUSION

The works discussed in this section provide you with heavily evaluated background information and inspire further avenues for your own inquiry. Though most of the sources found in this chapter are typical of those found in a library reference area and may therefore be noncirculating, they can be easily consulted. As you become grounded in your topic, these works can assist you in developing a broader sense of Canadian literature, its relationship to other national literatures, and its place in a global literary context. Critical materials published abroad offer insight into how Canadian authors are received and perceived outside of Canada. Chapter 3 will assist you in identifying individual titles to inform your research.

## NOTES

1. Doug Fetherling, review of *Canadian Literary Landmarks*, by John Robert Colombo, *Quill and Quire* 51 (January 1985): 22.
2. See page xi of William H. New's *Malcolm Lowry: A Reference Guide* for a chronology of Lowry's proclaimed literary affiliations.
3. Anthony Robertson, *West Coast Review* 7, no. 1 (June 1972): 57.
4. Robertson, *West Coast Review*, 57.

*Chapter Three*

# Library Catalogs

The purpose of this chapter is to discuss strategies and steps for identifying material relevant to your research through a library catalog. As time passes, people are less likely to have witnessed the era when libraries relied on card catalogs, drawers of paper records providing access to and describing library materials. Library patrons were quite limited in their searching options by these manual systems, and most books could only be located by author, subject, or title. Today, online systems allow for keyword searching of the millions of items in a university library collection, expediting our access to research and discovery. An online library catalog presents an interface for searching a library's full collection of materials, which today may include a range of formats, from e-books and DVDs to microform, mp3s, and even websites.

Library catalogs are often referred to as online public access catalogs, or OPACs, and usually also carry a name designated by the institution. For example, the Yale library refers to their OPAC as *Orbis*, while the University of Manitoba online catalog reflects the institution's mascot and carries the name *BISON*. Although library catalogs vary in design, name, and interface, the underlying principles for searching are fairly consistent.

In the face of shrinking library budgets and amid inflationary material costs, many libraries today are taking advantage of consortial alliances. Alliances allow libraries to share items from their circulating collections across geographic and institutional boundaries. Library consortiums can inform the selection of materials between institutions, and in some cases libraries are able to obtain consortial pricing of journals and database subscriptions through their membership. The University of Alberta, for example, belongs to the NEOS library consortium, which currently includes a mix of academic, medical, government, and public libraries.

Although there are some exceptions, libraries in Canada, the United States, and the United Kingdom each apply similar cataloging standards to ensure that consistent strategies and rules can be used to search any library catalog. Most libraries employ Library of Congress subject headings (LCSH), which promote the use of a standardized vocabulary across libraries and provide a list of subject headings for libraries to refer to when a new item is integrated into the library system. Catalogers who create the book records used in library catalogs may consult and even download records from the Library of Congress website.

While Library of Congress subject headings are the most commonly applied, Library and Archives Canada (LAC) maintains separate subject headings to describe documents and materials related specifically to Canadian culture, history, politics, economics, literature, and society. Canadian subject headings (CSH) are now only updated through CSH on the Web; however, the Bibliothèque de l'Université Laval does maintain a subscription-based French equivalent in Répertoire de vedettes-matière (RVM), now online as RVM Web (https://rvmweb.bibl.ulaval.ca). For the most part, the CSH are based on the published *Library of Congress Subject Headings*, with some variation to account for geographic, historical, governmental, cultural, and economic differences. Some people feel that subject headings are intensely reflective of a country's orientation toward a particular subject or group. For example, Library of Congress subject headings generally use the term *foreign speakers* to describe language learners, whereas Canadian subject headings more commonly employ the term *second language learners*.

There has been much discussion lately surrounding the concern that Library of Congress subject headings are Anglocentric, describing ethnic groups, issues, and historical events from a majority perspective. One critique of Library of Congress subject headings as they are applied to Native peoples is that they are outdated and inadequately represent indigenous communities. The Library of Congress uses *Indians of North America* as a standard subject heading for Native groups of North America. However, this designation is controversial, as some argue that it is not reflective of the terms used by indigenous groups to describe themselves. In an attempt to employ inclusive language, Library and Archives Canada has considered other terminology, including *First Nations*, *Native Peoples of Canada*, and *Aboriginal Peoples*. Canadian libraries run the risk of compromising the integrity of their library catalogs when LCSH and CSH differ for similar concepts. Consensus has not therefore been reached by the members of Canadian library associations regarding how to effectively deal with LCSH shortcomings in the terminology used to describe the Native peoples of Canada. For researchers using library catalogs in the United States, Library of Congress subject headings should be adhered to when performing a catalog subject search in order to ensure relevant results.

In the 1970s, a First Nations librarian and cataloger, Brian Deer, modified some areas of the Library of Congress system in order to provide a better foundation for describing indigenous issues, concerns, groups, history, and culture at the library where he worked. While Brian Deer's classification system was designed specifically for one site, other Canadian libraries with predominantly First Nations materials find the system useful in reflecting indigenous subjects. The Xwi7xwa Library at the University of British Columbia's First Nations House of Learning currently employs the Brian Deer Classification System to ensure that First Nations materials in the library's collections are adequately described and represented. Below are three author headings for First Nations author and actor Chief Dan George found within the University of British Columbia catalog. The first is the standard Library of Congress subject heading, the second heading reflects his title as chief of the Tsleil-Waututh nation, and the third includes his tribal affiliation with the same:

George, Dan, 1899–1981
George, Dan—Chief
George, Dan, (Tsleil-Waututh), 1899–1981

While the Library of Congress system generally uses one official authority heading, with "see" references to guide users away from variations, the above examples are illustrative of how an authority record may be modified for the purpose of a given library or site.

## EMERGING CATALOGS AND WEB 2.0 FUNCTIONALITY

Inspired perhaps by the popularity, interactivity, and functionality of online bookstores, many library consortiums are opting for a more seamless model of searching. Dalhousie currently uses the *WorldCat Local* interface, which facilitates simultaneous searching of local holdings, the holdings of the Novanet consortium to which Dalhousie belongs, as well as the *WorldCat* union catalog, which displays worldwide holdings of library books. The main search screen for the *WorldCat Local* interface is similar to the streamlined search box that you might find in a search engine, such as Google. The simple search interface considers books, articles, and Web content simultaneously, saving the user time that would have been spent using the library catalog and a variety of individual databases to locate information on a given topic.

Another new feature of many library catalog interfaces is the incorporation of instant-messaging widgets to facilitate contact with a librarian. This can be particularly useful if you are accessing the catalog from outside the library and are encountering difficulty with a given search. Though still in the experimental stages, libraries are taking advantage of social networking models and Web 2.0 technologies, for example, allowing users to apply tags to items in the library catalog. While tagging library items may seem controversial to those who consider Library of Congress subject headings to be the industry standard, a new generation of library patrons is inspiring shifts that are perhaps as controversial as the move from the manual card catalog to online systems.

Even as libraries adopt the one-search-box streamlined search interface, library catalogers who describe books for library users continue to rely on standards, such as the Library of Congress Authorities, to manage and organize library materials from behind the scenes. Although many academic library home pages offer the simple search interface, if you prefer to do a traditional search you may still be able to find a link to the local library catalog on the library home page. Traditional online library catalogs commonly offer not only field searches by author, title, or subject, but also allow full-text searching of library records through the keyword search. When you know a library's collection fairly well, you wish to limit your search to a particular format, and you expect to find a particular item in the library, the traditional search interface may still be the most efficient option.

## CATALOG SEARCH OPTIONS

Although library catalogs vary in appearance, design, and how searches are sorted and interpreted, the search information below should be applicable to most settings. Since differences exist between library catalogs, it can be useful to consult the catalog search tips before conducting a search. You may see either a help link or a search tips link from the catalog home page. These tip files should assist you in answering the following questions:

- How are the results sorted? By relevance, date, title, author? Are there options for changing how the results are displayed?
- Should phrases be placed in quotation marks?
- What symbol is recognized as the wildcard? Can search terms be truncated?
- Can Boolean operators be used? If so, should they be in uppercase letters?
- Are proximity searches possible? If so, which proximity operators are recognized, and how should proximity searches be constructed?

- What are some of the search limiters that may be applied? Location, format, language, year of publication, what else?

Many catalogs also offer the ability to limit your search results by format, including journals, electronic resources, and media materials. You may also be able to limit your results by language, publication year, and location. Depending on your search needs, limiting options can be very useful for narrowing your search.

## THE KEYWORD SEARCH

As addressed in chapter 1, keyword searches offer the most flexible search capability; however, they can also have their drawbacks. Since keyword searches are not based on standardized language, they are generally less precise than other search options and may be misinterpreted by the catalog. When a keyword search returns unanticipated results, these results are referred to as "false drops." An example of this would be if you did a keyword search for *L. M. Montgomery*, and the search returned an item on the *Montgomery* G.I. Bill, written by *L. M.* Russell. Another example of a false drop based on the *L. M. Montgomery* keyword search is illustrated in figure 3.1. Nevertheless, keyword searches are particularly useful when your query involves new terms and concepts, or if you are searching for something that is very specific.

KEYWORD | l.m. montgomery | View Entire Collection | Search

Did you mean lm montgomery? More Options »

38 results found. Sorted by **relevance** | date | title .

Result page:

**Title** **Magnesium [by] L. M. Pidgeon, J. C. Mathes, N. E. Woldman [and others] ... A series of five educational lectures on magnesium presented to members of the A.S.M. during the twenty-seventh national metal congress and exposition, Cleveland, February 4 to 8, 1946.**

**Imprint** [Cleveland, 1946]

| LOCATION | CALL NUMBER | STATUS |
|---|---|---|
| WSU Owen Dewey | 622.8 M274 | ON SHELF |

**Description** 2 p.l., 265 p. illus., diagrs. 24 cm.

**Bibliog.** Includes "References."

**Subject** Magnesium.

**Other Author** Pidgeon, L. M. (Lloyd Montgomery), 1903-1999.
American Society for Metals.

**Figure 3.1. Modified catalog record from the Washington State University Catalog illustrating a false drop resulting from a keyword search for *L. M. Montgomery*. Source: Washington State University Libraries Catalog.**

## AUTHOR SEARCHES AND EVALUATING RESULTS

An author search is the most straightforward method of searching when you know the name of the author. Since an author's name may vary, the Library of Congress maintains authority files to assist librarians in both Canada and the United States in selecting an authorized form of a name for a given author. The application of authority files, sometimes referred to as "authority control," helps to ensure that a standard author heading is used across libraries. Author names provide a good example of why authority control is important, as an author may undergo a name change, publish under a pseudonym, or use an abbreviated form of their full name for publishing purposes. If each library determined their own authority headings, searching would likely be chaotic, haphazard, and confusing, as a variety of name forms could potentially exist for a given author. The Library of Congress authority files guide users to the name applied by the Library of Congress for identifying a given author. In authority headings, authors' names are generally followed by their dates, which is particularly helpful in identifying the correct author when several authors have similar, or even the same, names.

Author searches should be constructed by typing the author's last name first. Despite the fact that an author may have published materials under several variations of their name, Library of Congress authority files will guide the user to the authorized name used in the library catalog. For example, if you were to do an author field search for *Montgomery, Lucy Maud*, the catalog may return a "see" reference directing you to the authority heading for the author, such as the following:

*Montgomery Lucy Maud 1874 1942*—See: Montgomery, L. M. (Lucy Maud), 1874–1942

Similarly, a search for *Emile Coderre* in the catalog will provide a "see" reference to the author's pen name, *Jean Narrache*, which is used as the authoritative Library of Congress heading:

*Coderre, Emile, 1893–1970*—See: Narrache, Jean, 1893–1970

Below are some additional examples of Library of Congress authority headings for Canadian authors:

Haliburton, Thomas Chandler, 1796–1865
Hart, Julia Catherine Beckwith, 1796–1867
McClung, Nellie L., 1873–1951

Nelligan, Émile, 1879–1941
Niven, Frederick, 1878–1944
Roy, Gabrielle, 1909–1983

Authority headings must be periodically updated, a process which is facilitated today by automation. Headings that do not include a date of death for an author known to be deceased were likely created before the author died. In such cases, it could be that these have not been revised, a common issue given the cost and intensity of updating library catalogs.

Corporate authors may also be located through an author field search. For example, if you were to search for the *Canadian Association of Journalists* or the *Canadian Authors' Association* as an author search, the results would include all of the published materials for which the organization assumes responsibility. Another example would be to search for the *National Film Board of Canada* in the author field in order to retrieve a list of your library's National Film Board (NFB) holdings, as illustrated in figure 3.2.

## LOCATING THE ELUSIVE AUTHOR

There are cases where an authority heading does not exist for a given author. New authors, headings for female and minority authors, and noncanonical authors may not have a consistent heading. If an author's work has only

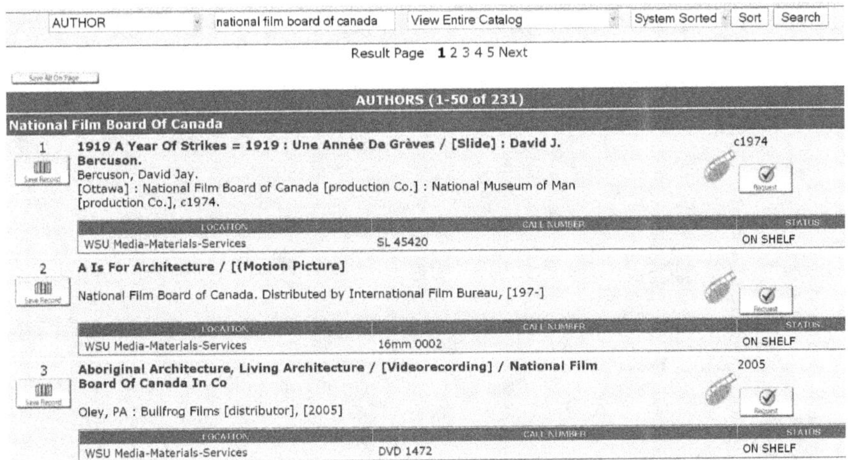


**Figure 3.2. Modified catalog results of an author search for *National Film Board of Canada*. Source: Washington State University Libraries Catalog.**

appeared in an anthology, which is common for authors of short stories, there may not be an authority heading for the author. Since authority headings clarify who is responsible for an item, this responsibility is often granted to the editor of the work in the case of anthologies. As works by new authors often appear within anthologies, performing a keyword search for your author may be more effective than doing an author field search. Another useful strategy would be to use the search terms *anthology* and *Canadian* as a keyword search, in combination with a third concept that is reflective of the author you are researching, such as *contemporary*, *women*, or *First Nations*, in order to direct you to anthologies that may contain the works of your writer. For example, a simple search using the terms *anthology*, *Canadian*, *poetry*, and *Asian* yields the title *Green Snow: Anthology of Canadian Poets of Asian Origin*, edited by Stephen Gill (figure 3.3). Since the catalog record for this item does not provide the names of the individual authors in the anthology, the item will have to be retrieved from the shelves and examined in order to confirm the appearance of a given author. In this case, a search for a specific poet included in the anthology would not have retrieved this title, as the catalog record did not incorporate this information.

As stated previously, searching is in many ways a conversation between you and the database, often mediated by an interface in the form of a search engine. When conducting an author search, note the authority heading used in the catalog. Once you have this information, if you do not seem to be able to locate a given work, or if you feel some of the author's works are missing from the results, try performing the search again, using the author's name as a keyword. If several editions of an author's work appear, closer examination of each item's publication information may prove useful in guiding you to the one that best meets your research needs. Oftentimes, a catalog search is only the first step, as items in the catalog are based on the cataloger's description. In retrieving material, whether physically from the library stacks or virtually

**Title** **Green snow : anthology of Canadian poets of Asian origin / edited, with an introd. by Stephen Gill.**
**Imprint** Cornwall, Ont. : Vesta Publications, 1976.

| LOCATION | CALL NUMBER | STATUS |
|---|---|---|
| WSU Holland & Terrell | PR9195.35.A8 G7 | ON SHELF |

**Description** 120 p. ; 21 cm.
**Subject** Canadian poetry -- Asian authors.
Canadian poetry -- 20th century.
**Other Author** Gill, Stephen M.
**ISBN** 0919806074 : $5.00
**Misc No** WSU000267888

**Figure 3.3. Modified catalog record returned on a keyword search for *anthology, Canadian, poetry,* and *Asian.* Source: Washington State University Libraries Catalog.**

as an e-book, you may discover information to further assist you in determining whether the item is in fact relevant to your research.

## TITLE SEARCHES

Just as with an author search, a title search is the most efficient search option when you know the exact title of a work. In the case of older works, a title may have undergone several title changes over time. For example, Thomas Chandler Haliburton's Clockmaker sketches were originally serialized between 1835 and 1836 in *The Nova Scotian*, a Halifax newspaper. The sketches have since been collected and published in various editions with the words "The Clockmaker" included in some variation of the title. The edition that is best for your needs will be determined by whether you are seeking the latest edition; an edition that more closely resembles the work at the time it was first published; a European, Canadian, or American edition; or perhaps an edition accompanied by critical material. For some works published more than fifty years ago, older editions may also be freely available online through *Google Books* and other such services. A search of *Google Books* reveals an 1848 printing of Haliburton's work held at the Bodleian Library, fully digitized with the following title appearing on the title page: *The Clockmaker; or, The Sayings and Doings of Samuel Slick, of Slickville.*

A *WorldCat* search for *As for Me and My House* by Sinclair Ross is illustrative of the variety of results you might obtain from doing a title field search. As seen in figure 3.4, the results of a title phrase search not only include Ross's work but also find the false drop *As for Me and My House: Crafting Your Marriage to Last*, by Walter Wangerin. Among the results pertaining to Ross's work, however, are collections of critical essays, a reader's guide, and various editions of the work published over the years. These additional results may actually be useful in helping you to identify further critical materials, surveys, and editions.

If you find that a title search returns too many irrelevant hits, you may try typing the title in quotations. As stated earlier, each library catalog interprets and sorts a search in a different way. Without quotations, a title search for *As for Me and My House* in the University of Manitoba's *BISON* catalog likewise returns the false drop *My House Is Killing Me!: The Home Guide for Families with Allergies and Asthma.* Before using quotations in your search, however, make sure that the catalog supports phrase searching. By repeating the above search as a phrase in the *BISON* catalog, fewer false drops were returned, along with critical editions, a contemporary edition, and a 1941 first edition of Ross's work.

**As for me and my house :**
crafting your marriage to last /

Walter Wangerin

1987
English Book 252 p. ; 24 cm.
Nashville : T. Nelson, ; ISBN: 0840754752 : 9780840754752

GET THIS ITEM

Availability: **Check the catalogs in your library.**
- Libraries worldwide that own item: 452
- Search the catalog at Washington State University Libraries

External Resources:
- Find It! at WSU Libraries
- Cite This Item

FIND RELATED

More Like This: Search for versions with same title and author | Advanced options ...

Find Items About: As for me and my house (20); Wangerin, Walter. (17)

Title: **As for me and my house : crafting your marriage to last /**

Author(s): Wangerin, Walter.

Publication: Nashville : T. Nelson,

Year: 1987

Description: 252 p. ; 24 cm.

Language: English

Standard No: ISBN: 0840754752 :; 9780840754752 LCCN: 87-5724

SUBJECT(S)

Descriptor: Marriage -- Religious aspects -- Christianity.

**Figure 3.4.** ***WorldCat*** **record for the false drop** ***As for Me and My House: Crafting Your Marriage to Last,*** **by Walter Wangerin. Source:** ***WorldCat.***

## SUBJECT SEARCHES

Subject searches help you to identify works on a given author, literary period, or theme. If you use the author's name as a subject search, the catalog may provide you with a list of works about the author, including criticism, biographies, autobiographies, anthologies, manuscripts, and papers. Using author Robert Kroetsch as an example, an author-as-subject search finds the author's name followed by subheadings to describe additional related areas of research.

Kroetsch, Robert, 1927–, Characters
Kroetsch, Robert, 1927–, Criticism and interpretation
Kroetsch, Robert, 1927–, Diaries
Kroetsch, Robert, 1927–, Interviews

Subject searches can also be helpful for identifying journals related to a given topic. By using limiting options available through your catalog's search interface, you can do a keyword search for *Canadian literature* and limit the results to journals for an indication of the related serials available through your institution. As you become familiar with your topic, it is unlikely that you will automatically know the exact terminology and construction of the Library of Congress subject headings that would apply to your searches. You might want to start by conducting several keyword searches first, noting the subject headings in the records of items that are relevant, and using them to link to further items that also carry the same subject headings.

Below are some examples of Library of Congress subject headings related to Canadian literary research:

Canadian literature—Inuit authors
Canadian literature—Prairie Provinces—History and criticism
Canadian literature—Ukrainian authors—History and criticism
Canadian fiction—20th century—History and criticism
Art and literature—Canada—History—20th century
National characteristics, Canadian, in literature
French-Canadians in literature
Authors, Canadian—20th century—Interviews
Authors, Canadian—19th century—Biography
Canadian drama—Stories, plots, etc.
Canadian poetry—American influences
Censorship—Canada

## UNION CATALOGS

*WorldCat*. Dublin, OH: OCLC. www.oclc.org/firstsearch.
*WorldCat.org*. Dublin, OH: OCLC. www.worldcat.org.

Currently, the most familiar acronym in Canadian, U.S., and British libraries is arguably OCLC (Online Computer Library Center), a nonprofit, cooperative organization which began in 1967, at the onset of the computer revolution. OCLC's ***WorldCat*** union catalog is updated and maintained by OCLC member institutions. This cooperative model allows libraries to share cataloging information, therefore maintaining common standards for library records, which in the end facilitates access for the user. With over 71,000 member libraries in 112 countries, OCLC currently boasts the world's largest library consortium. While library users may traditionally consult their local catalog for initial searches and then move to a union catalog in order to obtain a broader picture of books available through libraries worldwide, the *WorldCat Local* interface offers a more seamless searching environment. As stated earlier, the *WorldCat Local* interface allows users to view their local library holdings, the holdings of consortial catalogs, and the holdings of all *WorldCat* member libraries.

***WorldCat.org*** is an initiative that allows for searching of *WorldCat* records by users operating outside both physical and virtual library environments. Freely accessible via the Web, users can choose whether to perform their searches through a simple or an advanced Web interface. When search results are displayed, Web users can locate the owning library in closest proximity to them by entering their postal code. Users should be cautioned that only libraries who subscribe to *WorldCat* will be listed in the holdings. Partnerships with Google and social networking sites have afforded many enhancements to *WorldCat.org* content, including mobile phone applications. The ability to preview book titles found in *WorldCat* is available through a *Google Books* widget, and Amazon.com user reviews are likewise incorporated when available. A "cite this item" feature allows for the delivery of bibliographic citations in APA, Chicago, Harvard, Turabian, and MLA styles. Users can benefit from social networking enhancements, such as a *WorldCat* application for performing searches from within Facebook.

## NATIONAL CATALOGS AND PORTALS

*AMICUS: Canadian National Catalogue*. www.collectionscanada.gc.ca/amicus (accessed 30 June 2010).

Bibliothèque nationale de France. *Catalogue général*. http://catalogue.bnf.fr (accessed 30 June 2010).

British Library. *Integrated Catalogue*. www.bl.uk (accessed 30 June 2010).

Library of Congress. *Library of Congress Online Catalog*. http://catalog.loc.gov (accessed 30 June 2010).

*Theses Canada Portal*. www.collectionscanada.gc.ca/thesescanada/index-e.html (accessed 30 June 2010).

Charged with preserving Canada's documentary heritage through the Library and Archives of Canada Act, Library and Archives Canada promotes access to the nation's published works and archival materials, as well as electronic files and media. Library and Archives Canada boasts a suite of searchable databases and online collections that offer powerful resources for Canadian literary research. As part of Library and Archives Canada's collection of online resources, ***AMICUS: Canadian National Catalogue*** delivers over thirty million records from both Library and Archives Canada holdings, as well as the holdings of hundreds of libraries across the country. *AMICUS* holdings include monographs, magazines, newspapers, government documents, theses, sound recordings, maps, websites, and electronic sources. Providing both a basic- and advanced-search interface, items can be limited by format, publication date, language, target audience, and publication type. Browsing by subject allows you to see and compare the three subject heading systems incorporated within the database, including the Library of Congress subject headings (LCSH), Canadian subject headings (CSH), and Répertoire de vedettes-matière (RVM). Below are three examples of LCSH and CSH subject headings from *AMICUS* catalog searches and their RVM equivalents:

Example 1:
First Nations Confederacy—Periodicals (LCSH)
First Nations Confederacy—Périodiques (RVM)

Example 2:
Native youth—Canada—Poetry (CSH)
Jeunesse autochtone—Canada—Poésie (RVM)

Example 3:
Canadian literature (English)—Native authors (CSH)
Littérature canadienne-anglaise—Auteurs autochtones (RVM)

An *AMICUS* record (figure 3.5) further demonstrates the incorporation of LCSH, CSH, and RVM within the catalog.

The ***Theses Canada Portal*** is indicative of the Canadian government's efforts to promote and preserve the works of Canadian authors and researchers as they strive to acquire and provide access to Canadian theses and dissertations. Library and Archives Canada's *Theses Canada Portal* offers a separate search interface from the *AMICUS* catalog. Options include the ability to search by degree earned, degree-granting institution, and degree date, as well as full-text searching of electronic theses. Many older theses are available on microfilm from *Theses Canada* through interlibrary loan. Currently, over

**Full Record**

Introduction | Comments | AMICUS Help | My List
Go to Registered Service

Basic Search
Advanced Search

Previous | Next | Results | Save

AMICUS No. 2991148
Monograph

NLC COPIES: NL Stacks - PS8235 I6 V633 2004
Preserv - on site - B-65609 - Copy 2 - NO ILL
NAME(S): Broderick, Daniel, 1975-
TITLE(S): *Voices from the circle of aboriginal youth / [compiled by Daniel Broderick]
PUBLISHER: Toronto: On the Path Publications, 2004.
DESCRIPTION: 60 p.; 23 cm.
SERIES: Humanity in print
NUMBERS: Canadiana: 20049023772
ISBN: 0968762115
CLASSIFICATION: LC Class no.: PS8235*
LC Call no.: PS8235 I6 V638 2004
Dewey: C811/.60809283 22

SUBJECTS: Youths' writing, Canadian (English) *(CSH)*
Canadian poetry (English) – Native authors *(CSH)*
Canadian poetry (English) – 20th century *(CSH)*
Street youth – Canada -Poetry *(LCSH)*
Native youth – Canada - Poetry *(CSH)*
Écrits de jeunes canadiens-anglais *(RVM)*
Poésie canadienne-anglaise – Auteurs autochtones *(RVM)*
Poésie canadienne anglaise – 20e siècle *(RVM)*
Jeunes de la rue – Canada – Poésie *(RVM)*
Juenesse autochtone – Canada – Poésie *(RVM)*

**Figure 3.5.** ***AMICUS*** **record demonstrating LCSH, CSH, and RVM subject headings. Source:** ***AMICUS: Canadian National Catalogue.***

sixty-five Canadian universities participate in *Theses Canada*'s Electronic Theses and Dissertations (ETD) harvesting program, facilitating the country's efforts in promoting open access to published research.

Because of the ambiguous nationalities related to some Canadian authors, you may also want to search other national library catalogs, including the *Library of Congress Online Catalog*, the British Library *Integrated Catalogue*, and the Bibliothèque nationale de France *Catalogue général*, comparing your results with *AMICUS* searches. You will find that each offers a unique and somewhat different searching experience. The ***Library of Congress Online Catalog*** delivers exceptional content, with access to digital collections. The Library of Congress collections house close to 142 million items, including over 21 million cataloged books. Boasting the largest collection of rare books in the world, Library of Congress collections also feature over 63 million manuscripts. Users can search the *Library of Congress Online Catalog* through either a basic or a guided search interface.

As the depository library for the United Kingdom, the British Library currently holds over 150 items in a variety of formats. The British Library employs Library of Congress subject headings in the ***Integrated Catalogue***, which allows access to 14 million monograph records. Searches may be performed using either a simple search interface, or through the advanced search page, where language, year of publication, and format limiters can be applied.

The Bibliothèque nationale de France (BnF) actively collects works by and about Canadian authors, with particular emphasis on Quebec and francophone literature. The ***Catalogue général*** presents a simple search box, with an option to link to the "recherche simple classique" interface, where an author, title, or subject search may be selected. An advanced-search screen is likewise available, as is the ability to search specific areas of the collection, such as periodicals and audiovisual materials. The library has been involved in several large-scale digitization projects, with access to BnF collections through its digital library initiative, *Gallica*. The *Gallica* catalog conveniently provides permanent links to all of its digitized items. A search using the terms *Québec* and *littérature* produced a digitized copy of Jules S. LeSage's 1902 *Théorie du "merveilleux" dans la littérature française et canadienne, 17ième siècle* among the 192 results displayed. This same search also locates an 1882 edition of the *Oeuvres complètes de Octave Crémazie*. Keyword searches are best performed using French orthography, as an identical search using English equivalents produced only thirty-two results.

## CONCLUSION

Continued development of online catalogs and their further integration through Web 2.0 technologies provides unprecedented opportunities for the literary researcher. Searching is a process, and your skill will only improve with experience and experimentation. Examine the search options available through your library catalog, employing a combination of search strategies and trying variations of your initial search. Whether your academic institution offers a traditional catalog interface, a simple search model, or a consortial model, the library catalog will open your options for access to a variety of materials, from books, to journals, to e-content, and beyond.

## *Chapter Four*

# Print and Electronic Bibliographies, Indexes, and Annual Reviews

Bibliographies are vital to literary scholarship as tools for locating specific research on a given topic. Large electronic subscription bibliographies, such as the *Modern Language Association International Bibliography* (*MLAIB*), have been developing for some time, consistently improving in usability, convenience, and coverage. Specialized print bibliographies remain extremely valuable in the guidance they offer to narrower areas of study and are still regularly published. Both print and online bibliographies can deliver insight into an author's range, output, popularity, treatment, and critical reception. Another value of the bibliography lies in its use as a tool for identifying unexplored areas of critical treatment and analysis.

Bibliographies are often recognized as lists of works which either illuminate titles related to a common area of interest, or direct the reader to a selection of resources that authors consulted during the course of their own study. When delineated by a specified time period, a bibliography may be intended as a finite inventory. In other cases, a bibliography is expected to expand, such as the bibliography of a living author's primary works. Today, comprehensive electronic bibliographies, such as the *MLAIB*, represent an immense body of scholarship related to a broad category of study—in this case, literature. Large bibliographies, whether print or electronic, often function in tandem with an index.

In print form, indexes facilitate the reader's access to material within a book, offering a convenient listing of terms and subjects. In electronic form, an index can be a powerful tool for directing the researcher to items that pertain to their scholarly interests. The care that goes into selecting the indexed terms can be the deciding factor in the usefulness of an index. Database creators are keenly aware of the fact that the index is an important tool for interfacing a user's search with relevant item records. In electronic format, indexes and bibliographies are often intrinsically linked as research tools that operate together to improve access to the scholarly universe.

Annual reviews are a specialized form of bibliography that present a summary of the work published within secondary material, such as reviews, anthologies, journals, and critical editions, during the course of the previous year. Annual reviews are valuable in that they also offer an indication of the topics, controversies, discoveries, and concerns of a given period. Perusing past annual reviews can afford a convenient sense of the research climate and accomplishments of a specific year. The *Year's Work in English Studies* is an example of an annual review that may also give insight into sociocultural developments affecting a publishing period.

Bibliographers maintain vigilant awareness of the development and treatment of a given subject and embrace the painstaking task of piecing together the print history of an author's works. Many academic departments, researchers, literary societies, and book aficionados produce freely available online bibliographies. Such projects often represent a labor of love, but they vary in usability, searchability, and quality.

The Bibliographical Society of Canada/La Société bibliographique du Canada meets annually and publishes an attractive bulletin that is available online.[1] Named for Marie Tremaine, a librarian and bibliographer at the Toronto Public Library, the Society also annually awards the Tremaine Medal for outstanding service to Canadian bibliography. Tremaine completed several projects related to early Canadian imprints and served as the editor of the Arctic Bibliography Project. Past recipients of the award include Bruce Braden Peel (1975) and Ernie Ingles (1996).

## NATIONAL BIBLIOGRAPHIES

*Bibliothèque et Archives nationales du Québec* (*BAnQ*). Montréal: Bibliothèque et Archives nationales du Québec, 1968–. See www.banq.qc.ca/accueil/index.html (accessed 2 July 2010).

*Canadiana: The National Bibliography of Canada*. Ottawa: Library and Archives Canada, 1950–. Print edition discontinued after the December 1991 issue; microfiche discontinued after the December 1991 issue; final CD-ROM version appeared in 2007. Now published online as *Canadiana* and integrated into the *AMICUS* database. See www.collectionscanada.gc.ca/amicus/index-e.html (accessed 2 July 2010).

Overseen by Library and Archives Canada, ***Canadiana: The National Bibliography of Canada*** is charged with describing and collecting all published materials relevant to the country. Electronic books and digital media present new challenges for large-scale bibliography projects such as this. The incorporation of user-generated metadata, produced through venues such as blogs and wikis, proposes interesting considerations for Library and Archives Canada. The possibility exists that the general public may one day contribute to such endeavors, much in the same way that library catalogs currently facilitate user-generated tagging.

Once produced monthly in paper format, *Canadiana* is now integrated into, and available through, Library and Archives Canada's *AMICUS* database. Prior to online availability, the National Library of Canada offered the print version free to Canadian libraries, while charging other institutions an annual fee for their subscription. Essentially an enumerative bibliography, *Canadiana* ensures some permanency to titles that may otherwise fall into anonymity due to the limited print run of most Canadian publications. Items in the bibliography are generally restricted to those published in Canada, although titles printed abroad that are of significant interest to Canadians are also added to the bibliography. Materials listed in *Canadiana* encompass a variety of formats, from books and periodicals to sound recordings, microforms, theses, and electronic items.

The ***Bibliothèque et Archives nationales du Québec*** (***BAnQ***) serves as a legal depository for all material published in the province of Quebec, as well as foreign publications pertaining to the province. Collected items are searchable through *Iris* (http://iris.banq.qc.ca/iris.aspx), which offers both an English- and a French-language interface. The *BAnQ* also produces the *Bibliographie du Québec*, a monthly listing of all material published in the province, organized according to subject. The *Bibliographie* can be browsed according to year of publication but is also searchable by author, title, and subject heading.

## SELECTED ELECTRONIC BIBLIOGRAPHIES AND INDEXES

*Annual Bibliography of English Language and Literature* (*ABELL*). Leeds: Maney Publishing for the Modern Humanities Research Association, 1921–. Annually. www.chadwyck.com.

*Canadian Periodical Index Quarterly* (*CPI.Q*). Toronto: Gale, Canada, 1988–. Updated three times monthly. See www.gale.cengage.com.

*Humanities International Index*. Ipswich, MA: Whitston Publishing, 1929–. www.ebscohost.com.

*Modern Language Association International Bibliography* (*MLAIB*). New York: Modern Languages Association of America, 1922–. Annually.

Available online through multiple vendors; see www.mla.org/bib_dist_comparison.

While online bibliographies present search options that may seem complex, the ability to manipulate and combine elaborate combinations of search terms in querying an otherwise unmanageable number of records in fact affords the researcher significant opportunities and advantages over previous print versions.

As a major index for humanities research, most U.S. and Canadian university libraries subscribe to the ***Modern Language Association International Bibliography*** (***MLAIB***). The *MLAIB* indexes and presents citations for books, articles, dissertations, and scholarly websites that consider world literature, modern languages studies, folklore studies, and linguistics. Book reviews are not indexed. The bibliography is compiled by the staff of the Modern Language Association's Office of Bibliographic Information Services, with the assistance of over one hundred bibliographers who provide subject analysis for the citations. Currently, the *MLAIB* contains over 2.1 million records for materials published in over seventy languages.

The *MLAIB* began publication of the bibliography in 1922, producing a print version of the resource through the 2008 edition. To date, the online *MLAIB* includes access to the digitized version of the bibliography, from 1926 forward. The *MLAIB* partners with *JSTOR*, *Project Muse*, and *ProQuest Dissertation Abstracts* to allow full-text linking to articles through the citations. If your institution simultaneously subscribes to the *MLAIB* and one of these providers, you may be able to link directly to the full text of an article via the *MLAIB*. Electronic access to the *MLAIB* is available through several vendors, including EBSCO and CSA, each offering a slightly different search interface.

Searching the *MLAIB* is quite straightforward, with the ability for the user to employ advanced options to delineate more complex searching. Over fifteen thousand records in the *MLAIB* fall under the "Subject Literature = Canadian literature" classification. A general field search for *Canadian literature* will retrieve over twenty-three thousand records. Further search limiters in *MLAIB* include period and genre. Although subjects are not consistent with Library of Congress subject headings, the Modern Language Association based their development of subject descriptors on the language of literary and linguistic scholarship. In some ways, therefore, *MLAIB* descriptors may convey a richer appreciation of literary topics and terms than apparent in Library of Congress subject headings. As you become familiar with the *MLAIB*, you may want to begin with a few general searches, subsequently incorporating and applying the controlled vocabulary found within relevant results as you search further.

*MLAIB* bibliographers maintain a thesaurus to guide researchers to the preferred terms. Examples of some *MLAIB* descriptors related to literary research portray the range of specialized literary terms that can be employed:

Gothic conventions
Treatment of landscape
National identity
Postcolonial approach
Compared to Atwood, Margaret

Because of the bibliography's multilingual scope, literary researchers also seeking articles in French on French Canadian literature will find adequate coverage. For example, a subject search for *French Canadian literature* limited to "Language = French" retrieves over 6,200 results. The same search limited to "Publication Type = Journal Article" retrieves over 4,500 results. Other publication types by which you may limit your search include "book article," "dissertation abstract," "book collection," and "website."

Subscriptions to the *MLAIB* also encompass access to the *MLA Directory of Periodicals*, which provides detailed information on a particular periodical, such as place of publication, topics covered, whether a journal is peer reviewed, and information on the article submission and reviewing process.

Produced by the Modern Humanities Research Association, the ***Annual Bibliography of English Language and Literature*** (**ABELL**) lists books, periodical articles, critical editions of literary works, book reviews, collections of essays, and dissertations published worldwide from 1920 forward. The online version, now comprised of over 880,000 records, first appeared in 1997. While the bibliography's title may be misleading, content is not restricted to English-language research, and in fact encompasses scholarship in other languages from around the globe. Although *ABELL* is comparable to the *MLAIB*, variations in content do exist. If your aim is to be comprehensive, scholars familiar with the two services recommend that both bibliographies be searched. In examining pre-1956 Canadian works, *ABELL*'s content may better suit your needs, as up until 1956, the *MLAIB* focused only on U.S. scholarship. One often-cited advantage of *ABELL* over the *MLAIB* is that book reviews are indexed. For Canadian literary researchers familiar with the *MLAIB*, a distinct drawback of *ABELL* is that subject headings are not used to identify authors by nationality. Canadian content is therefore best discovered through an author-based search; in fact, a notable strength of the bibliography is that author-based content is easily revealed by typing the author's name (last, first) in the subject field. *ABELL* supports searching of keywords, title, subject, author/reviewer, publication details, journal title, and date fields;

searches can also be conveniently limited to articles, books, or reviews. Currently found within this database are over 1,200 book reviews from *Canadian literature*, content that would not be accessible through the *MLAIB*. Literary scholars regularly executing searches to uncover new research related to a selected subject will appreciate the ability to limit a query to "Last Update Only." Part of Chadwyck Healey's *Literature Online Complete Collection* (*LION*), *ABELL* continues to improve in usability, functionality, and content. Since *ABELL* has a reputation for being somewhat mystifying for the novice searcher, users who have never used this database should refer to the help links in order to ensure efficient searching.

Originally published jointly by the Canadian Library Association and the National Library of Canada, the *Canadian Periodical Index/Index de périodiques canadiens* is now also available electronically as the ***Canadian Periodical Index Quarterly*** (***CPI.Q***) through Gale publishers. Content is not limited to scholarly journals but also comprises Canadian newspapers, magazines, and selections from the *Toronto Globe and Mail*. The current online product offers coverage from 1980 forward in an attractive and usable interface. One advantage of the *CPI.Q* over more general indexes is that Canadian content abounds, from scholarly journals to popular newsmagazines, providing unprecedented insight into literary news, related current and political events, and Canadian culture. In contrast to the *MLAIB* and *ABELL*, the *CPI.Q* delivers full-text access to many specialized Canadian literary and scholarly journals, a convenient feature for the researcher. The Gale interface offers various limiters, such as a "target audience" selection, which consists of an "academic titles" designation. An additional option for the literary researcher is the ability to search only arts and humanities publications. Other limiters consider "country of publication" and "language of publication," with French and English as the only available language choices. In the advanced-search screen, a "document type" limiter indicates the variety of material available through the *CPI.Q*, from articles to blog entries. Other useful features include the ability to restrict the search to peer-reviewed articles, or to Canadian publications. In browsing search results, you will notice that abstracts are supplied for some, but not all, academic journals; other records contain only brief information, such as title, author, and date. The *CPI.Q* currently delivers full-text coverage of Gale reference works related to Canadian literature, such as *Contemporary Canadian Authors* and the *Native North American Almanac*. More specialized toward Canadian topics than the *MLAIB* or *ABELL*, the *CPI.Q* does in fact index some scholarly titles that are not offered in subject-specific humanities and literary databases. However, in addition to their broader scope and monograph coverage, users may still find that the *MLAIB* and *ABELL* better suit their needs by facilitating comparison with other national literatures.

Formerly published as the *American Humanities Index*, the ***Humanities International Index*** indexes more than 2,200 journals and offers over 2.71 million citations and abstracts for articles, book reviews, and essays appearing in scholarly books. Also available through Whitston Publishing is *Humanities International Complete*, a similar product but with full-text access to over one thousand journals, including *Canadian Literature* and the *Antigonish Review*. The database currently provides coverage dating back to 1929, affording comprehensive humanities content with special attention to the literary arts.

## READING AND EVALUATING AN *MLAIB* RECORD

Journal publishers often require authors to develop an abstract to highlight the scope of their article; in some cases, major bibliography projects recruit professional abstracters to write these summaries. Although many *MLAIB* records include an abstract, others offer only short entries or limited bibliographic information. In cases where an abstract is not available, you will have to use other clues to assist you in determining whether or not to pursue the full text of an article. The *MLAIB* via EBSCO record represented in figure 4.1 was found through a phrase keyword search for *nation building and Canadian literature*.

Since an abstract is not provided, we may want to consider whether the terms listed under General Subject Areas (*Subject Literature:* Canadian literature; *Period:* 1600–1999) and Subject Terms (relationship to *Cambridge Companion to Canadian Literature* [2004]) are representative of our topic. The information and experience that you bring may also be helpful to you, as in this case the author of the article, Eva-Marie Kröller, is a noted Canadian literary scholar. Although we might not have known that Kröller is also the editor of the *Cambridge Companion to Canadian Literature*, from the article title we can deduce that this narrative focuses on her activity in this capacity.

As you gain experience searching article databases for Canadian literary topics, you will also begin to familiarize yourself with journal titles related to Canadian themes. If you are not familiar with a particular journal, you may look up the title in the *MLA Directory of Periodicals*. In the above case, by consulting the *MLA Directory*, we learn that *Anglistik* is the official journal of the German Association of University Professors of English, publishing articles that pertain to English and American literature.

Title: Cultural Inventories and **Nation-Building**: Editing the *Cambridge Companion to **Canadian Literature***

Author(s): Kröller, Eva-Marie

Source: Anglistik 2004 Sept; 15 (2): 27-42.

Peer Reviewed: Yes

ISSN: 0947-0034

General Subject Areas:

*Subject Literature:* ***Canadian_literature***
*Period:* 1600-1999

Subject Terms: relationship to *Cambridge Companion to* ***Canadian Literature*** (2004)

Document Information:

*Publication Type:* journal article
*Language of Publication:* English
*Update Code:* 200401
*Sequence Numbers:* 2004-1-9301

Accession Number: 2004872242

Database: MLA International Bibliography

**Figure 4.1. *MLAIB* results for keyword search: *nation building and Canadian literature.* Source: *MLAIB* via EBSCO.**

To sum up our evaluation of the *MLAIB* citation, *Anglistik* is a notable, peer-reviewed, European publication, publishing articles that focus on literary theory and criticism. Although narrow in scope, the article is written by a well-known name in Canadian literary research. As editor of the *Cambridge Companion to Canadian Literature*, Eva-Marie Kröller will likely describe issues and challenges related to canon formation, literature, and nation building. As our goal is to research the concept of nation building as it relates to literature, this article could in fact present useful information relevant to our study.

Here are some ideas for evaluating abstracts and articles:

- Read through the abstract, if one is provided.
- If you can locate the full text of the article, read the introduction, conclusion, and section headings.
- Review the article's bibliography. What sources are being cited?
- Is the journal published by a reputable press?
- What are the author's affiliations? Is this article written by a notable scholar or on behalf of a creditable organization?

In online searching, one source often leads to another, and preliminary searches will inform subsequent queries. In this way, research using both online and print bibliographies can seem very much like detective work, as one source illuminates another, and your research results in unanticipated discoveries.

## ONLINE JOURNAL COLLECTIONS

*JSTOR: The Scholarly Journal Archive*. New York: JSTOR, 1996–. www.jstor.org.

*Project Muse*. Baltimore, MD: Johns Hopkins University Press, 1993–. http://muse.jhu.edu.

Founded in 1995 to facilitate access to and preservation of the scholarly record, ***JSTOR: The Scholarly Journal Archive*** provides full-text searchability and online retrieval of journal articles. Although recent content is not accessible (issues are not eligible for inclusion until they are three to five years old), as an online journal archive, *JSTOR* affords the liberating possibility of full-text access from anywhere an Internet connection is available. The accessibility of titles operates on the concept of what *JSTOR* calls the "moving wall," which describes the time period between when the latest issue of the journal was published and when the issue is actually added to the *JSTOR* archive. There are a few *JSTOR* titles that have a "zero" moving wall, meaning that the publisher allows *JSTOR* to offer immediate access to its journal issues.

Currently, specialized journals related directly to Canadian literature are not found within *JSTOR*; however, interdisciplinary titles such as *Twentieth Century Literature*, *Contemporary Literature*, *Comparative Literature*, the *French Review*, and the *Journal of Modern Literature* do periodically offer Canadian content. As *JSTOR* includes a mountainous quantity of book reviews, in looking specifically for articles, a search is best performed in the "Advanced Search" mode, which provides further limiting options. Articles are downloaded as PDF files, representing an electronic facsimile of the article as it would have appeared in the print version of the journal. While full-text articles must be downloaded, you can e-mail citations directly from *JSTOR*, or create a My*JSTOR* account where citations can be saved for future reference. Due to the limited inclusion of Canadian journals, unless your research specifically directs you to a title indexed in the collection, you will find that it is best to use the *MLAIB* or *ABELL* for searches requiring comprehensive coverage.

Offering an attractive interface, ***Project Muse*** provides full-text access to an impressive list of interdisciplinary journals. Titles of possible interest to the Canadian literary researcher are *Canadian Ethnic Studies*, *English Studies in Canada*, *Canadian Historical Review*, *Journal of Canadian Studies*, *Studies in American Indian Literatures*, *American Indian Studies*, *Comparative Literature Studies*, *Journal of Modern Literature*, *Postmodern Culture*, and *University of Toronto Quarterly*, in addition to other interdisciplinary titles. *Project Muse* content encompasses articles, reviews, poetry, drama, and fiction. A nice feature of the database is the ability to search by discipline, keeping in mind that this may exclude relevant multidisciplinary items from your search results. The interface is clean and usable, presenting a simple search interface with the option to build more complex queries through the "Advanced Article Search" screen. In addition to keyword, subject, author, and title field searching, *Project Muse* also offers "Author Reviewed" and "Title Reviewed" options. These can be especially valuable if your research includes book reviews. A "Title Reviewed" search for Randy Boyagoda's *Governor of the Northern Province* finds a review in the fall 2007 issue of *Canadian Ethnic Studies*. Additional search options allow you to limit the results to articles only, reviews only, as well as poetry, drama, and fiction. A convenient "What's New" link directs the user to recently published journal issues, and help links are concise yet informative.

## GENERAL PRINT BIBLIOGRAPHIES

Gerry, Thomas M. F. *Contemporary Canadian and U.S. Women of Letters: An Annotated Bibliography*. New York: Garland Publishing, 1993.

Ingles, Ernie, ed. *Bibliography of Canadian Bibliographies/Bibliographie des bibliographies canadiennes*. 3rd ed. Toronto: University of Toronto Press, 1994. Also available as an electronic book through the *Canadian Electronic Library*, Saint Lazare, Quebec, Gibson Library Connections.

Lecker, Robert, and Jack David, eds. *The Annotated Bibliography of Canada's Major Authors* (*ABCMA*). 8 vols. Downsview, Ontario: ECW Press, 1979–1994.

Tremaine, Marie. *A Bibliography of Canadian Imprints, 1751–1800*. Toronto: University of Toronto Press, 1999.

Watters, R. E. *A Checklist of Canadian Literature and Background Materials, 1628–1960*. 2nd ed. Toronto: University of Toronto Press, 1972.

Print bibliographies continue to be published for humanities research, often representing an exhaustive, inclusive list of materials related to a given research area, theme, or figure. As online subscription bibliographies evolve in functionality, print bibliographies have become underused, and their application underestimated. Critical bibliographies may contain useful annotations regarding the scope and application of the considered works. Additionally, bibliographies can also be valuable in exposing areas of uncharted research. The following serve to illustrate the structure of Library of Congress subject headings related to bibliographies:

Canadian literature—Bibliography
Canada—Bibliography
Canada—Bibliography—Catalogs
Dissertations, Academic—Canada—Bibliography
Munro, Alice—Bibliography
French-Canadian literature—Bibliography
French-Canadian literature—History and criticism—Bibliography
Canadian literature—Jewish authors—Bibliography

In common with other reference works, bibliographies represent a valuable initial point of departure to inform and delineate your specific research topic.

Although the introductory title indicates that ten volumes were originally planned (five devoted to poetry and five devoted to prose), volume 8, published in 1994, marks the end of ***The Annotated Bibliography of Canada's Major Authors*** (***ABCMA***). With each volume focusing on a short list of five authors, the series is designed to facilitate critical comparison, grouping writers who have achieved similar levels of notoriety. Volume 1 therefore covers Margaret Atwood, Margaret Laurence, Hugh MacLennan, Mordecai Richler, and Gabrielle Roy, bringing "together commentary on a group of writers who are explicitly modern in their concerns" (8). Although reviewers of the bibliography have criticized the arbitrary grouping of authors, the editors state that they had hoped the chosen format would facilitate comparison.

Each bibliography generally follows a consistent pattern of organization, treating the individual works according to categories of publication. For example, part 1, subsection A, of Margaret Atwood's bibliography considers "Books and Manuscripts" and is separated into subcategories such as "Fiction," "Criticism," "Children's Books," "Drama," and "Manuscripts." Subsection B provides "Contributions to Periodicals, Books, and Anthologies: Short Stories, Articles and Book Reviews, Published Graphic Work, Selected Anthology Contributions." Part 2, labeled subsection C, covers works on the author, including "Books, Articles and Sections of Books, Theses and Dissertations, Interviews, Awards and Honours." The annotations offer an impressive level of detail, bringing to light many titles that would otherwise be forgotten, even in the digital age. The annotations for "Selected Book Reviews" under subsection D are particularly helpful as they often use direct quotations to illustrate the reviewer's delight, or disdain, for the work in question. Found at entry D29 is a scathing review of Atwood's *Surfacing* published in the Vancouver publication *3 Cent Pulp*, characterizing the novel as "so relentlessly minor that you could play it at a funeral and everyone would fall asleep."[2] Practically an underground publication at the time the review was written, *3 Cent Pulp* is a precursor to *Geist*, a well-known Canadian literary journal. Given the following Atwood has cultivated over the years, today's critics might rail at such comments; still, the review does provide perspective on the early reception of an author who would ultimately help raise the status of Canadian literature around the world.

Volume 2 again considers Margaret Atwood, this time focusing on her poetry. Other poets treated in volume 2 include Leonard Cohen, Archibald Lampman, E. J. Pratt, and Al Purdy. Bruce Whiteman's bibliography of Leonard Cohen reveals that Michael Ondaatje published a study of Cohen's work in 1970, prior to the onset of Ondaatje's own literary fame.

Works are listed in chronological order of publication, allowing the reader to experience the waxing and waning of an author's literary production and critical treatment. An "Index to Critics Listed in the Bibliography" follows every individually authored entry, affording a convenient overview of the critics, both well and little known, who have reviewed the works of a given Canadian author. Another nice feature of the series is the provision of information on "Manuscripts" under part 1, subsection A, of each author bibliography, as applicable.

Because the bibliographies are individually authored, readers will see some variation in style and level of detail. George Wicken, for example, carefully combs through Archibald Lampman's critical treatment, quoting extensively from the works examined. An interesting reference is found at entry C9 for an 1891 article from the *Boston Evening Transcript* in which author Joseph Edgar Chamberlain seems to suggest that Lampman's association with Canada is a detriment to his career and that a move to Boston would liberate him from his "prosaic" employment at the Ottawa Post Office.[3] Another delightful quote is found at entry C59, where in a 1933 article from *The Canadian Forum*, the critic observes, "His devotion to the rag-tags of the poet's dictionary—the methinks, lo's, o'ers, begones, yesternights and yestereves—is dispiriting and trying."[4] Wicken's Lampman bibliography is engaging, encouraging the reader toward a newfound appreciation for the bibliographic format.

Other volumes in the series offer exceptional bibliographic studies for the following authors: Ernest Buckler, Robertson Davies, Raymond Knister, W. O. Mitchell, and Sinclair Ross (vol. 3); Earle Birney, Dorothy Livesay, F. R. Scott, and A. J. M. Smith (vol. 4); Morley Callaghan, Mavis Gallant, Hugh Hood, Alice Munro, and Ethel Wilson (vol. 5); Margaret Avison, John Newlove, Michael Ondaatje, Miriam (Dworkin) Waddington, and Phyllis Webb (vol. 6); Marian Engel, Anne Hebert, Robert Kroetsch, and Thomas H. Raddall (vol. 7); and poets Irving Layton, Dennis Lee, and Duncan Campbell Scott (vol. 8).

The ***Bibliography of Canadian Bibliographies/Bibliographie des bibliographies canadiennes*** (***BCB3***) builds on previous editions and continues a legacy of bibliography construction that began at the McGill University Library School in 1929. The interim between the publication of the second (1972) and third (1994) editions marks a dramatic rise in Canadian studies scholarship. As with other reference works related to Canadian studies, the editors establish the boundaries for "Canadian" within the "Inclusion/Exclusion Criteria" section of the introduction. Basically, works "which do not further our understanding of things, people, or events Canadian, or Canada's place in the world" (x) are not treated. Bibliographies published in Canada, devoid however of Canadian content or logical application to Canadian studies, are likewise left out. Further criteria stipulate that a work must be both published and available to the general public.

Formatting of entries is consistent with Danielle Thibault's 1989 *Bibliographic Style Manual/Guide de rédaction bibliographique* published by the National Library of Canada/Bibliothèque nationale du Canada. Descriptions are written in French for works published in the French language, and documents printed separately in both official languages may also be given a bilingual entry. Entries offer a detailed annotation expounding the extent and scope of the work's Canadian content, holding institutions, period of coverage, number of entries, and type of material. Other helpful information encompasses citations for previous editions and notes to indicate reprints. The *BCB3* is incredibly detailed, also citing bibliographies published in scholarly journals and periodicals. Serials that regularly publish bibliographies as recurring features are also incorporated. While researchers are likely to find other areas relevant to their studies, bibliographies related to Canadian literature are found under the "Arts and Humanities" subsections "Literature" and "Children's Literature." Publications are arranged chronologically, from the older to the more recent, in order to convey a historical understanding of the bibliographic endeavors completed within a given area. Access to items is facilitated by author, title, and subject indexes, as the work offers impressive coverage of Canadian bibliographies. Interesting citations include, for example, Dick Harrison's "Mountie Fiction: A Reader's Guide" in the October 1975 issue of *Royal Canadian Mounted Police Quarterly*.

Although not listed thematically, bibliographies of theses treating Canadian topics are located under the "Types of Material Bibliographies" subdivision "Theses." An example of a pertinent work from this section is Apollonia Steele's *Theses on English-Canadian Literature: A Bibliography of Research Produced in Canada and Elsewhere from 1903 Forward.* Aldrich Dyer's *Indian, Métis and Inuit of Canada in Theses and Dissertations, 1892–1987* also considers literary works. In 2008, the 1994 edition of the *Bibliography of Canadian Bibliographies* was simultaneously issued as an electronic book through the Canadian Electronic Library series from Gibson Library Connections, Inc.

A revised and enlarged edition of Watters' 1959 bibliography, ***A Checklist of Canadian Literature and Background Materials, 1628–1960***, attempts to comprehensively trace the development of English literature in Canada for the considered period. Entries are generally unannotated, and the title therefore constitutes an enumerative inventory of the country's anglophone literary output for the examined period. Although completeness is not his stated aim, Watters lists approximately sixteen thousand books written by over seven thousand authors. The bibliography is divided into such categories as poetry, biography, literary criticism, fiction, prose, scholarship, essays, and travel and description, among other topics, carefully selecting works that relate to literature, literary life, and literary culture. Although a subject index is not offered, Watters complements a "General Author Index" with an "Index of Anonymous Titles."

Marie Tremaine's retrospective ***A Bibliography of Canadian Imprints 1751–1800*** represents the early production of works published by the "little society" (xi) during a period when literary production was rather sparse. Mainly comprised of government documents, schoolbooks, and religious works, the introduction gives excellent background information on the publishing climate of the period. A master bibliographer, Tremaine incorporates monographs, including books, pamphlets, leaflets, and broadsheets, as well as a detailed section on newspapers and magazines.

As volume 21 in the Garland Bibliographies of Modern Critics and Critical Schools series, ***Contemporary Canadian and U.S. Women of Letters*** is a useful guide to significant female writers of the twentieth century. Written by Thomas Gerry, dean of Laurentian University at Georgian College, the title presents the opportunity for a comparative analysis of the selected Canadian and U.S. authors. Gerry chose to focus on writers who publish a variety of literary texts, including poetry, prose, criticism, and fiction, and a significant portion of the work is claimed by Canadian women of letters. Quebec authors are represented by Louky Bersianik and Nicole Brossard, and Gerry also provides annotated bibliographies for Janice Kulyk Keefer, Jay Macpherson, Australian-born Canadian writer Daphne Marlatt, Jean McKay, Jane Rule, Gail Scott, Lola Lemire Tostevin, and Aritha van Herk. In addition to Gerry's own bibliographical research, a section highlights existing bibliographies for Canadian authors Margaret Atwood, Gabrielle Roy, France Theoret, Miriam Waddington, and Phyllis Webb, in which the *Annotated Bibliography of Canada's Major Authors* (*ABCMA*) is a recurring citation. Gerry's enthusiasm for his subjects is infused throughout the work, both in his preface and in the thoughtful annotations he writes. Entries in all formats are arranged chronologically within each individual bibliography. In selecting authors who are somewhat out of the mainstream, Gerry fills a void in Canadian bibliographical research.

## GENRE, REGIONAL, AND BIBLIOGRAPHIES FOR SPECIAL TOPICS

Ball, John, and Richard Plant, eds. *Bibliography of Theatre History in Canada: The Beginnings through 1984*. Toronto: ECW Press, 1993. Also online at www.lib.unb.ca/Texts/Theatre/Bib/search.html.

Chartier, Daniel. *A Bibliography on the Imagined North: Arctic, Winter, Antarctic*. Montreal: Imaginaire/Nord, 2007.

Colombo, John Robert, Michael Richardson, John Bell, and Alexandre L. Amprimoz. *CDN SF & F: A Bibliography of Canadian Science Fiction and Fantasy*. Toronto: Hounslow Press, 1979.

Fee, Margery, and Ruth Cawker. *Canadian Fiction: An Annotated Bibliography*. Toronto: Peter Martin, 1976.

Francis, Flora (Blizzard). *A Black Canadian Bibliography*. Ottawa: Pan-African Publications, 2000.

Gerson, Carole. *Canada's Early Women Writers: Texts in English to 1859*. Ottawa: CRIAW/ICREF, 1994.

Havlice, Patricia Pate. *And So to Bed: A Bibliography of Diaries Published in English*. Metuchen, NJ: Scarecrow Press, 1987.

Ingles, Ernie B., and N. Merrill Distad, eds. *Peel's Bibliography of the Canadian Prairies to 1953*. Toronto: University of Toronto Press, 2003.

Maillet, Marguerite. *Bibliographie des publications de l'Acadie des provinces maritimes: livres et brochures, 1609–1995*. Moncton, New Brunswick: Les Éditions d'Acadie, 1997.

McQuarrie, Jane, Anne Mercer, and Gordon Ripley. *Index to Canadian Poetry in English*. Toronto: Reference Press, 1984.

Miska, John. *Ethnic and Native Canadian Literature: A Bibliography*. Toronto: University of Toronto Press, 1990.

National Library of Canada. *Indian-Inuit Authors: An Annotated Bibliography/Auteurs indiens et inuit: bibliographie annotée*. Ottawa: National Library of Canada, 1974.

Rome, David. *Jews in Canadian Literature: A Bibliography*. Montreal: Jewish Canadian Congress and the Jewish Public Library, 1962.

Wagner, Anton, ed. *The Brock Bibliography of Published Canadian Plays in English, 1766–1978*. Toronto: Playwright's Press, 1980.

Waldon, Freda Farrell. *Bibliography of Canadiana Published in Great Britain, 1519–1763*. Rev. and ed. William F. E. Morley. Ottawa: ECW Press, 1990.

Weiss, Allan. *A Comprehensive Bibliography of English-Canadian Short Stories: 1950–1983*. Toronto: ECW Press, 1988.

Though published over thirty years ago, Margery Fee and Ruth Cawker's ***Canadian Fiction: An Annotated Bibliography*** still remains a useful tool for Canadian literary research, treating both English Canadian and French Canadian authors and their works. Although introductions to similar reference works state the same in so many words, Fee and Cawker eloquently address the delimitations of "Canadian," explaining, "The large core of works about which there is no doubt is surrounded by a hazy aureole where lurk expatriates, landed immigrants, tourist and natives who write novels indistinguishable from any produced in New York or London" (ix). Erring on the side of "over-eager assimilation," the bibliography therefore incorporates authors whose Canadian identity is controversial, such as Malcolm Lowry. Fee and Cawker drew on *Canadian Books in Print 1974* to identify authors for inclusion, and the bibliography is therefore limited to works in print during 1973 and 1974. Conceived as a guide to assist secondary school teachers, colorful annotations enhance the work, as illustrated by the entry for Margaret Laurence's *The Fire-Dwellers*: "Alive with references to fire, hell and death, the novel deals with the strong feelings often held under the flabby, ordinary surface of life." (65) The first section enumerates a list of secondary sources useful for Canadian literary research, divided into "Bibliographic Sources," "Historical and Biographical Sources," "General Critical Works," and "Periodicals and Indexes," as well as a brief selection of works that consider Canadian films and film studies. Entries are organized alphabetically by author, with novel annotations comprising the bulk of the material. A section devoted to anthologies of short stories is organized alphabetically by title, and entries offer a list of works included within the various sources. A subject guide categorizes the citations under such headings as "Crime," "Canadian Identity," and "U.S. Influence." Author and title indexes are provided, separately treating the novels and short stories found in the bibliography.

For researchers of prairie writing, ***Peel's Bibliography of the Canadian Prairies to 1953*** is a key resource. As the Canadian West developed and grew, so did the literature produced in the region, and Peel's bibliography soon became a sought-after tool for tracing the development of written culture in the prairie provinces. The first edition of this work was published by the University of Toronto Press in 1956 and was augmented by a supplement in 1963. Begun as a graduate project for the University of Saskatchewan by Bruce Peel in 1946, the title entered into its second edition in 1973. Peel's bibliography focuses on the nineteenth and early twentieth centuries, and the terminal date of 1953 was selected to coincide with the beginning of the National Library of Canada's deposit program. Items are arranged chronologically, with the first entry being the journal of Henry Kelsey, dating from 1691 and published in 1928. Chronological arrangement enhances the appeal of the bibliography, aiding in tracing the progression of prairie history, thought, politics, and writing. Although Peel traveled around the world in search of the materials mentioned, he also indicates where an item was unseen, such as entry number 4, Thomas Bowery's *Dictionary of the Hudson's Bay Indian Language* (1701).[5] Subjects are organized by subheadings, such as "Red River Settlement," "Settling the West," and "Literary Works." Authors born outside of Canada whose works are nonetheless set in the prairies are considered. Title and author indexes are provided, with biographical notes for selected writers.

The work unarguably represents a labor of love, and the mystery behind Peel's drive to trace prairie writing is perhaps solved in his dedicatory note: "Dedicated to the homesteaders among whom were my father and my mother." The painstaking gathering of ephemera, such as limited-edition books and pamphlets, became a life's work for the bibliographer. The Canadian prairies, viewed as a featureless wasteland by some, are often the subject of derision by inhabitants of more prestigious provinces, cultivating perhaps a unique sense of pride in prairie dwellers. (Illustrative of the prairie identity, David Bouchard's *If You're Not from the Prairie* is a well-known picture book, evoking sensibilities comprehensible only perhaps to a person raised on the land. Written in verse, the story examines attributes of prairie life, including the wind, the sun, the crisp cold, and the sense of freedom embodied in the prairie landscape.)

In the foreword to the second edition, J. H. Archer commends Peel for his contribution to the development and celebration of western Canadian culture. The preface to the second edition also provides rich insight into the work of the bibliographer, as Peel recounts his travels around the world, digging through hundreds of archival boxes in search of elusive and ephemeral pamphlets. Peel describes his delight in the release of the "first document printed in Manitoba"[6] (1973, xii) when the cornerstone for Winnipeg's original city hall was finally reopened after the demolition of the old building itself. The notion that the work of a bibliographer is dull and isolating is dispelled as Peel refers to the many personal contacts he has established through his endeavors.

Peel's bibliography is an excellent example for the nonbibliographer as to the seductive nature of book history. Even if you are not interested in prairie writing, this work will ignite your curiosity. One nice feature for the ethnic studies scholar is that Peel incorporates entries related to writing both by and about specific cultural groups in his subject index. The entries on works pertaining to Ukrainians are particularly numerous and indicative of the level of detail that Peel exerts, with the inclusion of little-known titles such as Panteleimon Bozyk's rather obscure historical study, *Tserkov Ukrayintsiv v Kanadi* (The Church of the Ukrainians in Canada) (entry 3003), which was only recently translated into English.

University of Alberta scholars, Ingles and Distad took up Peel's lifework following his death in 1998. Their current, third edition of the bibliography has expanded to over 7,429 entries, significantly increasing the 2,769 entries found in the first edition. Ingles and Distad also developed a subject index to further facilitate research. In continuance of Bruce Peel's work, the University of Alberta hosts the website Peel's Prairie Provinces (http://peel.library.ualberta.ca/index.html), which provides access to over seven thousand digitized items related to the Canadian prairies.

Commissioned by the Social Sciences and Humanities Research Council of Canada to develop a research tool for the study of Canada's multicultural literature, John Miska authors ***Ethnic and Native Canadian Literature: A Bibliography***. Miska's bibliography provides over five thousand works published in over seventy languages. Part 1 examines general reference tools related to multicultural literature, such as bibliographies, directories, and anthologies. Part 2 considers literary works, critical treatment, and bibliographies relating to sixty-five different ethnic groups. Larger sections are divided into categories of writing, such as bibliographies, books, anthologies, and research papers. Part 3, "Minorities in Canadian Literature," focuses on theses, articles, research papers, and books related to the portrayal and characterization of cultural groups in mainstream Canadian writing. Divided into two sections, "The Immigrant in Canadian Literature" and "The Native in Canadian Literature," part 3 also lists biographies, poetry, fiction, and drama.

David Rome began work on ***Jews in Canadian Literature: A Bibliography*** as a project in partial fulfillment of his master's degree at the University of

Montreal, expanding the initial work to over six thousand entries related to Jewish Canadiana. The first part of the bibliography is organized according to authors and their works, with interesting biographical information and background notes. Rome, writing as the director of the Jewish Public Library in Montreal, and as curator of the Bronfman Collection of Jewish Canadiana, offers an excellent introduction to the history of Canadian Jewish writing. Other sections of the bibliography include Jewish authors who wrote for literary journals, literary criticism, and translation. Rome's bibliography delivers a historically illuminating discussion of early Canadian Jewish writing and examines A. M. Klein, Mordecai Richler, Eli Mandel, Adele Wiseman, and Leonard Cohen, among others.

Published as a joint project between the National Library of Canada and the Department of Indian Affairs and Northern Development, ***Indian-Inuit Authors: An Annotated Bibliography/Auteurs indiens et inuit: bibliographie annotée*** offers an interesting overview of the publication activity of northern writers up until 1972. Presented in both English and French, the annotations adequately describe a variety of texts, from literary to political. Intuitively organized, part 1, "Works by Canadian Indian and Métis Authors," is further subdivided into monographs, books by Native children, anthologies, collected works, poetry and songs, articles, addresses, conferences, reports, studies, theses, language, and texts. Items in part 2 "Works by Canadian Inuit Authors," are organized according to the following categories: books, anthologies, poetry and songs, articles, addresses, conferences, language, and Inuit periodicals. Although each category is arranged alphabetically by author, separate author indexes for parts 1 and 2 allow for easy identification of works. The literature of the North has developed significantly since 1972, as First Nations, Métis, and Inuit authors continue to flourish; an updated volume is therefore necessary. Despite this fact, the bibliography's organization, thoughtful annotations, and pleasing format ensure that it will continue to be consulted in the investigation of northern writing.

***A Bibliography of the Imagined North: Arctic, Winter, Antarctic*** is an impressive twelve-thousand-entry presentation of material on the territories of the North. Published in English, French, Swedish, and Icelandic, the first section of the bibliography arranges entries by territory, including Labrador, Nunavik, Nunavut, the Yukon, and the cultural territory of "Wintriness." The second section considers critical and theoretical perspectives of the North, such as traditional culture, spirituality, and travel and explorations. The various methodologies employed in researching the region are considered in the final section, including linguistics, women's studies, and postcolonialism. Sections are generally subdivided by books, articles, and documentary films; lacking an index, material pertinent to literary research is not easily identifiable.

Nevertheless, the attention given to northern themes guarantees that this bibliography will remain relevant to researchers of Canada's literary North.

Representing both French- and English-language works pertaining to the Maritime provinces, Maillet's ***Bibliographie des publications de l'Acadie des provinces maritimes: livres et brochures, 1609–1995*** offers many items of interest to the literary researcher. Arranged according to discipline, separate sections examine the arts, literature, linguistics, folklore, and biographical works. History, geography, the sciences, politics, law, economics, and education contribute to the multidisciplinary focus of this bibliography.

In her introduction to ***A Black Canadian Bibliography***, Flora Blizzard Francis outlines the major waves of immigration by black refugees and settlers of African heritage from the Caribbean, South America, the British West Indies, the United States, Haiti, Martinique, Guadeloupe, and over sixteen African countries. The first section of the bibliography examines all print materials, including books, journals, magazines, and newspaper articles, as well as entries from reference works, theses, and dissertations, arranging citations alphabetically by author. Audiovisual materials, such as musical contributions, are provided in the second part of the bibliography. The works of significant authors, such as M. NourbeSe Philip, Dionne Brand, Althea Prince, Austin Clark, and prolific children's author Tololwa Mollel, appear among lesser-known titles, for instance Raymond Spence's 1969 novel *Nothing Black but a Cadillac*. Although some may prefer to see the bibliography further arranged by type of material, subject and title indexes provide adequate direction. Flora Blizzard Francis's work has been critiqued for considering authors born abroad who may have resided briefly in Canada, but who ultimately took up residence outside of the country. In any case, Francis is not alone in the complex struggle to identify Canadianness and to delineate Canadianicity, topics with which all compilers of Canadian reference works must grapple.

Organized chronologically by century, ***The Brock Bibliography of Published Canadian Plays in English, 1766–1978*** draws and expands on previous scholarship related to theater bibliography in Canada. Under the Department of Drama at Brock University, twelve researchers contributed to this annotated work, seeking out all cited materials for in-hand examination. With each period further organized alphabetically by author, citation and informative plot summaries are provided for each entry. Production details, such as the number of acts and players, accompany each entry, as does information on the play's first production, where known. The first and only seventeenth-century citation is for Marc Lescarbot's *The Theatre of Neptune/Le théâtre de Neptune* (1606), and listed are all known published reprints of the play, such as a 1926 English translation found in *Queen's Quarterly*.

Like many bibliographies that revise earlier studies, Ball and Plant's ***Bibliography of Theatre History in Canada: The Beginnings through 1984*** fulfills a previous commitment to uncover works that were inadvertently omitted in the earlier version. A third of the additional content is comprised of titles that were in print at the time of the previous publication, while citations for newly published imprints make up another third of the updated volume. This revision to *A Bibliography of Canadian Theatre History 1583–1975* and its *Supplement 1975–1976* is augmented by a section on Native theater, found under “General Works.” This is a well-organized bibliography, as titles are arranged into fifteen sections, including such categories as “Little Theatre,” “Festivals,” “Radio and Television Drama,” and “Puppetry.” Each section is additionally arranged by period, region, language, and theme. A general index is well devised for excellent access to the bibliography’s almost eleven thousand citations, making this an essential work for Canadian theater research. The bibliography is now also accessible online and is augmented by Ball and Plant’s annual updates, as published in the Association for Canadian Theatre Research newsletter.

Since many Canadian short stories are first published in journals, periodicals, and specialized literary magazines, Allan Weiss’s ***A Comprehensive Bibliography of English-Canadian Short Stories: 1950–1983*** remains a relevant tool for locating short fiction for the examined period. Aiming to be exhaustive, Weiss lists a total of 14,314 short stories appearing in periodicals, anthologies, and even on CBC Radio’s *Anthology*. While working on his doctoral dissertation, Weiss found commercial indexing services to be inadequate for Canada’s vibrant production of little magazines, and he therefore set about the task of indexing an often obscured genre. In constructing the bibliography, Weiss surveyed Canadian short story writers in an attempt to cull all known works by the authors, in the process discovering pseudonymous titles that would otherwise have gone undetected. Weiss’s tenacity and unorthodox methods in tracking down information for the bibliography are likely a tribute to the passion and fervor of the young graduate student for his subject. Weiss consulted an impressive number of small-press periodicals, many of which are difficult to research even today with the advent of the Internet and consortial catalogs.

As the first bibliography to examine both English and French science fiction and fantasy writing, ***CDN SF & F: A Bibliography of Canadian Science Fiction and Fantasy*** is an interesting testimony to the country’s fascination with the genre. Although the majority of annotations are brief, the length and level of detail for each title listed is variable. Originally contrived as a checklist to be incorporated into the appendix of Colombo and Richardson’s *Other Canadas: An Anthology of Science Fiction and Fantasy*, additional assistance by Bell and Amprimoz allowed the initial conceptualization to develop into a separate bibliographic study. Among other collections, the bibliographers made use of the Toronto Public Library’s “Spaced Out Library,” which was renamed the

Merril Collection of Science Fiction, Speculation and Fantasy in 1991. With each section arranged alphabetically by author, the bibliography is organized into the following categories: "Science Fiction," "National Disaster Scenarios," "Polar Worlds," "Fantasy and Weird Tales," "French-Language Science Fiction and Fantasy," "Children's Literature," "Poetry and Plays," "Prose," "Collections and Criticism," and "Fanzines." The section on "Canadian Interest" encompasses works by expatriates and authors living abroad who nonetheless infuse their writing with Canadian settings and themes.

Havlice's ***And So to Bed: A Bibliography of Diaries Published in English*** annotates English-language diaries published in Canada, the United States, and Britain. Augmenting previous research conducted by Matthews in his three separate works *American Diaries*, *British Diaries*, and *Canadian Diaries*, some entries are also complemented by citations to book reviews. Havlice follows a chronological organization and then alphabetizes the entries according to the diarist's last name.

Carole Gerson's ***Canada's Early Women Writers: Texts in English to 1859*** culls otherwise elusive texts written by pioneers, immigrants, and visitors of colonial Canada. Although Gerson does examine life writing, such as published diaries and letters, excluded from the study are contributions by early female writers to newspapers and literary magazines. Another bibliography pertaining to Canada's early period is Freda Waldon's ***Bibliography of Canadiana Published in Great Britain, 1519–1763***. Compiled during the 1940s and 1950s while actively involved in the effort to establish a National Library of Canada, Waldon's work remained unpublished until the appearance of this ECW Press title in 1990. In preparing Waldon's manuscript for publication, William F. E. Morley revised and augmented the initial endeavor for the present, bilingual edition. Morley's meticulous verification of Waldon's painstaking bibliographic accomplishment reinforces this first-rate resource for researchers of early Canadiana.

With little introductory information, the ***Index to Canadian Poetry in English*** cites nearly seven thousand anthologized poems from the nineteenth and twentieth centuries. Translated French poetry is also considered, and three indexes facilitate discovery, including an index of titles and first lines in addition to author and subject indexes.

## QUEBEC AND FRANCOPHONE LITERATURE

Beaudoin, Réjean, Annette Hayward, and André Lamontagne. *Bibliographie de la critique de la littérature québécoise au Canada anglais (1939–1989)*. Québec: Éditions Nota Bene, 2004.

Dionne, René, and Pierre Cantin. *Bibliographie de la critique de la littérature québécoise et canadienne-française dans les revues canadiennes*. Ottawa: Les Presses de l'Université d'Ottawa, 1992.

Kandiuk, Mary. *French-Canadian Authors: A Bibliography of Their Works and of English Language Criticism*. Metuchen, NJ: Scarecrow Press, 1990.

Rinfret, G. Édouard. *Le théâtre canadien d'expression française: répertoire analytique des origines à nos jours*. Ottawa: Éditions Leméac, 1975.

Tougas, Gerard. *A Checklist of Printed Materials Relating to French-Canadian Literature, 1763–1968/Liste de référence d'imprimés relatifs à la littérature canadienne-française, 1763–1968*. 2nd ed. Vancouver: University of British Columbia Press, 1973.

Tremblay, Jean Pierre. *Bibliographie québécoise: Roman, théâtre, poésie, chanson; inventaire des écrits du Canada français*. Cap-Rouge, Québec: Éduco Média, 1973.

Although it received mixed reviews, Mary Kandiuk's ***French-Canadian Authors: A Bibliography of Their Works and of English Language Criticism*** is generally regarded as an easy-to-use resource. Kandiuk includes thirty-six authors in the bibliography, examining works both by and about the authors, as well as book reviews. The entry on Ringuet, for example, provides entries for articles from scholarly journals, magazines, and reference works, also indicating the specific pages of monographs that consider Ringuet's fiction. An interesting discovery is the critical reception afforded to Ringuet in the *New York Times Book Review* in 1939 and 1940, coinciding with the first English translation of *Trente Arpents/Thirty Acres*. Further examination of one *New York Times* review cited in the bibliography reveals the following insightful observation regarding the novel's protagonist: "Euchariste ('Charis) Moisan, like Lear, gives away his patrimony; but there is no Cordelia in his story."[7] If it is possible to describe a bibliography as elegant, Kandiuk's work is easily classified as such.

The University of Ottawa Press is an active publisher of bibliographies related to French Canadian and Quebec literature, and René Dionne has been a particularly prolific participant in such ventures. Dionne and Cantin's ***Bibliographie de la critique de la littérature québécoise et canadienne-française dans les revues canadiennes*** gives great insight into the critical treatment of French Canadian and Quebecois literature within Canada. In their introduction to the fourth volume, published in 1994, the editors explain that their plan to pursue two further volumes to cover 1900–1973 and 1987–1990, respectively, was inhibited by a lack of both financial funding and human resources. The four volumes of the series examine the following periods: 1974–1978 (vol. 1); 1979–1982 (vol. 2); 1760–1899 (vol. 3); and 1983–1986 (vol. 4). The introduction to volume 3 (1760–1899) explains that the periodicals of the era have little in common with the journals we see today, requiring careful selection of titles relevant to literary themes. Due to the common use of pseudonyms during the nineteenth century, verification of an author's true identity became a difficult part of the bibliographer's task. A flurry of French-language periodicals was published in Canada between 1760 and 1899, as 209 titles appeared to infuse the literary life of francophone Canada. A challenge of constructing this bibliography was the ephemeral nature of the periodicals of the period, as many titles enjoyed only a brief publication run. The bibliographies are divided into the following sections: "Part 1: Generalities" includes general texts that treat Quebecois and French Canadian literature; "Part 2: Genres" organizes the citations by novels, poetry, theater, short stories, essays, news, and oral tradition; and part 3 focuses on texts that deal with a specific author. Entries are unannotated and are listed in chronological order. Three indexes, including an author index, title index, and a year of publication index, complete each volume. The four volumes that materialized from the project represent an astounding collection of work that could only be accomplished through an intense and time-consuming research schedule. If your inquiry leads you to this source, you are fortunate to have the fruit of the authors' labors in this multivolume project.

Designed to facilitate, encourage, and inspire study of the genre, ***Le théâtre canadien d'expression française: répertoire analytique des origines à nos jours*** is a four-volume endeavor that arose from the 1961 Festival national d'art dramatique du Canada (National Festival of Dramatic Arts). In a very forthcoming introduction, G. Édouard Rinfret describes the sidewalk-pounding fervor with which he undertook the project, in the process discovering over three hundred unpublished plays which were subsequently deposited with the National Library. Rinfret recounts the serendipitous act of soliciting copies of plays from author Ernest Guimond for the National Library shortly before a house fire consumed the originals. Such anecdotes further confirm that the work of the bibliographer can read like an archeologist's adventure novel.

A bibliography eight years in the making, thorough publication and performance information is provided for the works listed. Entries are arranged alphabetically by author, qualifying the genre, number of acts and scenes, and estimated length in minutes, where available. Descriptive notes offer information on scenery, and a cast of characters is also listed. Rinfret's plot summaries are impressive and detailed enough to represent an interesting read in themselves. Synopses from French-language newspapers, such as *La Presse*, are occasionally used in place of Rinfret's own summaries. Volume 4 exclusively examines televised works (1952–1973) and dramas adapted for television. The indexes for the series are also found within the fourth volume, which ultimately concludes with a chronology of televised works. Rinfret's endeavor is a tribute to the bibliographer's craft, conveying an obsession for his subject, and is sure to inspire theater research for years to come.

Jean Pierre Tremblay's ***Bibliographie québécoise: Roman, théâtre, poésie, chanson; inventaire des écrits du Canada français*** begins with a series of introductory sections providing recommendations for background works related to French Canadian history and civilization. Tremblay also compiles a summary of the various periodizations applied to Quebec literature under "Les périodes de l'histoire littéraire," summarizing differing conceptualizations as applied in six surveys of French Canadian literary history. A section entitled "Un livre important" lists the table of contents to the four volumes of Pierre de Grandpré's *Histoire de la littérature française du Québec*, highlighting the work as one that belongs in the personal collections of all professors of Quebec literature. Other sections examine significant literary studies, including large surveys and important essay collections related to Quebec literature in French, French Canadian literature, and the Montreal School. The first part of Tremblay's work is organized in a manner different from the standard bibliographical format, and although most entries are unannotated, in reprinting the table of contents for the works selected, Tremblay offers adequate insight. The chronological organization of Tremblay's annotated "Manuel d'histoire de la littérature canadienne-française" highlights key pedagogical works for a given period. Other sections of the bibliography offer unannotated author/title entries for anthologies, novels, poetry, general works, theater, songs, critical essays, and monographs related to specific authors. In his introduction, Tremblay relates that his experience as a professor of Quebec literature informed his work, and as such, the bibliography serves as an enlightening survey of Quebec writing in French.

Beaudoin, Hayward, and Lamontagne's ***Bibliographie de la critique de la littérature québécoise au Canada anglais (1939–1989)*** began as a project between the University of British Columbia and Queen's University, comparing the critical reception of French Quebec literature in English-speaking Canada and French Quebec. The authors direct their work toward students, scholars, and anyone interested in Quebec literature in French to assist in illuminating similarities and differences in both critical treatment and canon formation. Citations also explore critical works written in French by writers who usually publish in English. The authors delineate the following periods to mark significant events or changes in Quebec literary history: 1939–1959, 1960–1969, 1970–1979, and 1979–1989. Chronological periods are organized by format, including monographs, book chapters, articles, essays, introductions and prefaces, articles in reference works, and anthologies. Over 2,700 entries assist the researcher in tracing English Canada's attention to Quebec authors, from the Second World War, through the Quiet Revolution, and up until the eve of the last decade of the twentieth century. The introduction provides graphs to illustrate the progression of critical treatment rendered to Quebec writing for the period covered, demonstrating a steady increase in interest. Additional graphical information illuminates Quebec authors, both living and deceased, who have garnered the most attention among anglophone critics, such as Anne Hébert, Marie-Claire Blais, Roch Carrier, and Hector de Saint-Denys Garneau.

As stated, this work serves to highlight disparities between a writer's critical reception in Quebec and inconsistent equivalents by English-speaking critics. The authors point out, for example, that Roch Carrier enjoys greater critical success in English Canadian criticism than he does in his native Quebec. Conversely, Jacques Poulin is received with lukewarm enthusiasm by English critics while enjoying significant critical acclaim in French literary circles. The authors state that general-interest Canadian literary magazines, such as *Quill and Quire*, have contributed to raising the status and awareness of Quebec literature within anglophone literary communities. An index of Quebec authors facilitates access to citations related to a particular writer, also exposing their level of critical treatment within English Canada. This bibliography concludes with a useful selection of reference titles and critical and theoretical studies related to Quebec literature.

First published in 1958, ***A Checklist of Printed Materials Relating to French-Canadian Literature, 1763–1968/Liste de référence d'imprimés relatifs à la littérature canadienne-française, 1763–1968*** is a standard title for the discovery of materials pertaining to the development of French Canadian literature. In his preface to the first edition, Tougas laments the lack of bibliographic studies to keep pace with the prolific literature of French Canada. The first section, "Works and Criticism," is organized alphabetically by author. In the second edition, Tougas augments his original study through the incorporation of theses and a brief list of other bibliographic studies related to the literature of Quebec and French Canada.

## BIBLIOGRAPHIES OF THESES

Naaman, Antoine. *Guide bibliographique des thèses littéraires canadiennes de 1921 à 1969*. Montréal: Éditions Cosmos, 1970.

Steele, Apollonia. *Theses on English-Canadian Literature: A Bibliography of Research Produced in Canada and Elsewhere from 1903 Forward.* Calgary, Alberta: University of Calgary Press, 1988. Also available online through NetLibrary.

In his preface to Naaman's guide, ***Guide bibliographique des thèses littéraires canadiennes de 1921 à 1969***, Jean Houpert explains the difficulties inherent in the selection of a thesis topic, pointing out that students have often had to piece together incomplete bibliographies published in disparate works. Naaman's guide is valuable for its retroactive completeness, dusting off the title pages of theses that perhaps had been long forgotten. Citing the fact that graduate-level researchers are often bilingual, and even polyglots, Naaman retains the title of each thesis in its original language. Organized into three sections, all of the theses listed were completed at Canadian institutions and focus on a literary topic. Canadian literary theses, written in either English or French, are only examined in part 1. Each part is further subdivided into "General Subjects" (Sujets généraux) and "Authors" (Auteurs). "General Subjects" is further broken down into the following subdivisions: "Civilization, Folklore and the Development of Thought," "Comparative Studies," "Literary Genres," "Literary History," and "Linguistics." Three indexes complete the title, including an analytical index of keywords found in the titles of theses, an index to authors and thesis directors, and an index of the authors treated.

The guide provides a fascinating overview of the status and variety of Canadian literary topics during an early period of the history of the literature. Thesis topics cover everything imaginable, from the memoirs of female pioneers, to writings for radio and television in French Canada, to the image of Toronto as portrayed in Canadian literature. The guide includes eleven theses written on Malcolm Lowry between 1965 and 1968, a further indication of the author's impact on the Canadian literary landscape.

Written by Apollonia Steele, a Special Collections librarian at the University of Calgary often named in the acknowledgments of works on Canadian literary studies, ***Theses on English-Canadian Literature: A Bibliography of Research Produced in Canada and Elsewhere from 1903 Forward*** attempts to comprehensively locate as many works as possible from around the world. The bibliography is organized according to thesis subject and thesis author, with several indexes promoting access to titles by university, degree earned, and date. Although the entries are unannotated, by listing the titles under well-devised subject terms, researchers should be able to assess the appropriateness of a given title to their own study. In comparison to Naaman's aforementioned work, Steele's bibliography uncovers twenty-five Lowry theses produced between 1965 and 1968.

## INDIVIDUAL AUTHOR BIBLIOGRAPHIES

Mazur, Carol. *Alice Munro: An Annotated Bibliography of Works and Criticism*, ed. Cathy Moulder. Lanham, MD: Scarecrow Press, 2007.

Oore, Irene. *Marie-Claire Blais: An Annotated Bibliography*. Toronto: ECW Press, 1998.

Panofsky, Ruth. *Adele Wiseman: An Annotated Bibliography*. Toronto: ECW Press, 1992.

Pollock, Zailig, Usher Caplan, and Linda Rozmovits. *A. M. Klein: An Annotated Bibliography*. Toronto: ECW Press, 1993.

Roberts, Carol, and Lynne Macdonald. *Timothy Findley: An Annotated Bibliography*. Toronto: ECW Press, 1990.

Spadoni, Carl. *A Bibliography of Stephen Leacock*. Toronto: ECW Press, 1998.

Vincent, Thomas B. *Basil King: A Bibliography of the Fiction*. 2nd ser., rev. Kingston, Ontario: Loyal Colonies Press, 2004.

Vincent, Thomas B. *E. Pauline Johnson: A Bibliography*. Kingston, Ontario: Loyal Colonies Press, 2006.

We can expect that bibliographers will continue to invigorate scholarship through the publication of author-specific studies related to Canadian writers. To find bibliographies in addition to those discussed below, consult your library catalog. If you find that a simple *WorldCat* search for *Robertson Davies* and *bibliography* is not an effective way to locate relevant results, use options available through field searching. An advanced search for subject *Davies, Robertson* and subject *bibliography*, for example, uncovers *Robertson Davies: Life, Work, and Criticism* by Lynne Diamond-Nigh. A review of the subject headings assigned to this title gives us, "Davies, Robertson,—1913–1995—Bibliography," which we can now use as a model for subsequent searches and serves as a link to additional Davies bibliographies.

Mazur's ***Alice Munro: An Annotated Bibliography of Works and Criticism*** is a thorough exploration, comprehensively covering both material by Munro and secondary works that treat her writing. Primary works encompass novels, short fiction, and media materials, including several CBC Radio interviews. Nonfiction pieces, such as essays, memoirs, and Munro's letters to editors are also exhaustively considered. Secondary works on Munro consist of theses and dissertations, numerous book reviews from both notable and lesser-known publications, critical titles, biographies, bibliographies, reference works, literary awards, conferences, and special journal issues devoted to the author. Mazur also provides a selective list of Internet sources. In her introduction, Mazur explains some of the challenges in compiling the bibliography, for example, the prevalence of non-English-language materials on Munro worldwide, consisting of a steady stream of criticism, anthologized works, and articles from periodicals in limited circulation. Mazur gives a thorough picture of Munro's literary reach in listing the numerous editions, reprints, and translations of the author's writing. Entries are arranged alphabetically versus chronologically. Interesting annotations surround Munro's nonfiction writings, as Mazur summarizes the author's many letters to the editor, allowing the reader insight into literary controversies and misunderstandings. For example, at entry P693, Munro responds to the censorship of Margaret Laurence's *The Diviners* by schools in Huron County, Ontario. In another letter at entry P688, Munro explains that she was misquoted in her characterization of Wingham, Ontario, clarifying that she "always found Wingham lively and interesting" (84). The 134 theses and dissertations found within the secondary works sections testify to the author's impact on Canadian scholars.

Following the conclusion of the *Annotated Bibliography of Canada's Major Authors* (*ABCMA*), ECW Press continued to deliver outstanding bibliographies of Canada's most notable authors. In the format of the *ABCMA*, each ECW title provides an introduction and organizes the content according to works by (part 1) and on (part 2) the selected author. Roberts and Macdonald convey in-depth knowledge of their subject in ***Timothy Findley: An Annotated Bibliography***. Annotations under "Works on Timothy Findley" carefully highlight significant statements regarding Findley's critical reception. In another ECW Press title, Pollock, Caplan, and Rozmovits collaborate to compile ***A. M. Klein: An Annotated Bibliography***. Aiming to be exhaustive in their pursuit of Canadian materials related to Klein, the bibliographers faithfully assemble the poet and writer's multitudinous articles, pamphlets, and essays. Ruth Panofsky's ***Adele Wiseman: An Annotated Bibliography*** likewise offers the same careful presentation as the two previous titles and follows the same basic organization as the *ABCMA*. In common with other ECW Press bibliographies, the bibliographer combs through manuscript collections to list all known Wiseman correspondence, drafts, and proofs. As an author whose papers are in disparate archival collections due to her contact with many well-known Canadian authors, this portion of the bibliography definitely contributes to a thorough study. The most recent ECW Press bibliography is ***Marie-Claire Blais: An Annotated Bibliography***. Communication with the publisher indicates that no further bibliographic titles are planned.

Spadoni's ***A Bibliography of Stephen Leacock*** is a fine example of descriptive bibliography. Restricted to Leacock's primary works, the bibliography enumerates the many editions of the author's books, as well as pamphlets, broadsides, sketches, commentaries, articles, letters to the editor, personal writings, and interviews, among other material. The early Canadian humorist, recruited by Bodley Head at the onset of his career, illustrates the transnational lifestyle that Canadian writers led during a period when the Canadian/U.S. border was far less restrictive. Leacock serves as an excellent subject for a descriptive bibliography, as his books were often reprinted in Canada, the United States, and England. Chronological organization of entries is followed within each category. An interesting addition to the bibliography is found in section L, "Lost Leads," which includes material that was not verifiable, either due to an ephemeral existence, or even perhaps because, despite Leacock's intentions, the item never did materialize in print. In his introduction, Spadoni offers significant detail regarding the location of Leacock's papers in archives at various institutions, such as McGill University and the Stephen Leacock Museum. A chronology highlights significant events in Leacock's personal and literary life.

Descriptive bibliographies are of exceptional value and use to book dealers, archivists, and librarians, as they examine the intimate publication details of the various editions, imprints, and translations. As a descriptive bibliography, Spadoni's investigation is incredibly detailed, providing title page information, binding variations, and the style of typeface for the various editions of Leacock's works. Spadoni builds on the labors of previous Leacock bibliographers, extending the comprehensiveness and detail of their inquiries.

As part of the Bibliofiles Project, authors are chosen from Watters' 1972 edition of *A Checklist of Canadian Literature and Background Materials, 1628–1960* for an in-depth accounting of the publishing history of selected early Canadian writers. To date, Loyal Colonies Press has published bibliographies for H. A. Cody, Basil King, W. A. Fraser, E. Pauline Johnson, and Arthur Stringer, as well as three volumes dedicated to Charles G. D. Roberts. ***Basil King: A Bibliography of the Fiction*** begins with an enumerative bibliography of King's writings, accompanied by annotations describing the unique features of the various editions and printings. Each item listed is further examined according to the norms of descriptive bibliography, with specifics for the item's title page, dedication page, dust jacket, and cover, among other bibliographic features. As such, the Loyal Colonies Press bibliographies are geared toward providing the level of detail that book dealers, special collections librarians, and Basil King scholars would find most useful. Another title in the series, ***E. Pauline Johnson: A Bibliography***, follows the same pattern of organization. The strength of the series is seen, for example, in the entries for Johnson's *Flint and Feather*, as the bibliographer lists and later describes in detail all fifty-six printings and editions from 1912 to 1997.

## EXAMPLES OF BIBLIOGRAPHIES PUBLISHED IN JOURNALS

Many scholarly and literary journals periodically print bibliographies related to a specific author, genre, or theme. Below is but a select sampling of the kinds of bibliographies that can be found within the pages of Canadian journals. In addition to the titles listed, publications regularly featuring bibliographies include the *Journal of Canadian Fiction* and *Modern Fiction Studies*.

"Appendix: Bibliography of Materials on L. M. Montgomery Published in *Canadian Children's Literature* 1975–2004." *Canadian Children's Literature* 113/114 (Spring/Summer 2004): 117–120.
Beauchemin, Melanie, and Nathalie Watteyne. "Bibliographie de Louise Dupré." *Voix et images* 34 (Spring 2009): 97–118.
"Canadian Ethnic Studies/Études ethniques au Canada." (Bibliography). *Canadian Ethnic Studies Journal* 36 (Fall 2004): 152–184.
"David Arnason: A Short Bibliography." *Prairie Fire*, Spring 2001, 8–9.
Saltman, Judith. "The Jewish Experience in *Canadian Children's Literature*." *Canadian Children's Literature* 115–116 (2004): 105–143.

## ANNUAL REVIEWS

*The Year's Work in English Studies*. Oxford: Oxford University Press, 1920–. http://ywes.oxfordjournals.org.

Annual reviews reveal invaluable information regarding the publication climate of a given year. The *Journal of Commonwealth Literature* publishes an annual bibliography of works, with a section devoted to Canadian Literature, and the *University of Toronto Quarterly* features an excellent annual "Letters in Canada" issue.

A wonderful resource for Canadian literary research, Canada receives unprejudiced coverage and careful treatment in ***The Year's Work in English Studies***. Entries are very readable and may elucidate new insights for further literary research. Discussion of Canadian literature comes under the section "New Literatures." Reviewers provide adequate detail on publication and reception of new reference, biographical, and critical works within the frameworks of "General literature," "Fiction," and "Poetry and Drama." Special issues of journals such as *Canadian Literature*, the *University of Toronto Quarterly*, and *Studies in Canadian Literature* are also highlighted. Journal articles and essays treating Canadian literature from interdisciplinary titles, such as *Revista Canaria de Estudios Ingleses*, the *Journal of Narrative Theory*, and *Modern Fiction Studies*, are also discussed. Canadian literature garners consideration in a variety of interdisciplinary, Commonwealth, and world literature journals, and *The Year's Work in English Studies* should therefore be seen as a valuable time-saving device for those trying to stay abreast of the field. The online version of the publication facilitates discovery, as it offers full-text searching of all published volumes, from January 1919 forward.

## CONCLUSION

The bibliographer's work is precious to literary researchers, as a bibliography can translate into a time-saving point of departure in the identification of materials relevant to their study. At times, the volume of information included in a bibliography can be overwhelming, and if you're striving for comprehensiveness, you may want to examine bibliographies in small, frequent doses. By their nature, bibliographies are exhaustive lists of works pertaining to a given topic or subject, so if you do find yourself overwhelmed by the amount of information available, find consolation in the fact that the compiler has likely saved you a great deal of time on the trail of otherwise esoteric resources.

General bibliographies, such as the *MLAIB*, though large in scope, can reveal unexpected insight, such as the interrelatedness of literatures, unprecedented comparative content, and unimagined research avenues. Specialized print bibliographies, such as *Peel's Bibliography of the Canadian Prairies*, likewise represent the bibliographer's focused and untiring pursuit of the literary universe related to a given subject. As you delve deeper into an area of research, you will find bibliographies, indexes, and annual reviews to be sources of information that can both launch and guide the inquiry process.

## NOTES

1. See www.library.utoronto.ca/bsc/bulletineng.html.
2. D. M. Fraser, "Margaret Atwood's *Surfacing*," *3 Cent Pulp* 2, no.1 (May 1, 1974): 1–4, cited in the *ABCMA*, p. 39.
3. Joseph Edgar Chamberlain, "The Listener," *Boston Evening Transcript*, August 12, 1891, 4, cited in the *ABCMA*, p. 116.
4. Leo Kennedy, "Canadian Writers of the Past: Archibald Lampman," *Canadian Forum* 14 (May 1933): 301–303, quoted in the *ABCMA*, p. 123.
5. To illustrate the changing nature of bibliographic research, this work is one which today Peel would have been able to conveniently inspect through Gale's *Eighteenth Century Collections Online*, discussed in chapter 7.
6. O. G. Corbett, *A Few Reasons for a Crown Colony* (Headingley, Manitoba: Headingley Press, 1859).
7. J. S. Southron, "Canadian Generation," review of *Trente Arpents*, by Ringuet, *New York Times*, October 13, 1940, p. 90.

## *Chapter Five*

# Scholarly Journals

This chapter will examine general scholarly journals covering Canadian authors and themes, as well as journals and newsletters devoted to individual authors. Scholarly journals provide humanities researchers with a platform for presenting their research, knowledge, and expertise. As a forum for discussion and information sharing, journals also offer an arena for discovery, insight, and new critical directions.

As scholarly journals continue their conversion to online formats, currently published print resources are becoming a thing of the past. Archival digitization projects are ongoing, converting issues that were once only available in print to electronic formats. In cases where a title has not been selected for retroactive digitization, the print journal is still a necessity for historical coverage. Many scholarly journals are in a transitive state, but the migration of small-press journals to the electronic world is still tenuous in some cases. Numerous libraries have not been able to meet the inflationary costs of academic journal subscriptions and have subsequently cut the number of journals to which they subscribe. Such actions create a ripple effect: as journals lose subscriptions, publishers may discontinue production in the face of financial challenges. While journal prices continue to rise, support for open-access models is also increasing. Your access to and ability to acquire an academic journal article will therefore vary according to several scenarios, for example,

- Does your institution have a current subscription? Does this subscription include both print and online access?
- If the subscription has been cancelled, what years did the subscription cover?

- In cases where your institution does not subscribe to a given journal, does your institution offer a free or fee-based "pay-per-view" service that may allow you to obtain a copy of the article?
- Does the journal publish under a full open-access, delayed open-access, or even a partial open-access model? Is there an embargo period for open access? (Some journals have an embargo period of a year or more in order to encourage readers to maintain their subscription.)
- Does open access include the ability to see all, or only certain sections, of the journal contents? (For example, in some cases, editor's remarks and introductions are only published in the print version or through a subscription model.)

Although you may find that your library is subscribing to fewer and fewer journals, your institution should still be able to acquire a copy of a journal article through an interlibrary loan service, which may facilitate electronic delivery of journal articles to your e-mail account. Where you do not have a subscription to a given journal, abstracts may be available through your institution's online databases, allowing you to at least surmise whether an article will be of use prior to requesting it through interlibrary loan.

For more detailed information on journals listed here, consult *Ulrich's Periodical Index* (http://ulrichsweb.com), which will provide additional information on journal pricing and circulation. Journal evaluations can often be found in review publications, such as *Quill and Quire* and the *Atlantic Provinces Book Review*. The *MLAIB* online includes access to the *MLA Directory of Periodicals*, which can clarify further information on a given journal, such as publisher details, circulation, journal scope, and frequency.

If you are fortunate enough to have a subscription to Gale's *CPI.Q* through your institution, you will find that most of the journals listed below are indexed via this service. Another key index for Canadian academic literary journals is the *MLAIB*, which covers many of the French- and English-language titles highlighted in this chapter. Indexing for the titles found below may also be available through other services, such as *Humanities International Index*, the *Arts and Humanities Citation Index*, and *ABELL*. Full-text access to some of the titles listed may likewise be available through online journal collections, such as *Project Muse* and *JSTOR*.

## GENERAL CANADIAN LITERATURE JOURNALS

*Canadian Literature*. Vancouver: University of British Columbia Press, 1959–. Quarterly. ISSN: 0008-4360. www.canlit.ca (accessed 25 June 2010).

*Essays on Canadian Writing*. Toronto: ECW Press, 1974–. 3/year. ISSN: 0316-0300.

*Studies in Canadian Literature/Études en littérature canadienne* (*SCL/ÉLC*). Fredericton: University of New Brunswick, 1976–. 2/year. ISSN: 0380-6995. www.lib.unb.ca/Texts/SCL (accessed 25 June 2010).

While there are many scholarly and literary journals that cover some aspect of Canadian literature, either from interdisciplinary perspectives or within world literatures, only a handful of journals are uniquely dedicated to Canadian literature, criticism, and analysis. Nonetheless, the few journals that fall into this category can be considered outstanding titles in their overall quality and eclectic approach. Covering all aspects of Canadian writing, the University of British Columbia's ***Canadian Literature*** is often regarded as the premier journal of the field. The journal's history is deeply grounded in the country's literary past, as prominent writer George Woodcock edited the journal's first seventy-three issues, from 1959 to 1977. W. H. New, a noted critic and prolific Canadian literary scholar, succeeded Woodcock from 1977 to 1995 and responded to Canada's burgeoning multicultural and aboriginal literatures during the course of his editorship. Attracting contributions from a virtual who's who of Canadian literature, including Margaret Atwood, Mordecai Richler, and Margaret Laurence, the journal has helped foster and solidify Canadian literature's standing as a distinct and national phenomenon. In 1988, *Canadian Literature* became the first and only journal to win the Gabrielle Roy Prize for best English book-length studies in Canadian and Quebec literary criticism. Reviewing the list of back issues, one obtains a very good sense of the multicultural orientation inherent in Canadian writing, as themed issues include coverage of francophone, South Asian, First Nations, black writing, Italian Canadian, and Slavic literatures, among many others. *Canadian Literature* is indexed in the *MLAIB* and *CPI.Q*.

While so many Canadian literary journals serve new writing, ***Essays on Canadian Writing*** is strictly devoted to literary criticism. Publishing submissions in both English and French, the journal provides a platform for critical literary essays, literary analysis, and book reviews. Interviews and bibliographies on Canadian literature are also published. The journal sponsors the George Wicken Prize in Canadian Literature, awarded annually to the best critical essay submitted by either a graduate or undergraduate student. Issues sometimes center around a theme, such as "Recent Canadian Fiction" (Spring 2001), "Race" (Winter 2002), or "Food, Cooking and Eating" (Winter 2003). Essays are often intriguingly unique, such as Michelle Hartley's "Does Shirley Temple Eat Chicken Feet? Consuming Ambivalence in Wayson Choy's *The Jade Peony*" (Winter 2003), or Wicken Prize winner

Lindsey McMaster's "The Urban Working Girl in Turn-of-the-Century Canadian Fiction" (Fall 2002). Similarly irresistible contributions include "'Git yr/eye off Canada/and onto internat criteria': Exploring the Influence of Ezra Pound on the Cultural Production of Louis Dudek" by Tony Tremblay (Fall 2001) and "Native Canadian Gothic Refigured: Reading Eden Robinson's *Monkey Beach*" by Jennifer Andrews (Spring 2001). Such content abounds in this gem of literary journals, attracting contributions the likes of which you will not find elsewhere. An added bonus to each issue is the cover artwork, featuring submissions from Canadian artists. *Essays on Canadian Writing* is indexed in the *MLAIB* and *CPI.Q*.

Hailing from the University of New Brunswick, ***Studies in Canadian Literature/Études en littérature canadienne*** delivers refereed essays, literary criticism, and book reviews covering an eclectic mix of Canadian writers and themes. Examples of contributions include "The Future of Racial Memory: Forgiveness, Reconciliation, and Redress in Joy Kogawa's Obasan and Itsuka" (Summer 2005) by Julie McGonegal. Special issues are published periodically; "Women in Motion" (Spring 2004) and "Past Matters: History and Canadian Fiction" (Spring 2002) are some examples. Although less structured than *Canadian Literature*, some full-text access to back issues is available online, and abstracts of more recent issues can be accessed through the journal's home page. This title is indexed in the *MLAIB* and *CPI.Q*.

## GENRE JOURNALS AND CANADIAN REGIONAL TITLES

*Canadian Poetry: Studies, Documents, Reviews*. London, Ontario: University of Western Ontario, 1977–. 2/year. ISSN: 0704-5646. www.canadianpoetry.ca (accessed 25 June 2010).

*Canadian Theatre Review*. Toronto: University of Toronto Press, 1974–. Quarterly. ISSN: 0315-0836. www.utpjournals.com/ctr/ctr.html (accessed 25 June 2010).

*Études françaises*. Montréal: Les Presses de l'Université de Montréal, 1965–. 3/year. ISSN: 0014-2085. www.erudit.org (accessed 25 June 2010).

*Jeunesse: Young People, Texts, Cultures*. Guelph, Ontario: University of Guelph, 1975–. 2/year. ISSN: 0319-0080. E-ISSN: 1703-6453. http://ccl.uwinnipeg.ca (accessed 25 June 2010).

*LittéRéalité*. Toronto: LittéRéalité Publications, 1989–2008. ISSN: 0843-4182.

*Prairie Journal: A Magazine of Canadian Literature*. Calgary, Alberta: Prairie Journal Trust, 1983–. Semiannually. ISSN: 0827-2921. www.geocities.com/prairiejournal (accessed 25 June 2010).

*Theatre Research in Canada/Recherches théâtrales au Canada*. Toronto: Graduate Centre for the Study of Drama, 1980–. 2/year. ISSN: 1196-1198. www.lib.unb.ca/Texts/TRIC (accessed 9 July 2010).

*Voix et images: littérature québécoise*. Montreal: Presses de l'Université du Québec, 1975–. 3/year. ISSN: 0318-9201. www.voixetimages.uqam.ca (accessed 25 June 2010).

Given the scale of Canada's publishing market, the prevalence and variety of specialized journals related to specific literatures, regions, and genres are indicative of the country's strong literary tradition. The journals in this section collectively convey the rich scholarly constituencies related to Canadian literature and literary production.

A perusal of the table of contents of the issues of ***Canadian Poetry: Studies, Documents, Reviews*** serves as a great testament to Canada's varied and notable poetic talent. Articles examine poets from Archibald Purdy, Leonard Cohen, Robert Service, and Gwendolyn MacEwen to bill bissett, Carl F. Klinck, and Mary di Michele, among many others. Previous issues are available full-text online; although a publisher's embargo restricts access to the more recent issues, these can be accessed through a subscription. Book reviews are commissioned. This title is indexed in the *MLAIB*; indexing is not available through *CPI.Q*.

Edited by renowned Canadian playwright, scholar, and critic Ric Knowles, ***Canadian Theatre Review*** publishes themed issues covering criticism, formerly unpublished works, and interviews with Canadian playwrights. Multicultural and ethnic topics figure prominently in the journal; the summer 2009 issue, for example, features an interview with innovative Cree performance artist Archer Pechawis as well as Floyd Favel's article "Poetry, Remnants and Ruins: Aboriginal Theatre in Canada." This title is indexed in the *MLAIB* and *CPI.Q*.

Covering French authors from around the globe, ***Études françaises*** provides a schema for positioning French Canadian and Quebec authors within the global context. Published in French, the journal presents themed issues on French literature, theory, and criticism from all literary eras and locales. Recent articles pertaining to Canadian writers include K. Tardif's "La bibliothèque imaginaire de l'humanité souffrante dans la trilogie Soifs de Marie-Claire Blais" (2008, no. 3) and M. H. LaRochelle's "Fuites et invectives dans les romans de Réjean Ducharme" (2008, no. 1). The journal's website delivers a great deal of full-text content; however, recent issues are restricted to subscribers. This title is indexed in the *MLAIB*; it is not indexed in *CPI.Q*.

A refereed journal publishing articles in English and French, ***Jeunesse: Young People, Texts, Cultures*** provides critical essays and reviews of texts for children published around the world. The journal, which once focused only on Canadian literary studies as *Canadian Children's Literature (CCL)/ Littérature canadienne pour la jeunesse (LCJ)*, underwent a title change in 2010 to reflect its new international scope. The journal examines the history of children's book publishing, as illustrated in Perry Nodelman's editorial essay "Where We've Come From, Where We Are Now, Where We're Going" (Spring 2005). Contributors approach children's literature from a variety of creative angles, delivering issues that are brimming with originality and fresh perspective. Examples of recently published articles include Judith Thistleton-Martin's "How Do Students in an Australian Classroom Construct Canadian Identity from Canadian Picture Books?" (Spring 2008). Margaret Mackey is among the notable children's literature scholars publishing regularly in the journal. Issues also include interviews with authors and illustrators. Book reviews are solicited. This title is indexed in the *MLAIB* and *CPI.Q*. The journal's bilingual English/French website also contains a searchable index of past articles.

Published out of York University, ***LittéRéalité*** had as its original mission the promotion of a vibrant Franco-Ontarian literature. Eventually, the journal extended its scope to represent international francophone literatures, publishing critical articles, reviews, unpublished poetry, and essays. Submissions are mainly written in French; however, English-language content is occasionally printed. Like other journals in the new millennium, the editorial for the fall/winter 2008 issue explains that *LittéRéalité* had unfortunately reached its final run. Longtime editor Sergio Villani laments the demise of Franco-Ontarian literature, attributing the cause to several factors, including a weak critical tradition, which he characterizes as "often partisan and incestuous."[1] *LittéRéalité* is indexed in the *MLAIB*; however, indexing is not available through *CPI.Q*.

Covering the literature of western Canada and supported by the Alberta Foundation for the Arts, ***Prairie Journal: A Magazine of Canadian Literature*** publishes poetry, short fiction, literary criticism, reviews, drama, essays, bibliographies, artwork, and interviews. Selected poetry and reviews are also available online through the journal's website. Essays include, for example, Carlotta Abrams's "A History of the Japanese Canadian Internment and Japanese Canadian Literature" (no. 33). A small publication with limited circulation, it nonetheless serves as a platform for Canadian prairie writing and criticism. Neither the *MLAIB* nor the *CPI.Q* offers indexing; however, *Prairie Journal* is actively indexed in the *Humanities International Index*.

***Theatre Research in Canada/Recherches théâtrales au Canada*** prints articles and book reviews to address Canadian theater history and criticism. Individual issues are guest edited and generally center on a particular theme, such as volume 30, the 2009 special double issue "Performing Intercultural Canada," edited by Ric Knowles. English- and French-language submissions are accepted. Access to past issues is freely available online, and the journal's website features a searchable index. This title is indexed in the *MLAIB* and *CPI.Q*.

A journal dedicated exclusively to the study of Quebec literature, ***Voix et images: littérature québécoise*** receives funding and support from both the FQRSC (Fonds québécois de recherche sur la société et la culture/Quebec Research Foundation for Society and Culture) and the Social Sciences and Humanities Research Council/Conseil de recherches en sciences humaines (SSHRC/CRSH). Publishing exclusively in French, submissions include essays, interviews, fiction, poetry, bibliographies, and book reviews. Individual issues focus on a given author or theme, such as the autumn 2008 issue featuring poet Pierre Nepveu and spring/summer 2009's "Trajectoires de l'auteur dans le théâtre contemporain." Access to all but the most recent issues is available through the Érudit consortium website (www.erudit.org/revue/). This title is indexed in the *MLAIB* and *CPI.Q*.

## INTERNATIONAL LITERATURE JOURNALS WITH CANADIAN CONTENT

*Antigonish Review*. Antigonish, Nova Scotia: Saint Francis Xavier University, 1970–. Quarterly. ISBN: 0003-5661. www.antigonishreview.com (accessed 25 June 2010).

*ARIEL: A Review of International English Literature*. Calgary, Alberta: University of Calgary Press, 1960–. Quarterly. ISSN: 0004-1327. http://english.ucalgary.ca/ariel (accessed 25 June 2010).

*International Fiction Review*. Fredericton, New Brunswick: International Fiction Association, 1974–. Semiannually. ISSN: 0315-4149. www.lib.unb.ca/Texts/IFR (accessed 25 June 2010).

*Journal of Commonwealth Literature*. London: Sage Publications, 1965–. Quarterly. ISSN: 0021-9894. http://jcl.sagepub.com (accessed 25 June 2010).

*Mosaic: A Journal for the Interdisciplinary Study of Literature*. Winnipeg, Manitoba: University of Manitoba Press, 1967–. Quarterly. ISSN: 0027-1276. www.umanitoba.ca/mosaic (accessed 25 June 2010).

Journals covering international and world literature will undoubtedly include some content on Canadian topics. Although you will not find Canadian subjects discussed in each and every issue of the titles listed below, staying current on the topics examined within these journals can afford a sense of Canada's place within the international context.

Hailing from Saint Francis Xavier University, an established undergraduate East Coast institution, the ***Antigonish Review*** publishes poetry, fiction, reviews, interviews, and critical essays from both Canada and abroad. A nice feature of the journal is the "Translations" section, offering side-by-side dual-language comparison of works printed in other languages. Book reviews, original poetry, and fiction make up the bulk of the material contributed. Some content, including critical essays from recent issues, can be accessed through the journal's website. Robert Edison Sandiford's book review of Yann Martel's *Life of Pi* (Winter 2003) is exemplary of the succinct clarity found within the *Review*'s pages. Issues also feature a selected artist, not only showcasing their artwork on the cover of the issue but throughout the selections. The *Antigonish Review* is indexed in the *MLAIB* and *CPI.Q*.

A well-established Canadian journal, ***ARIEL: A Review of International English Literature*** provides scholarly coverage of literatures in English from around the world. Topics related to colonial power and the impact of colonization on literature constitute a specific focus of the journal. *ARIEL* also examines relationships and intersections between new literatures and established canons. Articles on Canadian literature are at times few and far between; however, when included, they provide unique perspectives on cultural topics, such as Milan V. Dimic's "Language in Chinese Canadian Writing: Impact on Interpretation and Reception" (April/July 2006). Several book reviews are found in each issue, often selecting works that discuss colonial and postcolonial topics in world literature and cultures. New poetry is occasionally accepted for publication. *ARIEL* is indexed in the *MLAIB* and *CPI.Q*.

Published by the International Fiction Association, the ***International Fiction Review*** offers comprehensive coverage of world literature. Although Canadian fiction receives limited treatment due to the international scope of this journal, the Canadian works and literary topics featured convey the country's position within world literature. Book reviews of monographs published in Canada are more frequently printed than critical essays on Canadian literary themes. Nonetheless, among the uniquely Canadian contributions are "Temples and Tabernacles: Alternative Religions in the Fictional Microcosms of Robertson Davies, Margaret Laurence, and Alice Munro" (January 2004) and "Hearts of Stone: Quarrying the Canadian Shield in Recent Canadian Women's Writing" (January 2006), both by Nora Foster Stovel. The journal's website provides a searchable index of articles with some full-text access to recent issues. *International Fiction Review* is indexed in the *MLAIB* and *CPI.Q*.

While publishing articles pertaining to a variety of colonial nations, the ***Journal of Commonwealth Literature*** frequently has its eye on Canada. Recent submissions include "'Hello, Canada! It's Fine to Have You Here': Canadian Nationhood, Women and Popular Fiction during the Second World War" (2009), an examination of Canadian women's periodical publishing by Michelle Denise Smith. A notable feature is the journal's annual December issue, publishing the "Annual Bibliography of Commonwealth Literature," which offers a section devoted to Canada. The editor's introductions should not be overlooked within these special issues, as they provide a succinct synopsis of the developments, commonalities, and interdependencies related to Commonwealth literature during a given year. The current section for Canada has been compiled and introduced by Diana Chlebek since 2002; previous bibliographies were jointly written by William H. New and Moshie Dahms. A convenient feature of each bibliography is the listing of special journal issues related to Canadian literature appearing during the previous year. This title is indexed in the *MLAIB* but not in *CPI.Q*.

Published out of the University of Manitoba, ***Mosaic: A Journal for the Interdisciplinary Study of Literature*** has carved out its own niche as a unique journal of literary criticism and inquiry. Articles approach literature from unexpected angles, disciplines, and perspectives. Although contributions are not limited to Canadian literature, when included, they often explore original topics and untrodden critical territory. Take, for example, Laura Wright's "National Photographic: Images of Sensibility and the Nation in Margaret Atwood's *Surfacing* and Nadine Gordimer's *July's People*" (March 2005) or Cynthia Sugars' "The Anatomy of Influence: Robertson Davies' Psychosomatic Medicine" (December 2000). *Mosaic* attracts out-of-the-ordinary content and has set itself apart as an exceptional, in-depth, cross-cultural literary journal. Indexed in the *MLAIB* and *CPI.Q*, issues can also be searched through the journal's website.

## INTERDISCIPLINARY AND CANADIAN STUDIES JOURNALS COVERING CANADIAN LITERATURE

*American Review of Canadian Studies*. Washington, DC: Association for Canadian Studies in the United States, 1971–. Quarterly. ISSN: 0272-2011. www.acsus.org (accessed 25 June 2010).

*Arachne: Interdisciplinary Journal of the Humanities/Revue interdisciplinaire de langue et de littérature*. Sudbury, Ontario: Laurentian University, 1994–2000. Ceased. ISSN: 1192-3474.

*Canadian Journal of Native Studies*. Brandon, Manitoba: Brandon University, 1981–. Semiannually. ISSN: 0715-3244. www2.brandonu.ca/Library/cjns (accessed 25 June 2010).

*Dalhousie Review: A Canadian Journal of Literature and Opinion*. Halifax, Nova Scotia: Dalhousie University, 1921–. 3/year. ISSN: 0011-5827. http://dalhousiereview.dal.ca/index.html (accessed 25 June 2010).

*International Journal of Canadian Studies/Revue internationale d'études canadiennes*. Ottawa: International Council for Canadian Studies, 1990–. Semiannually. ISSN: 1180-3991. www.iccs-ciec.ca (accessed 25 June 2010).

*Journal of Canadian Studies (JCS)/Revue d'études canadiennes (REC)*. Peterborough, Ontario: Trent University, 1966–. 3/year. ISSN: 0021-9495. www.utpjournals.com/jcs/jcs.html (accessed 25 June 2010).

*Québec Studies*. Burlington: University of Vermont, 1983–. 2/year. ISSN: 0737-3759. www.acqs.org/qc_studies_journal (accessed 25 June 2010).

*Queen's Quarterly: A Canadian Review*. Kingston, Ontario: Queen's University, 1893–. Quarterly. ISSN: 0033-6041. www.queensu.ca/quarterly (accessed 25 June 2010).

*University of Toronto Quarterly: A Canadian Journal of the Humanities*. Toronto: University of Toronto Press, 1931–. Quarterly. ISBN: 0042-0247. www.utpjournals.com/utq/utq.html (accessed 25 June 2010).

Subjects pertaining to Canadian literature appear in the pages of many interdisciplinary journals. The ***American Review of Canadian Studies*** is a multidisciplinary journal, printing articles devoted to Canadian history, politics, art, film, music, and literature. The variety of subjects covered makes this journal a great resource for staying current on Canadian issues and themes. Recently published articles related to Canadian literature include Cinda Gault's "Grooving the Nation: 1965–1980 as a Literary Era in Canada" (Autumn 2008), and Jane Moss's "Francophone Theater of Western Canada: Dramatic Tales of Disappearing Francophones" (March 2009). Issues feature book reviews from all disciplines; however, Canadian novels and critical literary works are particularly well covered. Indexing is provided by the *MLAIB* and *CPI.Q*.

Featuring essays from the current Arachne at Rutgers, ***Arachne: Interdisciplinary Journal of the Humanities/Revue interdisciplinaire de langue et de littérature*** had its finger on the pulse of a certain element of creative scholarship. Articles addressed topics from outside the mainstream, an approach that some appreciated and others found inaccessible. Publication ceased in 2000, and the journal should not be confused with the title *Arachne at Rutgers*: *Journal of Iberian and Latin American Cultural Studies*, which began in 2001. An impassioned introduction to the final two issues by editor Tom Gerry explains that under Laurentian University's business model, publication of an unprofitable journal was simply no longer feasible. As an interdisciplinary journal, *Arachne* featured only a handful of articles devoted to Canadian literature between 1994 and 2000, the records for which can easily be accessed in a search of the *MLAIB*.

As the official publication of the Canadian Indian/Native Studies Association, the ***Canadian Journal of Native Studies*** prints articles, bibliographies, and book reviews pertaining to all aspects of Native Studies and First Nations peoples. Among the unique submissions related to literature is James Forsythe's "The Plains Cree Grotowski" (2001, no. 2), which examines aboriginal performance principles. In partnership with the University of Saskatchewan Libraries, the journal currently provides full-text access to nearly all of its issues through its website. This title is indexed in the *MLAIB* and *CPI.Q*.

The ***Dalhousie Review: A Canadian Journal of Literature and Opinion*** is an interdisciplinary journal presenting articles in literature, history, political science, philosophy, sociology, popular culture, visual culture, short fiction, verse, and commissioned book reviews. It is an established journal from one of Canada's oldest universities, also the largest postsecondary educational institution in the Maritimes. Critical literary essays and articles focusing on Canadian literature occasionally appear. Some examples are Carrie Dawson's "Under Scrutiny, Under Siege: The Nation in Contemporary Canadian Literary Criticism" (Summer 2003) and John LePage's "William Henry Drumond's 'Habitants' and the Quebec of My Youth" (Spring 2008). This title is indexed in the *MLAIB* and *CPI.Q*.

As a multidisciplinary publication, articles pertaining directly to Canadian literature appear only occasionally in the ***International Journal of Canadian Studies/Revue internationale d'études canadiennes***. Online content is available through the journal's website, providing access to all issues through the assistance of the University of Alberta. Publishing articles in both English and French, submissions often reflect the country's linguistic duality. Catherine Khordoc's "Reconsidérer Babel: appropriation du mythe de Babel dans quelques textes québécois et franco-ontariens" (Fall 2004) receives a thorough bilingual introduction from editor Marta Dvorak. Another fascinating contribution is Pamela Banting's "How Rural Settings Can Unsettle Prairie Critics: Deconstructing the Politics of Location" (Fall 2005), printed in the journal's annual "Open-Topic Issue." The advisory board for the publication reads like a United Nations roster, in this journal that caters to Canadian studies scholars around the world. This title is indexed in the *CPI.Q*.

A multidisciplinary and interdisciplinary serial, the ***Journal of Canadian Studies/Revue d'études canadiennes*** quite frequently prints essays relating to

Canadian literature. The spring 2006 issue, devoted to Canadian archives and archival studies, includes, for example, Oriel C. L. MacLennan's "Boundaries, Borders, and Barriers: Marie-Claire Blais and the Archival Adventure." This title is indexed in the *MLAIB* and *CPI.Q*.

Published by the American Council for Quebec Studies (ACQS), ***Québec Studies*** offers articles in English and French on Quebec literature, politics, business and economics, history, film, and culture. Book reviews are solicited. The ACQS also sponsors a biennial conference, with the venue alternating between the United States and Quebec. Individual issues may contain special sections on literature and literary studies, and recent dossiers have included headings such as "Contemporary Acadian Literature," "Re-reading Roy and Hébert," and "Writing Montreal." *Quebec Studies* is indexed in the *MLAIB* and *CPI.Q*.

Though publishing articles related to a variety of Canadian topics, ***Queen's Quarterly: A Canadian Review*** remains an important platform for Canadian literature. Attractively produced, with colored artwork and photos rarely found in scholarly journals, literary considerations include new poetry, short stories, author interviews, literary articles, editorials, and book reviews. Though articles directly related to literary criticism are scarce, when featured they are worth waiting for. Robert Fulford's "Furtive Autobiography: the Peterborough Journalism of Robertson Davies" (Spring 2007) is among the critical essays found within this title. *Queen's Quarterly* frequently appears in the *Globe and Mail*'s "On the Stand: A Weekly Roundup of the Best Magazine Reads on the Rack." This title is indexed in the *MLAIB* and *CPI.Q*.

The ***University of Toronto Quarterly: A Canadian Journal of the Humanities*** provides interdisciplinary coverage of all areas of the humanities, printing articles in both English and French. An excellent "Letters in Canada" issue is featured annually, offering reviews of the previous year's work in Canadian fiction, poetry, drama, and translations, in addition to book reviews of monographs with a humanities focus. Canadian literary scholars wishing to keep abreast of annual developments should not miss this special issue. Although often themed, issues are not limited to Canadian subjects. This title is indexed in the *MLAIB* and *CPI.Q*.

## CANADA'S LITERARY HYBRIDS

*Brick: A Literary Journal*. Toronto: Brick, 1977–. 3/year. ISSN: 0382-8565. www.brickmag.com (accessed 25 May 2010).

*Lettres québécoises: revue de l'actualité littéraire*. Montreal: Productions Valmont, 1976–. Quarterly. ISSN: 0382-084X. www.lettresquebecoises.qc.ca (accessed 25 May 2010).

Canada has long had a tradition of publishing literary periodicals that blur the boundaries between scholarly journal and literary magazine. A 2004 article in the *Globe and Mail* noted the increasing popularity of the "academag" and the "scholazine,"[2] classifying *Queen's Quarterly* as a premier journal among such formats. While *Queen's Quarterly* is in fact considered a scholarly, peer-reviewed journal, publishing articles appealing to both the academic and the general reader, other unorthodox titles remain more difficult to classify. Perhaps the best known among such publications is ***Brick: A Literary Journal***. Originally published mainly as a vehicle for book reviews, *Brick* attracts premier literati from around the globe in its articles, interviews, reviews, new poetry, and fiction. Award-winning author and playwright Michael Redhill assumed publishing responsibility in 2003, along with a stated commitment to showcasing "newer voices." While difficult to define, *Brick* bends the common rules of peer review for art's sake, in the process producing an exceptionally unique literary product. Although not formally considered an academic journal, perhaps Rebecca Caldwell sums it up best, saying, "Despite of, or perhaps because of, its non-scholarly approach, *Brick* is largely considered the finest literary journal in Canada."[3] Canada's literary elite maintain a loyal patronage to the publication, and Atwood, Munro, and Martel have all graced *Brick*'s pages. Covering both Canadian and international literatures, *Brick* has innovatively, and even iconoclastically, forged its own niche as a literary journal/magazine.

Although not classified as a scholarly journal and published in a magazine-style format, ***Lettres québécoises: Revue de l'actualité littéraire*** has forged its own path as a review dedicated to Quebec literature in French. Examining all genres of Quebec writing, including poetry, biography, critical editions, novels, and memoirs, selected content is also available online. This title is indexed in the *MLAIB* and *CPI.Q*.

## AUTHOR JOURNALS

*Malcolm Lowry Newsletter*. Waterloo, Ontario: Wilfrid Laurier University, 1977–1984. ISSN: 0228-8427.

*The Malcolm Lowry Review*. Waterloo, Ontario: Wilfrid Laurier University, 1984–2002. 2/year. ISSN: 0828-5020.

*Margaret Atwood Studies*. Ashland, VA: Margaret Atwood Society, 2007–. 2/year. ISSN: 2772-8102.

*Newsletter of the Margaret Atwood Society*. Tampa, FL: Margaret Atwood Society, 1984–2007. Annually. ISSN: 1081-9622.

After publishing thirty-six issues, the ***Newsletter of the Margaret Atwood Society*** underwent a metamorphosis from periodical to scholarly journal. Under the editorship of Theodore F. Scheckels, ***Margaret Atwood Studies*** debuted in September 2007. Publishing refereed scholarly articles related to the author and her works, the journal provides in-depth essays on Atwood's poetry, prose, nonfiction, and literary celebrity. In the newsletter portion of the publication, *Margaret Atwood Studies* also prints the minutes of the meetings of the Margaret Atwood Society as well as updates on conferences and events. Expanding on their work *Margaret Atwood: A Reference Guide, 1988–2005*, discussed in chapter 2, authors Ashley Thomson and Shannon Hengen contribute an "Annual Checklist" of Atwood output and scholarship.

As in the case of the *Newsletter of the Margaret Atwood Society*, the ***Malcolm Lowry Newsletter*** underwent a similar transition when the publication became ***The Malcolm Lowry Review*** in 1984. In common with *Margaret Atwood Studies*, the transformed *Review* retained some features of the *Newsletter*, including a section entitled "Notes and Announcements," with informative updates from the Lowry scholarly community. The *Review* also updated Norman Amor's *Malcolm Lowry: A Checklist* with occasional supplements. Interesting articles included Michael Ballin's "Reward and Punishment: The Cultural Role of the Alcoholic in Budd Schullberg's *The Disenchanted* and Malcolm Lowry's *Under the Volcano*" (fall 2000/spring 2001). The *Review* would have been a welcome refuge and source of inspiration for Lowry scholars, and it is therefore sad to read guest editor Chris Ackerley's comments in the final issue, fall 2001/spring 2002. Like so many other smaller academic journals that represent a labor of love for the scholars that support and contribute to them, the *Review* folded amid funding challenges. Though publication has ceased, Lowryeans can continue to discover gems of Lowry scholarship in this delightful publication. Past issues of the journal are indexed in the *MLAIB*.

## CONCLUSION

While some scholarly journals are devoted entirely to criticism and literary analysis, many Canadian titles are at least in part devoted to giving exposure to forthcoming Canadian authors. Although readership for scholarly journals dedicated to Canadian literature is modest in comparison to titles focusing on American literature geared toward a U.S. audience, smaller models tend to result in an eclectic mix of experiences, viewpoints, styles, and perspectives. Canadian literary journals impart a sense of uniqueness, accessibility, and novelty, often absent from larger publishing scenes.

## NOTES

1. Sergio Villani, "Fin d'une revue littéraire," *LittéRéalité* 20, no. 2 (Winter 2008): 5.
2. John Fraser, "Big Ideas, Slick Packages: It's the . . . Academag? Scholazine? *Globe and Mail*, December 4, 2004, F9.
3. Rebecca Caldwell, "Brick Celebrates 25th in Its Eclectic Tradition: First and Foremost a Literary Journal, the Magazine Never Had Designs on Becoming a Scholarly Publication," *Globe and Mail*, May 31, 2003, R13.

# *Chapter Six*

# Periodicals, Newspapers, and Reviews

While scholarly journals offer well-researched coverage of Canadian literary authors, topics, and themes, Canadian periodicals maintain vigilant awareness of literary trends, debates, and issues. Canadian literary magazines have a firm commitment to showcasing new voices, a practice which has created a rich, if not democratic, literary community, providing a steady stream of eclectic work from a variety of backgrounds and perspectives. Canadian writers contribute their time, talents, and expertise to maintaining an impressive and diverse number of publications. Many literary magazines have benefited from government publishing programs aimed at promoting Canadian content and elevating the status of the national literature.

Although the first Canadian literary magazines (litmags) appeared in the mid-1800s, a small publishing market, coupled with the country's widespread population and a harsh frontier environment, contributed to a unique set of challenges for nascent titles. While government assistance in the twentieth century alleviated some of these demographic and logistical issues, proposed changes to publishing programs threaten the current periodical environment. In the past, many of Canada's literary magazines relied on funding from both the Canada Magazine Fund and the Publications Assistance Program; however, under a new program, the Canadian Periodical Fund, financial assistance is no longer extended to titles circulating less than five thousand total copies annually. Articles such as Jason McBride's September 2009 *Quill and Quire* piece, "The Plight of Small Magazines," discuss the future of Canada's litmags. As McBride relates, "With the circulation of virtually all Canadian literary and arts magazines falling well below that threshold, such a shift could mean the demise of dozens of small cultural magazines distributed by Magazines Canada."[1] Although the changes affect the large majority of Canada's literary and arts magazines, some small-press titles are successfully making the transition to the Web in order to remain relevant and to offset publishing costs. Through an entirely online presence, litmags such as Toronto-based *Joyland: A Hub for Short Fiction* (www.joyland.ca) have emerged and are managing to survive independently of government funding, maximizing their reach through opportunities presented by social networking, RSS feeds, and Web 2.0 applications.

The present chapter will not only provide you with some background information on Canadian periodicals, newspapers, and little magazines but should also be useful in identifying both print and online sources for book reviews. Scholarly journals regularly publishing book reviews have been discussed in chapter 5, and online bibliographies, discussed in chapter 4, such as *JSTOR* and *Project Muse*, will facilitate access to academic reviews. Since Canadian literary magazines are not comprehensively indexed by any one service, you may have to consult a variety of sources. In the case of some titles, indexes are not readily available, and perusal of individual issues may be required. Access to many early periodicals is facilitated through online databases such as Canadiana.org's *Early Canadiana Online*, which will be discussed in chapter 7, "Microform and Digital Collections."

## FROM BELLES LETTRES TO LITERARY MAGAZINES

Bissell, Claude T. "Literary Taste in Central Canada during the Late Nineteenth Century." *Canadian Historical Review* 31, no. 3 (September 1950): 237–251.

*Literary Garland.* Montreal: Lovell & Gibson, 1838–1851.

Norris, Ken. *The Little Magazine in Canada, 1925–1980.* Toronto: ECW Press, 1984.

*The Week: A Canadian Journal of Politics, Society, and Literature.* Toronto: C. Blackett Robinson, 1883–1896.

There are few comprehensive surveys providing historical background for Canadian literary magazines; however, Claude T. Bissell's 1950 article **"Literary Taste in Central Canada during the Late Nineteenth Century"** from the *Canadian Historical Review* offers an excellent introduction to the significance and influence of early titles. Canada's strong legacy of literary periodicals dates to preconfederation times, and titles that grew out of a British Victorian tradition such as the ***Literary Garland*** gave voice to many pioneer writers. Published between 1838 and 1851, the *Garland* printed tales of travels in the new world while expressing nostalgia for a life left behind. In contrast to the perils of frontier life and the political traumas faced by the emerging nation, the *Garland* offered the ultimate form of literary escape. While the *Garland* may have served as an antidote to harsh environments, the influence of the magazine in setting the groundwork for the Canadian literary tradition cannot be underestimated. The *Garland*'s most prolific contributor, Susanna Moodie (publishing as "Mrs. Moodie"), offered accounts of early life in Canada and launched "survival" as a persistent Canadian literary theme.

A host of notable early authors, such as Archibald Lampman, Bliss Carman, Duncan Campbell Scott, Charles G. D. Roberts, and Sara Jeannette Duncan, were found on the pages of another early title, ***The Week: A Canadian Journal of Politics, Society, and Literature*** (1883–1896). Publishing out of Toronto, *The Week* may be regarded as the first example of a Canadian publication which, through a participatory model, blurred the lines between the scholarly and the literary. Of *The Week*, Bissell observes the following:

> In its pages one finds a synthesis of the academic and the literary that has since broken down with the split between the learned journal and the little magazine, on the one hand, and the general magazine designed for careless reading, on the other. It is admittedly the vehicle of the intellectuals and the high-brows, but it is not the effusion of a coterie nor the unbending spokesman of the learned.[2]

As Bissell explains, the early part of the twentieth century would see the rise of many university-based scholarly journals that survive to this day, including the *Dalhousie Review*, *University of Toronto Quarterly*, and *Queen's Quarterly*. Without the sponsorship of academic institutions, little magazines faced a far more ephemeral existence, falling prey to economic circumstances, changing literary sentiments, and shifting schools of thought. Scholarly publications and literary magazines would continue their separate trajectories over the first part of the century, into the late 1950s. The 1960s and 1970s would mark a new era in the history of Canadian literary magazines and academic journals. A generation of little magazines, such as *Tish* and *Open Letter*, benefited from the participation of up-and-coming authors, attracting the attention of established writers and academics. During this period, the rift between the literary and the scholarly was in part reconciled, as little magazines became a meeting ground for the creative and the academic, a trend which continues into present times. For more on the development of small-press publications in Canada, Ken Norris provides an excellent overview in ***The Little Magazine in Canada, 1925–1980***. Tracing the roots of the little magazine to the American modernist movement, Norris describes Canada's unique interpretation of U.S. models, examining the fascinating history of a singular publishing scene and its players. The work concludes with a bibliography of Canadian little magazines and their publishing runs, as well as a list of secondary sources pertaining to the genre.

## THE *TISH* MOVEMENT AND CANADA'S LITMAG TRADITION

Davey, Frank, ed. *Tish: 1–19*. Vancouver, British Columbia: Talonbooks, 1975.

*Open Letter*. Strathroy, Ontario: Frank Davey, 1965–. 3/year.

*Tish*. Vancouver: University of British Columbia Press, 1961–1969.

Started by a group of University of British Columbia (UBC) English students, Frank Davey, George Bowering, Fred Wah, James Reid, and David Dawson, ***Tish*** was published between 1961 and 1969. The young editors eventually settled on categorizing the publication as a "poetry newsletter," influenced by avant-garde American little magazines of the period, including *Origin*, *The Floating Bear*, and *Black Mountain Review*. Seeking to provide an authentic account of the activities of the contributors, the editors of *Tish* preserved "every roughness, insight, and stupidity that this activity enclosed."[3] The magazine's founding members had been inspired by their UBC English professor, Warren Tallman, who was instrumental in exposing his students to the San Francisco poetry scene. At his students' urging, Tallman would organize lectures and visits by American poets, including Robert Duncan and Allen Ginsburg, further stimulating the creative fuel of his impassioned students.

*Tish* articles and reviews sparked both laudatory and negative sentiments from a variety of familiar names, such as Al Purdy, John Robert Colombo, Lionel Kearns, and Denise Levertov. *Tish* editors were not afraid to print intensely critical reactions to the magazine's publishing format, as demonstrated in this entertaining letter of issue 5, written by New York artist Marian Zazeela and illustrative of the open concept that *Tish* espoused:

> Gee, for a rag that shd be perpetually at least OPEN to influences comin IN fr/ outside yr town (& I know you don't deny yr sources, Olson, Whalen, McClure, the Bear mentioned somewhere every issue,) you sure get painfully ingrown toe-nail, snail-like, creep pace. Why is it you all feed on each others' derivative little drippings? Don't you have minds of your own? Can't you function independently at least of each other? Given yr present dependence on what paths there are, thru the jungle, for all of us to follow.
>
> I dig that yr most likely a bunch of young innarested guys, trying to (modestly, etc) scare up a little light in yr corner of the globe, but OPEN THE WINDOWS. No flames ignite without air.[4]

Early issues of *Tish* mainly served as a publishing platform for new poetry, but also included letters, book reviews, and the occasional essay. In contrast to their Canadian predecessors, *Tish* contributors were radically unself-conscious, and what remains is an unadulterated and unrestrained record of these influential

Vancouver poets at the start of their careers. While many Canadian poets were still operating under a neo-Victorian model, *Tish* editors strove to produce poetry in contrast to what George Bowering refers to as "professor poems." Seeing their poetry as works in progress, *Tish* writers did not aim for literary perfection in the romantic tradition, instead elevating experimentation and creativity over a polished product. In issue 20, the final installment of what is now known as the "first run" of *Tish*, Bowering explains that the founders were dispersing to locales outside of Vancouver and that editorship was being transferred to Dave Dawson. Under new leadership, *Tish* would continue publication until 1969. Since an index to *Tish* does not exist, probably the best way to review the title is to sift through the published issues, the first nineteen of which were conveniently reissued in 1975 by Talonbooks as ***Tish: 1–19***.

Upon arriving in Victoria, founding *Tish* editor, Frank Davey, laid the groundwork for a new publication, ***Open Letter***, maintaining the original principles of what is now referred to as the "*Tish* movement." In the introductory issue of *Open Letter*, Davey expresses that over the years, *Tish* had strayed from his original vision, and that his new magazine would therefore revert to his original concept. Although *Open Letter* was started in the tradition of other undergrounds of the 1960s, the publication has since evolved into a polished journal that enjoys the continued involvement of its original editors. Recent special issues include spring 2007's "Into the Looking-Glass Labyrinth: Myths and Mystery in Canadian Literature," guest edited by Heliane Ventura and featuring Frank Davey's "Canadian Revisions of the Labyrinth." Despite the scholarly content, issues still offer a selection of eclectic poetry, printing submissions by Frank Wah and George Bowering, whose work appeared in *Open Letter*'s very first issues.

The journal has published several special issues dedicated to the influential Canadian poet bpNichol, a former regular contributor to *Open Letter*. Spring 2009's "bpNichol+21" commemorates the twentieth anniversary of the writer's death and features a series of inspired essays on the experimental poet who has come to symbolize a generation of Canadian authors. The journal remains true to its small-press publishing roots and a commitment to showcasing the work of visual artists, as this same special issue includes cover artwork that was quite literally "hand-stamped by Dan Waber."

Enjoying a fascinating trajectory as a uniquely Canadian publication, *Open Letter* continues to be cutting-edge, without trying too hard. Issues are well focused, as each submission contributes to the collective impact of the theme at hand. While now scholarly in concept, contributors are given a creative license that brings a vein of freshness to the journal, shaking off the usual norms and restrictions of academic publication. *Open Letter* is indexed in the *MLAIB* and *CPI.Q*.

## PRINT INDEXES FOR MAGAZINES

Brown, Mary Markham. *An Index to the Literary Garland, Montreal, 1838–1851*. Toronto: Bibliographic Society of Canada, 1962.

Heggie, Grace F., and G. R. Adshead. *An Index to Saturday Night: The First Fifty Years, 1887–1937*. Toronto: Micromedia, 1987.

Heggie, Grace F., and Anne McGaughey. *The University Magazine, 1901–1920: An Annotated Index*. Teeswater, Ontario: Reference Press, 1997.

MacDonald, Mary Lu. "An Index to the *Literary Garland* Updated." *Papers of the Bibliographical Society of Canada* 19 (1980): 79–83.

Sader, Marion, ed. *Comprehensive Index to English-Language Little Magazines: 1890–1970, Series One*. 8 vols. Millwood, NY: Kraus-Thomson Organization, 1976.

Woodsworth, A. *The "Alternative" Press in Canada: A Checklist of Underground, Revolutionary, Radical, and Other Alternative Serials from 1960*. Toronto: University of Toronto Press, 1972.

Although online subscription databases offer great usability and convenience over print titles, indexing of Canadian periodicals is still spotty, particularly for older issues. The print titles described below should assist you in researching early Canadian literary and little magazines and serve as supplements to online databases such as the *CPI.Q*.

Mary Markham Brown's ***An Index to the Literary Garland, Montreal, 1838–1851*** is an important reference work for access to Canada's first major literary magazine. The index is prefaced by an essay discussing the literary climate under which the magazine was produced, highlighting several of its most important contributors. Mary Lu MacDonald's article "**An Index to the *Literary Garland* Updated**" is a necessary read for users of the index as it lists several errors inherent in Brown's work, clarifying the identity of several authors and listing additional overlooked items. MacDonald's article also provides the reader with practical information concerning the publication norms of the *Literary Garland* and the publishing atmosphere of nineteenth-century Canada.

With the first issue appearing on December 3, 1887, *Saturday Night* holds the title as Canada's longest-running magazine. Printed in Toronto, *Saturday Night* began as a weekly report on current affairs and the arts, eventually serving the country as a general-interest periodical. In 2000, after over one hundred years of publication, the magazine emerged as a weekend supplement in Canada's *National Post*. However, a lack of advertising support eventually caused the venture to fold, and the final issue appeared in 2005. The remnants of the title still survive as a website (www.saturdaynight.ca), and there is always the possibility that it may again one day be revived as a print publication.

A host of well-known literati have contributed to the pages of *Saturday Night* over the years, and a young Robertson Davies served as literary editor from 1940 to 1942. The periodical maintained a watchful eye on Canada's literary notables, debating the talents and virtues of writers such as Bliss Carman and Stephen Leacock in the early part of the twentieth century. Grace Heggie and G. R. Adshead's ***An Index to Saturday Night: The First Fifty Years, 1887–1937*** is an excellent resource for researchers who wish to investigate literary trends and issues of the period. Book reviews published between 1887 and 1937 are also indexed, and those seeking to shed light on Canada's reception of British and American works will find *Saturday Night* to be a fruitful resource. Reviews of Ernest Hemingway, Sir Arthur Conan Doyle, and Theodore Dreiser are found among Canadian writers, such as Frederick Philip Grove, E. Pauline Johnson, and Lucy Maud Montgomery. For more recent issues, EBSCO provides electronic indexing and full-text access to *Saturday Night* content from December 1993 to March 2000 through the *MasterFILE Premier Database*. Coverage through the *CPI.Q* additionally offers indexing from January 1965 to March 2000, and full-text coverage from February 1994 to March 2000.

Coauthored with Anne McGaughey, Grace F. Heggie again facilitates access to Canada's early periodical literature through ***The University Magazine, 1901–1920: An Annotated Index***. Formerly published as the *McGill University Magazine* (1901–1906), the periodical was not limited to literary topics; however, many of Canada's early writers contributed their creativity and insight to the quarterly. The first issue includes Stephen Leacock's whimsical and irreverent parody "A Children's Corner," the contents of which testify to the fact that humorous jabs at the inapplicability of a university education are not necessarily new. Pretending to reprint a letter from recent McGill graduate Tiny Teddie, Leacock writes, "Since I took my degree I have got a job opening gates at a railway crossing, and am doing well, as I have just the touch required. When I get a little older I may get a job at a tollgate."[5] In their index, Heggie and McGaughey deliver a fine instrument for locating materials in an early publication which enjoyed nearly a twenty-year run.

Although the eight-volume title does not specifically address Canadian publications, the ***Comprehensive Index to English-Language Little Magazines: 1890–1970, Series One*** still affords some usefulness in identifying the reception of authors such as Lucy Maud Montgomery and Frank Davey within alternative press publications in the United States and Britain. This source should be used in addition to materials providing better coverage of Canadian literary considerations. Despite the lack of Canadian content, the index includes an impressive list of one hundred little magazines, both familiar and obscure.

Although now quite dated, ***The "Alternative" Press in Canada: A Checklist of Underground, Revolutionary, Radical, and Other Alternative Serials from 1960*** offers a convenient listing of little-known undergrounds. Two helpful indexes further organize the 413 identified titles of the period by geographic region and by subject.

## A SELECTION OF NOTABLE CANADIAN LITERARY PERIODICALS

*Arc: Canada's National Poetry Magazine*. Ottawa: Arc Poetry Society, 1978–. 2/year. ISSN: 1910-3239. www.arcpoetry.ca (accessed 25 June 2010).

*BC BookWorld*. Vancouver, British Columbia: BC Bookworld, 1987–. Quarterly. ISSN: 0847-7728. www.bcbookworld.com (accessed 25 June 2010).

*Canadian Fiction*. Kingston, Ontario: Quarry Press, 1971–2000. 2/year. ISSN: 1495-243.

*Canadian Notes and Queries*. Emeryville, Ontario: Biblioasis, 1968–. Semiannually. ISSN: 0576-5803. www.notesandqueries.ca (accessed 25 June 2010).

*Descant*. Toronto: Descant Arts and Letters Foundation, 1970–. Quarterly. ISSN: 0382-909X. www.descant.ca (accessed 25 June 2010).

*The Fiddlehead*. Fredericton, New Brunswick: University of New Brunswick, 1945–. Quarterly. ISSN: 0015-0630. www.thefiddlehead.ca (accessed 25 June 2010).

*Geist: Canadian Ideas, Canadian Culture*. Vancouver: Geist Foundation, 1990–. Quarterly. ISSN: 1181-6554. www.geist.com (accessed 25 June 2010).

*Literary Review of Canada*. Toronto: Literary Review of Canada, 1991–. 10/year. ISSN: 1188-7494. http://reviewcanada.ca (accessed 25 June 2010).

*Lurelu*. Montréal: Association Lurelu, 1978–. 3/year. ISSN: 0705-6567. www.lurelu.net (accessed 10 July 2010).

*On-Spec: The Canadian Magazine of the Fantastic*. Edmonton, Alberta: Copper Pig Writers' Society, 1989–. Quarterly. ISSN: 0843-476X. www.onspec.ca (accessed 25 June 2010).

*Prairie Fire: A Canadian Magazine of New Writing*. Winnipeg, Manitoba: Prairie Fire Press, 1978–. www.prairiefire.ca (accessed 25 June 2010).

*Prism International: Contemporary Writing from Canada and around the World*. Vancouver: University of British Columbia Press, 1959–. Quarterly. ISSN: 0032-8790. http://prism.arts.ubc.ca (accessed 25 June 2010).

*Quill and Quire: Canada's Magazine of Books News and Reviews*. Toronto: Saint Joseph Media, 1935–. 12/year. ISSN: 0033-6491. www.quilland quire.com (accessed 25 June 2010).

Many Canadian literary magazines offer a mix of articles, essays, reviews, and creative writing. Most of the literary magazines listed below focus on publishing new poetry and short fiction, but they also print interviews and encourage continued literary production through prizes and innovative contests. Some of these periodicals are difficult to classify, and the *MLAIB* and *CPI.Q* may differ in their categorization of these titles as magazines or scholarly journals. For clarification of a journal's status, you may want to consult *Ulrich's Periodicals Directory*, an online database of bibliographic and publisher information for over three hundred thousand academic, scholarly, and popular periodicals. The titles listed below mainly publish new poetry, short fiction, drama, book reviews, and industry news.

Though sometimes printing articles and reviews, ***Arc: Canada's National Poetry Magazine*** is mainly dedicated to presenting new works and criticism. Attractively published, the magazine sponsors several contests, including Poem of the Year and the Confederation Poets Prize. *Arc* has developed a strong online presence, and a digital edition is available through subscription.

Self-described as a newspaper about books of "middle-brow usefulness," ***BC BookWorld*** strives to appeal to the average reader in British Columbia. The newspaper maintains a well-presented and searchable database of over nine thousand British Columbia authors. Online entries provide useful author biographies and some supplementary material, including selections from *BC Bookworld* articles and reviews pertaining to the author. Additional Web content is available through the *BC Bookworld* archive on its affiliate site (http://abcbookworld.com), with access to downloadable PDF versions of past issues. The publication annually sponsors the George Woodcock Lifetime Achievement Award to an established British Columbia writer.

Published twice a year, ***Canadian Fiction*** printed mainly short fiction, as well as "manifestoes, reviews, graphics, photos, and interviews." Originally titled *Canadian Fiction Magazine*, a student publication of the University of British Columbia, the journal offered an eclectic selection of new fiction from across the country. Under the Canadian Fiction Anthology series, Quarry Press also reprints short fiction that originally appeared in the pages of the periodical, such as the 1999 *Pop Goes the Story*, examining the influence of pop culture on fiction. Literary interviews with noteworthy authors have long been featured on the pages of the journal. With George Hancock at the helm as general editor from 1976 to 1997, each individual issue was subsequently overseen by a guest editor. The final issue, published in 2000, is dedicated to

Canadian horror, with Bram Stoker Prize winner Edo Van Belkom penning the introduction. Submissions were accepted by both Canadian writers living abroad and authors living in Canada.

Originally modeled on *British Notes and Queries* and founded as a publication of the Antiquarian Bookseller's Association of Canada, ***Canadian Notes and Queries*** today offers interesting features that allow for thoughtful yet fearless criticism of the Canadian literary world. Also printing short fiction, poetry, and reviews, the magazine has an impressive Web presence.

A literary journal, ***Descant*** publishes poetry, fiction, plays, essays, musical scores, and visual art. Issues are generally centered on a theme, such as "Immanence/Transcendence" (Fall 2009) and "Writers in Prison" (Fall 2010). As with *Open Letter*, what began as a mimeographed little magazine has developed into a polished literary journal, attracting both established authors and promising newcomers.

Published out of the University of New Brunswick, ***The Fiddlehead*** prints poetry, short fiction, and reviews. A long-running literary magazine, *The Fiddlehead* also sponsors an annual contest, with awards for best story and best poem.

Billed as a magazine that fosters "plain talking" and "the offbeat," ***Geist: Canadian Ideas, Canadian Culture*** continues the tradition set by founder Stephen Osborne in his underground Vancouver magazine of the 1970s, *3 Cent Pulp*. Publishing a mix of fiction, nonfiction, poetry, reviews, visual art, and "little-known facts of interest," *Geist* also sponsors several innovative writing contests.

Focusing its efforts on reviewing new Canadian fiction and nonfiction, the ***Literary Review of Canada*** also publishes essays examining Canadian history, politics, culture, and current events. Issues showcase an eclectic mix of original poetry.

Described as the only French-language Quebec magazine exclusively dedicated to youth literature, ***Lurelu*** is an enjoyable literary periodical with over thirty years of publishing history. Exploring various aspects of children's literature, issues of this publication incorporate editorials, dossiers, interviews, critiques, and featured research articles, such as Suzanne Pouliot's "Le livre, la lecture et les bibliothèques dans les romans pour jeunes" (Spring/Summer 2003). A special dossier in the same issue brings awareness to English Canadian authors whose works have been translated into French, such as Norah McClintock, Monica Hughes, and Linda Bailey. "Critiques" provides reviews of picture books, audiobooks, novellas, novels, poetry, story collections, comic books, nonfiction, activity books, biographies, reference works, magazines, and recently received titles. *Lurindex*, an index to the first twenty-five years of publication is available on CD-ROM and indexes all book reviews printed in the title. *Lurelu* incorporates wonderful features such as M. Jean-Claude Boivin's "Petites pages," a bulletin highlighting notable books for infants.

Founded in 1989, ***On-Spec: The Canadian Magazine of the Fantastic*** accepts submissions of fiction and poetry written in the speculative tradition. Issues feature author and artist interviews, as well as special tributes to Canadian fantasy, science fiction, and horror writers.

Formerly published as *Writers News Manitoba*, ***Prairie Fire*** is an attractive periodical consisting mainly of new fiction but also featuring poetry and creative nonfiction. As the journal's name suggests, prairie authors receive considerable attention; however, contributions are not limited to prairie writing. The journal's website offers access to the *Prairie Fire Review of Books*, a searchable database of reviews that vary in length and format and that are not published in the print version. The magazine sponsors a writing contest for authors of poetry, short fiction, and creative nonfiction, the winners of which appear in the journal's summer issue. Although certain authors and contributors tend to be repeatedly included, *Prairie Fire* remains committed to providing a platform for new and emerging writers. Issues occasionally contain author interviews, such as Robyn Maharaj's "'Arc of a Whole Life': A Telephone Interview with Carol Shields." (Winter 2002).

A publication of the University of British Columbia's Creative Writing Program, ***Prism International*** prints contemporary fiction, poetry, drama, creative nonfiction, and translations. Billed as western Canada's oldest literary magazine, *Prism* also sponsors several writing contests, including the Earle Birney Prize for Poetry.

Publishing industry news, trends, and author interviews, ***Quill and Quire: Canada's Magazine of Books News and Reviews*** has long been a Canadian literary staple. Aside from its extensive book reviews, unique and interesting pieces, such as "Exposing Family Secrets: Six Authors Reflect on Navigating the Personal Minefield of Memoir Writing" by Sarah Trevleaven (September 2009), ensure a dedicated readership.

## CONTEMPORARY CANADIAN LITTLE MAGAZINES

*Broken Pencil: The Magazine of Zine Culture and the Independent Arts*. Toronto: Broken Pencil, 1995–. 4/year. ISSN: 1201-8996. www.brokenpencil.com (accessed 25 June 2010).

*The Capilano Review*. Vancouver: Capilano Press Society, 1972–. 3/year. ISSN: 0315-3754. www.thecapilanoreview.ca (accessed 28 June 2010).

*filling Station*. Calgary, Alberta: Filling Station Publications Society, 1994–. 3/year. ISSN: 1198-0060. www.fillingstation.ca (accessed 28 June 2010).

*Jeu: Revue de théâtre*. Montreal: Jeu, Inc., 1976–. Quarterly. ISSN: 0382-0335. www.revuejeu.org (accessed 28 June 2010).

*Joyland: A Hub for Short Fiction*. www.joyland.ca (accessed 25 June 2010).

*Matrix*. Montreal: Matrix Magazine, 1975–. 4/year. ISSN: 0318-3610. www.matrixmagazine.org (accessed 28 June 2010).

*Sub-Terrain*. Vancouver: Sub-Terrain Magazine, 1988–. 3/year. ISSN: 0840-7533. www.subterrain.ca (accessed 28 June 2010).

As small-press titles face funding obstacles, alternative press and underground magazines are becoming increasingly creative in their approach to soliciting submissions, recruiting authors, and navigating the transition to an online presence. Although the titles listed below may not self-describe as "little magazines," they maintain similar elements of the little magazine tradition, through experimentation, exposure of new voices, and creative content. Most of the titles listed below feature varying levels of Web material, and many make use of social networking technologies.

With its finger on the pulse of Canadian publishing trends, accomplishments, fiascos, and calamities, ***Broken Pencil: The Magazine of Zine Culture and the Independent Arts*** traces Canadian literary life with charming candidness and irreverence. Cutting edge and self-described as a cross between *Utne Reader* and "an underground *Reader's Digest*," *Broken Pencil* reviews books, magazines, websites, and digital media. Maintaining a strong Web presence, issues also include reprints from the underground press, interviews, and original fiction. The magazine sponsors the Indie Writers Deathmatch, an annual contest that publishes selected submissions online to vie for top position, as voted on by *Broken Pencil* readers.

Publishing short fiction, poetry, creative nonfiction, reviews, interviews, articles, drama, and visual art, ***filling Station*** began in 1994 as a literary magazine, rebilling itself in 2006 as a "literary and arts magazine." Produced entirely through the assistance of volunteers, *filling Station* is planning on augmenting their Web presence with social networking opportunities and online content. Although submissions are not restricted to prairie authors, new Alberta voices are often showcased.

Based in Toronto, ***Joyland: A Hub for Short Fiction*** has editorial centers in several Canadian and U.S. cities, including Los Angeles, Chicago, New York, San Francisco, Montreal, and Vancouver. Entirely dedicated to new short fiction, *Joyland* offers innovative enhancements, such as "*Joyland* for Cellphones," delivering selected stories to mobile devices. Operating under a Creative Commons license, *Joyland* distributes material free of charge and survives without government assistance.

***Matrix*** publishes fiction, essays, poems, short articles, and book reviews. Some downloadable content is available on the *Matrix* website, including audio files of performed poetry. The November 2009 issue, dedicated to "The New Vancouver," features an interview with *Open Letter* founder, Frank Davey.

In the style of avant-garde undergrounds, ***Sub-Terrain*** contains a mix of fiction, poetry, photography, and graphic illustrations from rising Canadian and international authors and artists.

Publishing work by well-known authors such as August Kleinzahler, Daphne Marlatt, Michael Ondaatje, and Fred Wah, ***The Capilano Review*** prints poetry, fiction, fine art, and drama from both Canada and abroad. Committed to promoting new authors, the periodical frequently produces special issues on creative topics, such as "Artifice and Intelligence" (Fall 2006).

Dedicated to contemporary Quebec theater, ***Jeu: Revue de théâtre*** is also the only North American French-language publication focusing on the dramatic arts. Printing news, interviews, and reviews, content covers all aspects of theater production, including puppetry, scenography, translation, and dance. Limited content, such as editorials and selected reviews, is available on the magazine's website.

## CANADIAN NEWSPAPERS: HISTORICAL SURVEYS

Distad, N. Merrill, with the assistance of Linda M. Distad. "Canada." In *Periodicals of Queen Victoria's Empire*, ed. J. Don Vann and Rosemary T. VanArsdel. Toronto: University of Toronto Press, 1996.

Fetherling, Douglas. *The Rise of the Canadian Newspaper*. Toronto: Oxford University Press, 1990.

Kesterton, W. H. *A History of Journalism in Canada*. Toronto: McClelland and Stewart Limited, 1967.

Sotiron, Minko. *From Politics to Profit: The Commercialization of Canadian Daily Newspapers, 1890–1920*. Montreal: McGill-Queen's University Press, 1997.

The newspaper, central to Canadian identity, is often credited for its role in creating a cohesive society, in spite of the country's vast geography. Early publications, such as the *Halifax Gazette* (1752–1756) and William Lyon MacKenzie's *Colonial Advocate* (1824–1834) were printed using handpresses and mainly served as vehicles for political apologetics.[6] Newspapers, with their broad appeal to a range of topics and tastes, have in general enjoyed greater success than the Canadian magazine industry. As N. Merrill Distad states, "The history of Canadian magazines has largely been a story of attrition and failure. By contrast, the newspaper press, though not without its many casualties, grew to unprecedented size and power by adapting more successfully to the economic necessities of mass sales and distribution."[7] Mass-audience publications focusing on local, national, and international news did not develop until the 1880s, with the appearance of titles such as Montreal's *La Presse* (1884–) and Ottawa's *Journal* (1885–). N. Merrill Distad presents a survey of Canada's earliest newspaper and periodical publishing industry in a thoroughly researched essay, **"Canada,"** found in Vann and VanArsdel's *Periodicals of Queen Victoria's Empire*. A section of his study specifically examines "Literary/Cultural (Regional)" titles, among which he cites *The Montreal Tattler* (1844) and *Sporting and Dramatic Review* (1899).

Part of the Perspectives on Canadian Culture series, ***The Rise of the Canadian Newspaper*** traces the progression of Canadian journalism from Bushell's 1752 *Halifax Gazette* to contemporary times. In clearly written prose, Fetherling describes the struggles faced by early publishers, the print battles between the Tories and the Whigs, the spread of journalism in the West, and the emergence of the contemporary press. A selected bibliography suggests related works, including numerous memoirs, to inform further research.

While there are several works examining contemporary print culture, Kesterton's ***A History of Journalism in Canada*** thoroughly considers the early period, from 1752 through the mid-1960s. Chapter 5, "Journals and Journalism," is devoted to the individual histories of national and regional publications, such as the *Globe and Mail*, *La Presse*, *Le Devoir*, and the *Vancouver Province*. Another well-researched work, Sotiron ***From Politics to Profit: The Commercialization of Canadian Daily Newspapers, 1890–1920*** enthusiastically describes the role of the newspaper in shaping Canadian politics and the development of a national consciousness. An extensive bibliography identifies archival collections related to notable figures in the history of Canadian journalism, as well as sources for additional research.

## CANADIAN NEWSPAPERS INDEXES

*B.C. Newspaper Index, 1991–2007*. Vancouver: Legislative Library of British Columbia, 1991–2007. www.llbcnews.leg.bc.ca/#focus (accessed 28 June 2010).

*Canadian Newsstand Complete*. Ann Arbor, MI: ProQuest, 1977–. www.proquest.com (accessed 28 June 2010).

*Canadian Periodical Index* (*CPI.Q*). New York: Gale, Canada, 1988–. www.gale.cengage.com (accessed 28 June 2010).

*Manitobia Life and Times Newspapers*. Winnipeg: Manitoba Library Consortium. http://manitobia.ca/cocoon/launch/en/newspapers (accessed 28 June 2010).

*Saskatchewan News Index, 1884–2000*. Saskatoon: University of Saskatchewan Libraries. http://library2.usask.ca/sni (accessed 28 June 2010).

*Toronto Star Pages of the Past*. Toronto: Toronto Star, 1894–. http://thestar.pagesofthepast.ca (accessed 28 June 2010).

Newspapers, due to their range of topics and frequency of publication, present complex indexing issues. Indexes for Canadian newspapers are generally found in three varieties: large-scale commercial projects, such as ProQuest's *Canadian Newsstand Complete*; searchable databases of digitized print indexes often executed through provincial library consortia; and thematic newspaper digitization projects, such as Manitobia.ca. Some commercial titles, for example the *Toronto Star*, also offer a range of subscription options for access to their individual archives. The **Canadian Periodical Index (CPI.Q)**, discussed in chapter 4, indexes select content from the *National Post*, with coverage from November 1998 forward. Likewise, *CPI.Q*'s full-text access to the Toronto *Globe and Mail*, from January 1997 onward, further facilitates literary research.

Of the sources discussed in this section, ProQuest's ***Canadian Newsstand Complete*** represents the most comprehensive coverage. A subscription database with full-text access to over 170 titles, the *Globe and Mail* (1977–), *The Gazette* (1985–), *Ottawa Citizen* (1985–), *The Province* (1989–), and the *Winnipeg Free Press* (2006–) are among the significant newspapers found within this convenient product. ProQuest offers several versions of the database, including *Canadian Newsstand Major Dailies* (leading national and regional titles), as well as regional packages (New Brunswick, Ontario, Pacific, Prairies, and Quebec).

With options for basic and advanced searches, the ***B.C. Newspaper Index, 1991–2007*** is a freely available database maintained by the Legislative Library of British Columbia. The index represents a continuation of two microform indexes, the *B.C. Newspaper Index (1900–1990)* and *BCARS (British Columbia Archives and Records Services) Newspaper Index (1858–1900)*. While this service is devoid of digitized content, users will appreciate the ability to conduct keyword, author, headline, subject, and series searches of important British Columbia publications, such as the *Vancouver Sun* and the *Province*.

Maintained by the University of Saskatchewan Libraries, ***Saskatchewan News Index, 1884–2000*** represents the digitization of several indexes previously available only in print. With limited coverage of several prairie newspapers, including the *Saskatoon Phoenix* (1902–1908) and the *Regina Leader-Post* (1935–1943), title, subject, keyword, source, and date are among the available search terms.

The Manitobia.ca project (a combination of the province's name and the word "utopia"), an initiative of the Manitoba Library Consortium, hosts ***Manitobia Life and Times Newspapers***, offering full-text searching of several historical provincial newspapers. The website also supports browsing of individual titles, such as the *Daily Nor'Wester* (1894–1898) and *Le Métis* (1871–1881).

A subscription-based service, ***Toronto Star Pages of the Past*** presents the digitized pages of the newspaper from 1894 forward. The search interface allows the ability to search by "Page Content," of which "Books/Weekly Review" is one option.

## PRINT AND ONLINE RESOURCES FOR LOCATING ARTICLES AND REVIEWS

*Book Review Digest Plus*. New York: H. W. Wilson, 1905–. www.hwwilson.com/Databases/brdig.htm.

*Book Review Digest Retrospective*. New York: H. W. Wilson, 2000. www.hwwilson.com/Databases/brdig_retro.htm.

*Canadian Book Review Annual* (*CBRA*). Toronto: CBRA, 1975–.

*Canadian Book Review Annual Online*. Toronto: CBRA Online. www.cbraonline.com.

*Periodicals Archive Online*. Alexandria, VA: Chadwyck-Healey (multiple sources with multiple date ranges). http://pao.chadwyck.com.

*Periodicals Index Online*. Alexandria, VA: Chadwyck-Healey (multiple sources with multiple date ranges). http://pio.chadwyck.com.

*Readers' Guide to Periodical Literature*. New York: H. W. Wilson, 1983–. www.hwwilson.com/Databases/Readersg.htm#Literature.

*Readers' Guide Retrospective, 1890–1982*. New York: H. W. Wilson, 1890–1982. www.hwwilson.com/Databases/rdgretro.htm.

*Repère: Index analytique d'articles de périodiques de la langue française*. Montréal: Bibliothèque et Archives nationales du Québec, 1984–. Also available electronically; see http://repere.sdm.qc.ca/#focus.

Book reviews represent the pulse of the country's literary life and are a collective endeavor of writers, scholars, and journalists. Aside from printing the works of new writers, Canadian literary magazines have also been very committed to reviewing material published by new authors. Since book reviews appear in scholarly journals, periodicals, magazines, and newspapers, as well as online, the following is only a selective list of possible print and electronic resources for identifying published reviews.

The first edition of ***Canadian Book Review Annual*** (***CBRA***) appeared in 1976, printing original, two-hundred-to-four-hundred-word reviews of Canadian trade books published in the preceding year. In the print version, reviews are arranged by subject, with literature subdivided into categories such as novels, short stories, poetry, drama, anthologies, criticism, and children's literature. An electronic version of the resource was launched in 2009 as ***Canadian Book Review Annual Online***, delivering content from all of the previous editions, augmented by current reviews that are updated monthly. Materials reviewed in the *CBRA* are restricted to titles written by Canadian authors and editors.

***Book Review Digest Plus*** is a database of reviews of contemporary English-language fiction and nonfiction published in North America. Although Canadian works are considered, *Book Review Digest* adheres to strict criteria that may eliminate many Canadian imprints as candidates for inclusion. In order to be indexed, a work of fiction must have been reviewed by three of the periodicals in the *Book Review Digest Plus* selection list. Due to Canada's small publishing scene, this criterion weeds out many small-press titles and new authors, limiting the indexing of book reviews to works by well-known writers who are more likely to garner critical attention in established reviewing journals. Book reviews may be searched by either author or reviewing author; other useful limiters are country of publication and language of the document. Canadian publications found in the selection list include *Quill and Quire* and *Canadian Literature*. The *Times Literary Supplement*, the *New York Times Book Review*, and the *London Review of Books* are among the notable American and British periodicals indexed in this database. Complementing *Book Review Digest*, another service, ***Book Review Digest Retrospective***, provides coverage of book reviews for the period 1905–1982.

Published by the Bibliothèque et Archives nationales du Québec (BAnQ), ***Repère: Index analytique d'articles de périodiques de la langue française*** exclusively covers French-language magazines and journals. Formerly *Périodex: Index analytique de périodiques de langue française*, subscription via the Internet is now offered as an alternative to the print version. The online version available through EBSCO has close to five hundred thousand entries from 1980 forward, with full-text access to nearly twenty-five thousand articles. The print edition provides a separate index for book reviews, organized separately by author, title, and subject. While *Repère* is multidisciplinary in scope, Canadian, francophone, and Quebec literatures are all represented, and titles indexed include *Lettres québécoises*, *Jeu*, *Voix et images*, and *Lurelu*.

Accessible in both print and online format, H. W. Wilson's ***Readers' Guide to Periodical Literature*** indexes many Canadian periodicals. For indexing prior to 1983, researchers should consult ***Readers' Guide Retrospective: 1890–1982***. If your institution does not have a subscription to the online version, print copies will still prove useful.

***Periodicals Index Online*** (***PIO***) presents over three hundred years of fully indexed articles for the arts, social sciences, and humanities. The database currently delivers over fifteen million articles from over 4,700 journals dating back to 1665. Presenting the user with an almost identical interface, ***Periodicals Archive Online*** (***PAO***) is the full-text counterpart to *PIO*, providing users with digitized versions of the original articles and on-screen highlighting of their query term. Searches within both databases can be restricted to articles or book reviews, and keyword, author, journal title, and journal subject searches are all supported. When combined, the *Index* and *Archives* represent an excellent source for book reviews written in over forty languages, published in journals worldwide.

## CONCLUSION

Literary researchers will find Canadian literary magazines to be rich resources for new fiction, outspoken criticism, and current awareness. Although periodical publishing faces financial obstacles, Canada continues its strong tradition of culturally relevant little magazines, which are brimming with creativity, insightful, and accessible to new writers.

Indexes to individual titles are however scarce and, where they do exist, are often still spotty in their coverage. The resources discussed in this chapter will assist you in locating and identifying material printed in literary magazines and periodicals. While large subscription databases, such as the *CPI.Q*, offer some coverage of literary periodicals, keep in mind that a perusal of individual issues may still be the best way to research some of these titles.

## NOTES

1. Jason McBride, "The Plight of Small Magazines," *Quill and Quire*, September 2009, 18.
2. Claude T. Bissell, "Literary Taste in Central Canada during the Late Nineteenth Century," *Canadian Historical Review* 31, no. 3 (September 1950): 242.
3. Frank Davey, ed., *Tish: 1–19* (Vancouver, British Columbia: Talonbooks, 1975), 7.
4. Davey, *Tish: 1–19*, 93.

5. Stephen Leacock, "A Children's Corner," *The University Magazine* 1, no. 1 (December 1901): 81.

6. For more information on early Canadian newspaper publishing, see Merrill Distad's "Newspapers, Magazines, and Commercial Journals," in *Encyclopedia of Literature in Canada*, ed. William H. New (Toronto: University of Toronto Press, 2002), 807–813.

7. Distad, "Newspapers," 808.

## *Chapter Seven*

# Microform and Digital Collections

Although differentiated by separate eras of technological improvement, microform and digital collections serve a similar purpose. Both offer the possibility of preserving rare and fragile works, converting them to a format that is accessible and easily distributed. While digital collections fulfill this mission in a manner that was unimaginable at the advent of microform, for its time the latter format was an equally revolutionary solution.

Despite an increasing number of digitization projects, microform has not gone entirely by the wayside. Current collections are generally comprised of one of two formats: microfilm or microfiche. While microfilm entails long reels of continuous film, microfiche refers to small translucent sheets, about the size of an index card. One fiche can hold multiple pages of text, and special readers are used to enlarge the filmed images. It is possible that you might also come across older formats during your research, including microcards; however, these are not common. During a transitionary period, as large-scale projects are sure to produce an increasing amount of digital content, hard-copy microform persists as a relevant format, despite its outdated reputation. Although users of microform are confined to special equipment, libraries and institutions are likely to continue to rely on the format, at least for the immediate future.

Often sold as a large, coherent collection of works, some entities may also market and sell individual microform titles separately. Microform offers several advantages, such as the ability to make available elusive materials through an easily replicated and distributable format. Some libraries have initiated their own filming projects as a way to both back up and lessen the handling of precious materials. As many libraries struggle with space issues, condensed storage is another attractive advantage of microform. While using the format may at first seem inconvenient and daunting, library staff should be able to assist you in learning to handle the specialized equipment required to view the material. Additionally, your library might have a printer connected to its microform readers, or may offer scanners and software to facilitate microform-to-PDF conversion.

A disadvantage of microform is that older film may be difficult to read, as the format faces similar deterioration concerns as print items. Secondly, depending on where and when the microfilming of the material was completed, some projects may not have been well executed, and variability in the quality and legibility of film is common. Another drawback of microform is that individual collections are not necessarily accompanied by an index, making identification of relevant items extremely difficult. While microform in and of itself is a cost-effective option, thorough indexing remains an expensive enterprise, though essential to the usability of a collection.

Digitization projects continue to decrease the role of microform. Since indexes to microform are not always available, a great advantage of digitization is that electronic documents often allow for full-text searching. Instead of scrolling through reels of film in pursuit of an item of interest, electronic formats afford researchers the convenience of online access. With many microform collections to choose from, institutions often prioritize their work according to collections that will serve the greatest number of users. Library and Archives Canada (LAC) is in the process of migrating its microform collections to the online environment. Two large-scale microfilm collections completed by LAC are *Border Entry Records, 1919–1924* and the *School Files Series, 1879–1953*.[1] While these collections are not directly related to literature, they serve as examples of future projects that may soon cover other areas of interest. A unique feature of these digitized LAC collections is that they mimic the experience of reading microform on traditional reels or fiche. Navigation links allow the user to scroll forward or backward through the microform, with the ability to skip to a specific page in the series. Images are presented as JPEGs; however, PDF options are also available, allowing the user to print, zoom, and rotate images.

The Canadian Institute for Historical Microreproductions (CIHM, later becoming Canadiana.org) began in 1978 as a nonprofit entity with a mission to preserve and distribute material relevant to Canadian culture, politics, and history. CIHM's microfilming endeavors first targeted early titles about Canada (including those published abroad), works by Canadian authors, and Canadian imprints. Between 1978 and 2008, CIHM oversaw five major microfilming projects, facilitating access to early printed materials, such as pre-1920 monographs and serials. CIHM collections have been purchased and distributed to libraries around the world, and while your library may not own certain items, holdings may be available through interlibrary loan.

Literary researchers will benefit from CIHM's broad initiatives to identify, locate, and film early Canadian imprints. As one of the main bodies conducting large-scale microfilming of early Canadiana, the majority of microfilm relevant to the study of Canadian literature is available through CIHM. During the late 1970s and early 1980s, CIHM researchers visited libraries across Canada seeking rare and relevant material. Further work was conducted in the collections of the British Library, and the Library of Congress served as a filming site during the processing of the CIHM's first project, *Pre-1900 Monographs*. CIHM was committed to providing quality cataloging for its collections, and subscribers now have access to downloadable records through Canadiana.org. As the main distributor of its own collections, Canadiana.org keeps careful track of CIHM holding institutions. Many major Canadian universities own full collections of CIHM microform; however, Princeton is listed as the only U.S. institution with comprehensive holdings. Literature is only one of many subjects that CIHM projects encompass, as other broad areas of coverage include government publications, history, Native studies, and political science. A "Series Title" search for *CIHM/ICMH Microfiche series* in *WorldCat* returns over three hundred thousand results, reflecting the many projects that the entity has tirelessly developed. The same search, adding the keyword *literature*, returns 6,182 records. To identify institutions holding specific CIHM collections, a *WorldCat* search will prove useful. Figure 7.1 provides a modified *WorldCat* record returned for a search where *An Ode for the Queen's Birthday* and *CIHM* are used as search terms.

The record indicates that twenty-seven OCLC member libraries hold this particular item, a CIHM microfiche of a poem by anthropologist Alexander Francis Chamberlain, originally appearing in *The Week* on May 29, 1891. The "Series" field indicates that the item is part of the *CIHM/ICHM Microfiche* series and that this particular item is found on reel 11868. The "Material Type" field tells us that this item is available as a microfiche. Additionally, the "Notes" field contains information on the source document used by CIHM for microfilming: "Reproduction of original in: National Library of Canada." Although individual titles can be purchased from Canadiana.org, both large-scale microform collections and thematic subject collections will be discussed in the next section.

## CIHM'S EARLY CANADIANA RESEARCH COLLECTIONS ON MICROFICHE

*Monographs, 1900–1920*. 56,387 fiche. Ottawa, Ontario: Canadian Institute for Historical Microreproductions, 1994–2000.

*Pre-1900 Canadian Periodicals*. 62,221 fiche. Ottawa, Ontario: Canadian Institute for Historical Microreproductions, 1989–1994.
*Pre-1900 Monographs*. 132,374 fiche. Ottawa, Ontario: Canadian Institute for Historical Microreproductions, 1979–1986.

Filming for the inaugural CIHM collection, ***Pre-1900 Monographs***, was completed between 1979 and 1986. The entire collection, including supplements, boasts over sixty-five thousand titles. A large-scale, labor-intensive endeavor, surveyors inspected bibliographies and visited holding institutions for on-site viewing of potential items. Frances Brooke's *The History of Emily Montague* (1769), considered to be the first Canadian novel, is an example of the literary items found in the collection. Due to the bulk of material identified during the intervening years, CIHM began work on an addition to the initial collection, *Pre-1900 Monographs, Supplement 1*. Published bibliographies served in guiding the developers of the supplement, including Patricia Fleming's *Upper Canadian Imprints, 1801–1841*.[2]

In 1989, CIHM began filming for ***Pre-1900 Canadian Periodicals***, basing initial identification and selection of items on Linda Jones's *Preliminary Checklist of Pre-1900 Canadian Serials*.[3] Although *Pre-1900 Periodicals* is

• Libraries worldwide that own item: 27

| | |
|---|---|
| **Title:** | **An ode for the Queen's birthday** |
| **Author(s):** | Chamberlain, Alexander Francis, 1865-1914. |
| **Publication:** | [Toronto? : s.n., |
| **Year:** | 1891 |
| **Description:** | 12 p. |
| **Language:** | English |
| **Series:** | **Variation:** CIHM/ICMH Microfiche series ;; no. 11868. |
| **Standard No:** | **ISBN:** 0665118686; 9780665118685; **Stock no:** CL0070000005; **National Library:** 826110959 |
| | **SUBJECT(S)** |
| **Named Corp:** | Catholic Church -- Controversial literature -- Protestant authors. |
| **Note(s):** | "Reprinted from the 'Week', May 29, 1891"--verso of t.p./ Reproduction of original in: National Library of Canada./ **Reproduction:** Microfiche./ Ottawa :/ Canadian Institute for Historical Microreproductions,/ 1981./ 1 microfiche (10 fr.) ; 11 x 15 cm./ (CIHM/ICMH Microfiche series = CIHM/ICMH collection de microfiches ; no. 11868) |
| **Class Descriptors:** | **LC:** PS1289; **Dewey:** 811.4 |
| **Other Titles:** | Week.; May 29, 1891. |
| **Responsibility:** | by A.F. Chamberlain. |
| **Material Type:** | Microfiche (mfc); Master microform (mmc) |
| **Document Type:** | Book |

Figure 7.1. Modified *WorldCat* record for *An Ode for the Queen's Birthday* and *CIHM*. Source: *WorldCat*.

a multidisciplinary collection of 1,389 titles, over thirty important literary serials form a part of this collection. A bibliography is available for purchase from Canadiana.org.

Initiated in 1994, ***Monographs 1900–1920*** encompasses works by Canadian authors, both published in Canada and abroad. Peel's *Bibliography of the Prairie Provinces* and the *Dictionnaire des oeuvres littéraires du Québec II: 1900–1939* were among the titles initially consulted to identify potential items for filming. *Monographs 1900–1920* encompasses a large number of literary items, with over 2,900 titles. Due to the fact that many titles in this collection are still under copyright, CIHM went to great lengths to locate rights holders prior to filming. Works by many notable writers of the period, for example Bliss Carman, L. M. Montgomery, and Robert Service, contribute to the richness of this collection.

Since completing the broad-scale projects listed above, CIHM has also conceptualized and made available smaller thematic sets. The following literary collections are all derived from the *Pre-1900 Monographs* series, and bibliographies for many of these collections can be purchased from Canadiana .org: *Canadian Women's History*; *Children's Literature: A Feast of Titles*; *English Canadian Language and Literature*; *French Canadian Language and Literature*; *Native Studies*; *Literature (general), Language and Bibliography*; *Children's Literature.*

*Literature (general), Language and Bibliography* represents a collection of over 5,600 titles related to fiction, poetry, children's literature, language, and drama. *English Canadian Language and Literature* is a focused collection consisting of both literary titles and a supplement. Fiction, poetry, and drama form the core collection of over 2,370 titles, while the supplement is comprised of an additional 8,999 works, from travel and exploration to letters and memoirs. *Early Canadiana Online* (*ECO*) provides open access to eight hundred titles from *English Canadian Language and Literature. French Canadian Language and Literature* is similarly organized by a core collection of 517 titles along with supplementary literatures including songs, speeches, and exploration narratives, totaling over 2,500 works. Available as a separate collection of nineteenth-century titles by both English and French Canadian authors, *Children's Literature: A Feast of Titles*, is composed of 642 works on over 2,000 fiches.

CIHM's *Native Studies* collection presents monographs, pamphlets, and reports covering all aspects of Native culture and life, including legends, traditions, customs, eyewitness accounts, and biographies. Over 900 of the 1,900 titles in this collection are available as open-access items through *Early Canadiana Online*. Memoirs, diaries, letters, exploration narratives, travel writing, theater, and political pamphlets are among the material found in *Canadian Women's History*, a collection of 1,742 titles related to nineteenth-century women authors, their works, and women's experiences.

Although indexed CIHM bibliographies are available for many of the above titles, individual works may also be searched using *WorldCat*. Generally, conducting your search using the author, title, or keyword field, in addition to *CIHM* as a keyword, should retrieve the title you seek. Many of these collections are now available online, and searching for individual titles may also be conducted through Canadiana.org's digital initiatives, discussed in the next section.

## CANADIANA.ORG'S DIGITAL INITIATIVES

*Early Canadiana Online* (*ECO*). Ottawa: Canadiana.org, 1999–. www.canadiana.org/ECO (accessed 25 June 2010).

*Early Canadian Periodicals* (*ECP*). Ottawa: Canadiana.org, 2006–. www1.canadiana.org/en/co/eco#ecp1920 (accessed 1 July 2010).

In 2008, the Canadian Institute for Historical Microreproductions and the Canadian Association of Research Libraries' Alouette Canada initiative merged their digitization, access, and preservation efforts under a new program, Canadiana.org. The resulting alliance is supported by the participation of provincial and national institutions, such as libraries, archives, and museums, all contributing to a collective online initiative. Aside from the convenience of online access, Canadiana.org's collections benefit from optical character recognition (OCR) indexing, which offers full-text searching, a convenience unrealizable with microform formats. Canadiana.org maintains a close relationship with libraries and scholarly organizations, soliciting input on proposed projects and future endeavors.

Currently comprised of seven online collections, ***Early Canadiana Online* (*ECO*)** offers full-text, digitized access to material originating from the arrival of Canada's first settlers until the early part of the twentieth century. The advanced-search interface provides year of publication and language limiters; a browse feature is also available. Access points include author, title, subject, publisher, date, collection, notes, metadata, and document text. Search results display links to each of the documents containing matches, along with direct links to the individual pages of the item containing your search term. A search for *Pauline Johnson*, for example, returned 145 pages in 105 documents. Results related to Johnson encompass poetry collections, Canadian women's history, biographical surveys, and historical works on the Iroquois, among other considerations. Since all items filmed by CIHM and digitized by Canadiana.org were borrowed from various libraries and institutions, individual item records also give the name of the document source. The interface is clean and user-friendly, culling otherwise difficult-to-acquire

DIARY WRITTEN IN THE PROVINCIAL LUNATIC ASYLUM

View Cover View Page: Technical Data Sheet Go

| | |
|---|---|
| **Title:** | Diary written in the Provincial Lunatic Asylum |
| **Principal Author:** | Pengilly, Mary Huestis. |
| **Imprint:** | [St. John, N.B.?] : M.H. Pengilly, 1885. |
| **General Note:** | "The prison doors are open--I am free ..." |
| | Title from title screen. |
| **Document Source:** | Scanned from a CIHM microfiche of the original publication held by the National Library of Canada. |
| **Subject:** | Provincial Lunatic Asylum (N.B.) |
| | Mentally ill -- Care -- New Brunswick. |
| **Collection:** | Women's History |
| **CIHM no.:** | 11978 |
| **Page Count:** | 30 |

**Figure 7.2. Modified *Early Canadiana Online* record for *Diary Written in the Provincial Lunatic Asylum*. Source: Canadiana.org.**

resources and placing them at the fingertips of the researcher. With close to sixty thousand documents totaling over three million pages of digitized material, *Early Canadiana Online* continues to develop and grow.

In 2006, Canadiana.org began a six-year project to digitize the *Pre-1920 Canadian Periodicals* microform collection. The grand plan of the multiyear ***Early Canadian Periodicals*** project is ultimately to digitize all pre-1920 Canadian periodicals, and content will subsequently be added to the *Early Canadiana Online* library. The collection boasts a rich selection of literary titles, such as *The Literary Garland*, *Punch in Canada*, *The Amaranth*, and the nineteenth-century French Canadian magazine *Les Soirées canadiennes*. As discussed in chapter 6, Canadiana.org is the main entity providing digitization of early Canadian periodicals and documents. Many nascent titles can therefore be found through *Early Canadian Periodicals*.

Canadiana.org's digitization projects are ambitious, and the results of their efforts translate into unprecedented convenience for the researcher seeking early Canadian texts. Although the organization depends heavily on subscriptions, a commitment to the principles of open access grants users a fair amount of *Early Canadiana Online* content. Mary Huestis Pengilly's 1885 *Diary Written in the Provincial Lunatic Asylum* is one item freely available through the site. Visitors to the Canadiana.org website can view the entire book, digitally reproduced from a copy held at Library and Archives Canada (formerly the National Library of Canada). Figure 7.2 illustrates an *Early Canadiana Online* record for Pengilly's biography.

## DIGITAL COLLECTIONS

*Canadian Poetry*. Ann Arbor, MI: Jointly published by Chadwyck-Healey and the Electronic Text Centre at the University of New Brunswick Libraries, 1999–. http://collections.chadwyck.co.uk/marketing/home_cp.jsp (accessed 10 July 2010).

*Canadian Writers/Écrivains et écrivaines du Canada*. Ottawa: Library and Archives Canada. www.collectionscanada.gc.ca/writers (accessed 12 July 2010).

*Canadiana Discovery Portal*. Ottawa: Canadiana.org. http://search.alouettecanada.ca/search (accessed 10 July 2010).

*CBC Digital Archives*. Toronto: Canadian Broadcasting Company. http://archives.cbc.ca (accessed 12 July 2010).

*Early English Books Online* (*EEBO*). Ann Arbor, MI: Chadwyck-Healey, 1473–1700. http://eebo.chadwyck.com (accessed 10 July 2010).

*Eighteenth Century Collections Online* (*ECCO*). Detroit, MI: Gale. www.gale.com/EighteenthCentury.

*Érudit*. Montréal: Consortium Érudit, 1998. www.erudit.org (accessed 10 July 2010).

*Internet Archive Canada*. www.archive.org/details/toronto (accessed 10 July 2010).

*Multicultural Canada*. www.multiculturalcanada.ca (accessed 10 July 2010).

*North American Women's Drama*. Alexandria, VA: Alexander Street Press. http://solomon.wodr.alexanderstreet.com (accessed 10 July 2010).

*North American Women's Letters and Diaries*. Alexandria, VA: Alexander Street Press. http://solomon.nwld.alexanderstreet.com (accessed 10 July 2010).

*Synergies: Canada's Social Sciences and Humanities Research Infrastructure*. 2009–. www.synergiescanada.org (accessed 25 June 2010).

With the exception of large-scale digital projects that aim toward comprehensiveness, many digital collections represent a focused attempt to provide electronic access to material representing a common genre, subject, or theme. The ***Canadiana Discovery Portal*** is a fascinating site that serves as a searchable access point to a variety of digital collections from across Canada. Initially conceptualized by the Canadian Association of Research Libraries' Alouette Canada initiative, access is now available through the Canadiana.org website. Given the number of individual digital projects undertaken by separate entities, the need for such gateway sites cannot be overstated. Aside from merely providing links to various subject-oriented digital collections, the *Canadiana Discovery Portal* also offers a search feature. The advanced-search interface allows users to limit results by contributing institution, and to specific formats, such as audio, images, text, and video. The *Portal*'s collections are particularly strong in access to both ephemera and to oral history projects encompassing audio files and transcripts.

The ***CBC Digital Archives*** is a website featuring searchable video and audio clips from the archives of the Canadian Broadcasting Corporation (CBC). Special programs, reports, and author interviews are among the materials presented. Audio from the awarding of the first Giller Prize, presented by Mordecai Richler to M. G. Vassanji on November 3, 1994, is available through the site. Additionally, a young Leonard Cohen can be heard reading his poetry in an April 22, 1958, radio performance from the long-running CBC program *Anthology*. The site affords excellent historical perspective on several Canadian authors, such as Hubert Aquin, Guy Vanderhaeghe, Maria Campbell, Irving Layton, and Miriam Toews, while demonstrating the country's commitment to promoting their accomplishments and works. A candid clip from the literary news program *Hot Type* presents host Evan Solomon's December 10, 2000, interview with Margaret Atwood. Advanced-search features offer the ability to limit results to radio or television clips. Thematic browsing is also available, with categories such as literature, poetry, theater, humor, and the visual arts. A search for Alice Munro, for example, returns ten items, including radio and television clips spanning her career from 1974 to 2007.

Launched in 2009, ***Synergies: Canada's Social Sciences and Humanities Research Infrastructure*** is a "national network for the production, storage, and access to digitized knowledge produced in Canada." With member institutions from each of Canada's geographic regions, *Synergies* affiliates include the University of Montreal, the University of New Brunswick, the University of Toronto, the University of Calgary, and Simon Fraser University. Although founded in 1998, ***Érudit*** is now affiliated with and described as the "Quebec node" of *Synergies*, offering a searchable platform of open-access journals, e-books, conference proceedings, and a growing collection of University of Montreal theses. Users are able to query several literary journals, including *Voix et images*, *Études littéraires*, *Cahiers franco-canadiens de l'Ouest*, *Studies in Canadian Literature*, and *Theatre Research in Canada*. Similar to *JSTOR*, *Érudit* uses the "moving wall" concept, restricting article access for the most recent years of publication to journal subscribers. *Érudit* content is currently more developed than other *Synergies* projects and offers a strong francophone component. A search for "Marie-Claire Blais," for example, returns ninety journal articles, two book articles, and three theses. A multi-institutional publishing consortium, *Érudit* partners include the Université de Montréal, the Université Laval, and the Université de Québec à Montréal. The *Synergies* concept is one which we are likely to see replicated as academic institutions seek open-access and institutional repository models to both draw attention to research and to counteract inflationary publishing costs.

***Multicultural Canada*** is a digital collection of newspapers, books, manuscripts, documents, photographs, and audio files organized by ethnic community. Individual collections provide a wealth of materials that exhibit cultural interests, challenges, and sentiments of the period. Materials contributed by research institutions, such as Simon Frasier University Library and the University of Calgary Library, related to the French Canadian ethnic press, children's literature, oral history, drama, and poetry are found within the collections. Ephemera, calendars, and meeting minutes offer insight into the day-to-day lives of specific cultural communities. While items appear in small windows that require considerable scrolling, advanced display options are also accessible.

Library and Archives Canada has developed many sites to highlight its rich holdings. ***Canadian Writers/Écrivains et écrivaines du Canada***, curated by several University of Ottawa professors, uses examples from LAC's Literary Manuscript Collection to illustrate the creative process. Unpublished materials by notable writers, including rough drafts, manuscripts, typescripts, illustrations, correspondence, notebooks, journal entries, and ephemera, contribute to an understanding of the craft of writing. The "Manuscript Gallery" for Hector de Saint-Denys Garneau, for example, showcases items that demonstrate the French Canadian poet's simultaneous passion for both art and writing. Materials span the course of Saint-Denys Garneau's career, displaying examples of his earliest attempts, along with later, more polished pieces. Likewise, the Jane Urquhart gallery offers beautifully illustrated pages from the author's diary, in addition to her manuscript notebooks. While the collection may develop further, other writers examined to date are Marie-Claire Blais, Jacques Brault, Roger Lemelin, Carol Shields, Elizabeth Smart, and Michel Tremblay. A "Cultural Context" write-up is presented for each author, contextualizing the digitized items in the manuscript gallery. Although *Canadian Writers* does not encompass the entirety of LAC's archival collections, the items selected present a richer view of each writer examined.

Founded in San Francisco in 1996, the *Internet Archive* facilitates access to historical collections in digital format. Robert Service's *Songs of a Sourdough*, donated for scanning by the Thomas Fisher Rare Book Library at the University of Toronto, represents the two hundred thousandth text to be added to the Canadian arm of the project. Items in the ***Internet Archive Canada*** include periodicals, books, literary handbooks, theses, bibliographies, and catalogs. *Internet Archive* records clarify an item's copyright status, as well as the name of the originating institution. Material can be downloaded in a variety of formats, and the scanning quality is pristine. Library and Archives Canada and McMaster University are among the institutions contributing material to the project.

Thus far, the digital collections we have discussed are mostly freely available or at least offer some open-access content. We will now examine a few commercial collections developed by publishers and sold through database vendors. Alexander Street Press has been a leader in developing extensive digital collections with unprecedented coverage of otherwise elusive material. ***North American Women's Drama*** reports full-text access to over 1,500 plays by 330 female writers. However, of the material included, only 102 of the plays are written by Canadian playwrights. Although content is overwhelmingly American, the following Canadians are represented: Carol Bolt, Kia Corthron, Maria Campbell, Marianne Ackerman, Nancy Jo Cullen, Colleen Curran, Margaretta Faugères, Linda Griffiths, Louisa J. Hall, Mrs. Marriott, Yvette Nolan, Gail Nyoka, Sharon Pollock, Rose Scollard, Flora Stohr-Danziger, and Rachel Wyatt. Many of the plays, such as Gail Nyoka's *Mella Mella*, have not been previously published. The interface supports performing searches by genre, theater name, production company, author nationality, author race, and author age when writing, among other limiters.

Another Alexander Street Press product, ***North American Women's Letters and Diaries***, is a 150,000-page collection of material from over one thousand sources. Of the 1,325 women writers included, twenty-seven are Canadian. The advanced-search interface presents an impressive array of limiting options, such as the age of the author when writing, their marital status when writing, age at marriage, race, and religion. Limiting the information to Canadian content is easy, as results can also be searched according to "Where Written," with several cities and provinces available as terms. Susanna Strickland Moodie, Letitia MacTavish Hargrave, Mary Georgina Hall, Catherine Parr Traill, and Rachel Bowman Cormany are among the writers and diarists found in this exceptional collection. A search limiting the results to documents written in Canada retrieves 894 items. Other limiters include "Historical Events," "Personal Events," and "Number of Marriages."

***Early English Books Online* (*EEBO*)** is a major digital resource for works printed in England, Scotland, Ireland, Wales, and British North America, as well as titles written in English and published elsewhere, for the period covering 1473 to 1700. Since titles pertaining to Canada published during this period are mainly comprised of exploration narratives and missionary accounts, there may be little content in this fascinating collection pertaining to "Canadian literature." Despite this, if your research entails examination of English historical texts for the period, *EEBO* will facilitate your endeavors. One of the earliest *EEBO* titles relevant to Canada is a 1580 imprint of Jacques Cartier's *A Short and Brief Narration*, originally appearing in Paris as *Bref récit* in 1545. Richard Hakluyt's anthology of exploration history, *The Principall Navigations, Voiages and Discoveries of the English Nation*

(1589), which Iain M. Higgins refers to as having "some claim to being a work of proto-English-Canadian literature,"[4] is also accessible through this collection. Other early works include a 1609 imprint of Marc Lescarbot's *Noua Francia*, of which the 1609 French version is freely available through Canadiana.org.

***Eighteenth Century Collections Online* (*ECCO*)** is a collection of digitized books printed in Great Britain during the eighteenth century, including titles from the Americas. *ECCO* encompasses an early period for Canadian writing, but it may likewise have little application for Canadian literary research. As Guy LaFleche points out in his discussion of the colonial literature of New France, "This culture had no time to develop a literature of its own. Only a few major works can be numbered from a literary life that remained embryonic."[5] The collections can be queried using either the basic or advanced-search interface, and date of publication and subject limiters can be applied. Searches can also be performed by author, title, full text, front matter, main text, back-of-book indexes, publisher, and place of publication. The place of publication limiter is useful for searching Canadian imprints; for example, a search limited to *Montreal* produces six results, including *A Primer for the Use of the Mohawk Children* (1781) by Daniel Claus. Browsing by author or published work is also an option. *ECCO* allows for full-text searching, and content is enhanced by a growing library of images. *ECCO*'s twenty-six million pages of text are based on the *English Short Title Catalog*, representing 136,000 works. The recently added "Eighteenth Century Collections Online, Part II: New Editions" portion of *ECCO* increases these numbers to thirty-three million pages of text, representing 180,000 titles. Titles of interest within this collection include several editions of Frances Brooke's *The History of Emily Montague*. In common with *Early English Books Online*, exploration narratives related to Canada are likewise in abundance. Two editions of Samuel Hearne's *A Journey from Prince of Wales' Fort in Hudson's Bay to the Northern Ocean* (1795) are found within *ECCO*. Another item of interest is a review of Alexander MacKenzie's *Voyages from Montreal through the Continent of North America to the Frozen and Pacific Oceans* printed in *The European Magazine, and London Review*.[6]

Created and published in collaboration with the Electronic Text Centre at the University of New Brunswick Libraries, Chadwyck-Healey's ***Canadian Poetry*** is a digital collection of nineteen thousand poems by over 177 Canadian writers. The collection essentially represents the entire corpus of English-language Canadian poetry, from the seventeenth century to the early twentieth. The search interface allows for full-text keyword queries, first line/title searches, as well as author searching. Additional features offer application of "Gender," "Period," and "Living in the Year" limiters.

## CONCLUSION

Just as microform collections diverge in quality and readability, you will find similar issues while exploring digital collections. Variations in document download speed, display options, and licensing can be significant. Digital collections depend heavily on a sustained commitment from the entities responsible for their development. It can be disappointing to learn, upon revisiting a site, that a project has been abandoned or discontinued. Portal sites to freely available digital collections are often plagued by broken links, calling into question the relevance and usefulness of the collection itself. Some electronic collections derive digitized materials from microform copies, improving accessibility, but not necessarily the readability of the items. Despite some of these issues, as digital collections continue to be developed, we are likely to witness unprecedented access to previously inaccessible material.

## NOTES

1. For more information, consult www.collectionscanada.gc.ca/microform-digitization (accessed 2 July 2010).
2. Patricia Fleming, *Upper Canadian Imprints, 1801–1841: A Bibliography* (Toronto: University of Toronto Press, 1988).
3. Linda Jones, *Preliminary Checklist of Pre-1900 Canadian Serials* (Ottawa: Canadian Institute for Historical Microreproductions, 1986).
4. Iain Higgins, "White Writing before Canada, 1000–1600," in *History of Literature in Canada: English-Canadian and French-Canadian*, ed. Reingard M. Nischik (Rochester, NY: Camden House, 2008), 41.
5. Guy LaFleche, "Colonial Literature in New France," in *History of Literature in Canada: English-Canadian and French-Canadian*, ed. Reingard M. Nischik (Rochester, NY: Camden House, 2008), 66.
6. "MacKenzie's Voyages from Montreal to the Frozen and Pacific Oceans," *The European Magazine, and London Review* 41 (January–June 1802): 113, 198, 282.

# *Chapter Eight*

# Manuscripts and Archives

Archives and manuscript collections hold unique materials that can contribute to a stimulating research environment. Insight into the writer's creative process can be discovered through manuscript collections, and archival investigation, though time consuming, can provide rich perspective. The dispersion of archival materials related to Canadian writers testifies to the itinerant and international nature of the Canadian author in the twentieth century, as collections related to Canadian authors may be located in Canada, the United States, and abroad. With the potential for online accessibility, archival collections are in a state of flux, and archival acquisition today encompasses elaborate issues related to copyright, access, permissions for digitization, and the protection and management of intellectual property. Despite such complexities, as electronic archives develop, unpublished documents may be as readily accessible as published items.

Many archives rely on donors who maintain and collect relevant materials. Canadian writers and literary aficionados have been active contributors to special collections across Canada, and the relationship between author, archivist, and researcher is mutually dependent. As such, archivists who are directly involved with a particular collection are often mentioned in the introductions of reference works, acknowledging their assistance and expertise. Some recognizable names from works both past and present include Jennifer Toews, for her involvement with the Margaret Atwood papers at the University of Toronto, and Apollonia Steele, who contributed to many archival research projects through her position at the University of Calgary.

In the past, researchers depended heavily on print guides and archival directories, which could be in themselves difficult to access. A lack of guides and finding aids prompts the following statement from the archival introduction to *The Mordecai Richler Papers*: "Unfortunately, since awareness of and access to primary materials are prerequisites for many other research projects, including traditional bibliographies, editions of letters, critical studies and biographies, archives are seen as sources of frustration almost as often as they are seen as sources of information."[1] Online accessibility has revolutionized the archival environment, as the electronic availability of finding aids and collection descriptions has increased the scholar's awareness of specific materials. In addition to the existence and location of author papers, researchers are often readily aware of specialized collections pertaining to particular areas of interest, such as the University of British Columbia's Canadian children's literature collection, and the Thomas Fisher Rare Book Library's extensive acquisition of little magazines.

Archival considerations occasionally inspire special journal issues, such as *Canadian Literature*'s "What the Archives Reveal" (Summer 1989) and the *Journal of Canadian Studies* "Turning the Knobs on Writers' Closets: Archives and Canadian Literature in the 21st Century" (Spring 2006). For a thorough survey of current archival topics, you may wish to consult *Archivaria: The Journal of the Canadian Association of Archivists*. Published semiannually since 1975, the journal is available as an open-access publication through Simon Fraser University (http://journals.sfu.ca/archivar/index.php/archivaria/index).

Just as catalog records describe library holdings, archivists create specialized descriptions of collections known as "finding aids" to facilitate access to archival materials. Many institutions have made their finding aids available online, and archival collections are often integrated into the online catalogs of large libraries. If you have never used an archival collection in your research, you may want to familiarize yourself with some of the specialized terminology used by archivists. The University of Calgary provides a succinct online glossary (http://archives.ucalgary.ca/glossary) clarifying many common archival terms that you may encounter during your inquiry. One term often used in archival research in Canada is *fonds*, which describes a collection of archival materials, regardless of format, originating from the same source. For example, later in this chapter we will discuss the W. H. New fonds at the University of British Columbia Archives, representing 29.93 meters of materials collected and donated by New upon his retirement in 2003.

## EXPLORING CANADIAN REPOSITORIES

Ash, Lee, and William G. Miller, comps. *Subject Collections: A Guide to Special Book Collections and Subject Emphases as Reported by University, College, Public, and Special Libraries and Museums in the United*

*States and Canada*. 2 vols. 7th ed., rev. and enl. New Providence, NJ: R. R. Bowker, 1993.

Gordon, Robert S., dir., and E. Grace Maurice, ed. *Union List of Manuscripts in Canadian Repositories/Catalogue collectif des manuscrits conservés dans les dépôts d'archives canadiens*. 2 vols. Rev. ed. Ottawa: Public Archives of Canada, 1975.

Library and Archives Canada. *Literary Archives: A Guide to the Literary Fonds at Library and Archives Canada*. Ottawa: Library and Archives Canada, 2001–. www.lac-bac.gc.ca/literaryarchives/index-e.html (accessed 10 July 2010).

Moore, Jean, comp., Marlys Chevrefils, and Apollonia Steele, eds. *Mapping the Territory: A Guide to the Archival Holdings, Special Collections, University of Calgary Library*. Calgary, Alberta: University of Calgary Press, 1994.

National Library of Canada. *Research Collections in Canadian Libraries*. 2 vols. Ottawa: National Library of Canada, 1973.

Public Archives of Canada, Manuscript Division. *General Inventory: Manuscripts/Inventaire général: Manuscrits*. 8 vols. Ottawa: Public Archives of Canada, Manuscript Division, 1971–1977.

University of Calgary Libraries, Special Collections Division. *Canadian Archival Inventories Series: Literary Papers*. Multiple vols. Calgary, Alberta: University of Calgary Press, 1986–.

Wood, Donna, ed. *International Research Centers Directory*. Farmington Hills, MI: Gale Research Company, 1981–.

The appearance of published archival guides was of great significance to patrons of special collections during the latter part of the twentieth century. However, online venues now facilitate streamlined and time-saving access to finding aids and serve to advertise the existence of a particular collection. Materials that were previously regularly updated in monographic form have largely migrated to electronic formats; nevertheless, traditional print resources may still offer unreplicated information and historical perspective.

Public Archives Canada originally began publishing the ***Union List of Manuscripts in Canadian Repositories/Catalogue collectif des manuscrits conservés dans les dépôts d'archives canadiens*** in order to assist researchers in determining whether a collection would warrant travel to the holding institution. The project began in 1961 as a joint venture between the Public Archives of Canada and the Humanities Research Council of Canada, when 124 repositories contributed eleven thousand entries of archival holdings to the 1968 volume. When the revised version appeared in 1975, the number of participating institutions had increased to 171. Collection-level entries in the print version are organized by person, corporate entity, or government agency responsible for creating or accumulating the items. The union list demonstrates that archival manuscript collections can be comprised of a great variety of formats, including holographic documents, transcripts, photocopies, typescripts, carbon copies, photographs, slides, and microfilm. Brief descriptions offer information such as the title, extent, provenance, date, and type of materials in the collection. A feature of the 1975 edition is the "Catalogue by Repositories" listing; this rundown of archival holdings by institution allows perspective on whether additional collections of interest might also be held at the same site. The *Union List* provides a wonderful sense of the country's rich printed history, the fields from which many of Canada's secondary documents of literary and historical research have sprung. The commitment of the individual entities, both large and small, that safeguarded these items for future generations is also apparent. While your own archival research may be a solitary experience, the curation of materials is a team effort. As project director Robert S. Gordon explains in the introduction to the revised 1975 edition, "It should be stressed that the *Union List* is the collective achievement of archivists, historians, curators and librarians, including support staff, in one hundred and seventy-one Canadian repositories who tirelessly prepared the entries which form the basis of the *List*" (v).

During the 1970s, Public Archives Canada published the eight-volume ***General Inventory: Manuscripts/Inventaire général: Manuscrits***. While such print listings may seem dated, they served as precursors to online guides and were regarded as indispensable time-saving resources for researchers. A review of volume 2 of the *General Inventory* by T. D. Regehr in the winter 1976 issue of *Archivaria* reminds us of the importance of such projects at the time of their publication: "With this inventory the need for nice scholarly research junkets to London will probably disappear for many students of Canadian history. . . . Inventories of the kind under review here are one of the reasons for this development."[2]

In 1972, the National Library of Canada (now Library and Archives Canada, or LAC) began publishing ***Research Collections in Canadian Libraries***. The Universities series consists of six parts and examines library collections by region, with separate issues dedicated to the "Prairie Provinces," the "Atlantic Provinces," British Columbia, Ontario, and Quebec. An excellent survey of theater-related materials is found in volume 2, issue 1, of the Special Studies series, *Theatre Resources in Canadian Collections*. Reflecting the theater-related holdings of 114 institutions across Canada, special collections and nonbook formats here receive careful consideration, as surveys of published written materials were already reflected in the general National Library of Canada catalog. This study therefore considers photos, diaries, financial documents, unpublished materials, and newspaper reviews, among other nonmonographic items. Aside from soliciting input from over three hundred libraries and archival collections, the authors of this volume also visited many of the sites discussed. Annotations carefully explore the collections, selection policies, and holdings of materials pertaining to the performing arts from Canadian libraries, archives, and special collections. The annotation for Calgary's Glenbow-Alberta Institute, for example, illuminates the Chautauqua movement, a form of prairie theater that began in the United States but became popularized in Canada circa 1917. It is apparent that the authors combed through the rich and varied holdings of the institutions as a labor of love in honor of Canadian theater history. The inventory is organized according to the holdings of federal, provincial, and university libraries, as well as "University Theatre Departments, Theatre Schools," "Theatre Organizations, Ballet, Opera and Theatre Companies," "Public Libraries, Municipal Archives," "Museums and Galleries," "Special Collections," "Private Collections," "Cinema Collections," and "Theatre Archives outside Canada." Additional sections offer an overall "Assessment," as well as "Observations" and "Recommendations" for Canadian theater collections.

In an aim to contribute to the Social Sciences and Humanities Research Council of Canada's Canadian Studies Research Tools Program, the University of Calgary Press has been active in producing the ***Canadian Archival Inventories Series: Literary Papers***, with volumes dedicated to numerous authors, including W. O. Mitchell, Alice Munro, and children's author Christie Harris. The stated goals of the series are to stimulate interest and to supply off-site researchers with an adequate description of the archival materials available at the University of Calgary so that they might be able to determine whether an in-person visit would be advantageous. With over twenty publications in the series to date, some variability is found within the presentation of ancillary information in each individually authored title. Nevertheless, the series adheres to the Rules of Archival Description (RAD), following the standards set by the Canadian archival community. The major sections of the individual titles present a biocritical essay, an archival introduction, an inventory, and both alphabetical and chronological listings of written letters.

Published in 1994, ***Mapping the Territory: A Guide to the Archival Holdings, Special Collections, University of Calgary Library*** complements and serves as a general handbook to the individual titles of the aforementioned *Canadian Archival Inventories Series* while incorporating descriptions of additional University of Calgary collections. This resource is divided into three areas, with descriptive entries for archival collections comprising the bulk of the work. Other sections provide a subject index and a guide to names in the described collections.

Ash and Miller's ***Subject Collections: A Guide to Special Book Collections and Subject Emphases as Reported by University, College, Public,***

***and Special Libraries and Museums in the United States and Canada*** is an example of a major research guide that has been overshadowed by Web accessibility. Nevertheless, the listings by subject are convenient and are not elsewhere replicated. If you do consult this 1993 imprint, you will want to consider it as only a preliminary step to alert you to the existence of materials at a given repository, further checking online for updates and changes to a particular collection. Information for the two-volume work was solicited from the holding institutions via a questionnaire, and the guide employs Library of Congress subject headings, with some modifications.

Organized by subject, entries in the ***International Research Centers Directory*** provide information on an institution's founding year, number of staff, research areas, on-site resources, publications, sponsored workshops and conferences, and library holdings, where applicable. Collection descriptions include the extent, material format, as well as scope and contents notes, highlighting unique or unusual aspects of the collection. Literature is considered under "Humanities and Religion," section 14, and entries are further arranged alphabetically by research institution. Entry 8946, for example, highlights Carleton University's Institute of Comparative Studies in Literature, Art, and Culture. In addition to a master index, the directory is complemented by three additional indexes, including a personal name index, a country index, and a subject index, with cross-referencing. Your institution may have online access to this resource through the Gale Directory Library.

Library and Archives Canada's ***Literary Archives: A Guide to the Literary Fonds at Library and Archives Canada*** serves as an excellent example of a resource that was once published in print form but is today exclusively and freely available online. The guide is useful for the novice researcher in that it not only serves to clarify LAC's archival collections for literary research, but also supplies explanations of archival terms and structures through the "About the Guide" link. LAC's literary collections encompass the fonds of writers, editors, and illustrators, in addition to those of periodicals and small Canadian literary presses, such as Tundra Books and *Arc Magazine*. The entry for Jane Urquhart, for example, offers a biographical sketch, scope and content notes, the source of acquisition, collection restrictions, and the availability of finding aids.

## ONLINE CATALOGS AND GATEWAYS FOR ARCHIVAL RESEARCH

Canadian Council of Archives. *ArchivesCanada.ca: Canadian Archival Information Network.* www.archivescanada.ca (accessed 10 July 2010).

Library and Archives Canada. *Library and Archives Canada*. www.collectionscanada.gc.ca/index-e.html (accessed 10 July 2010).

In 1987, the Public Archives of Canada became the National Archives of Canada and is now called Library and Archives Canada, reflecting the merger of the National Library and National Archives. Aside from government materials, Library and Archives Canada retains relevant historical, cultural, and political items of importance to the Canadian people. Since the 1970s, Canadian archives have subscribed to a "total archives" mission, collecting and preserving material in all formats, from both public and private entities, in order to build a rich picture of Canadian history and culture.[3] A second aspect of the "total archives" concept is that materials should be accessible to the public, a goal which is today facilitated by the Web. The information contained in many of the Public Archives and National Archives of Canada titles listed in the previous section is now available and augmented online through the ***Library and Archives Canada*** website. Online functionality offers many advantages, significantly improving the level of detail over print listings while maintaining original LAC grouping systems. LAC's archival descriptions are well written and provide a significant amount of detail, such as excellent scope and content notes, thorough information on restrictions of access and terms of use, provenance, and links to related finding aids. An example of the interface for a search of textual material related to Gabrielle Roy is shown in figure 8.1.

The basic search interface allows you to limit by material type, using "Textual Material" as a criterion in the example in figure 8.1. Other material-type limiters available include photographic, sound recordings, and film and video. The "Hierarchical Level" limiter refers to the organization of LAC's archival materials and will be most useful for the researcher who is already familiar with a particular collection. Limiters found under this option are "Fonds/Collections," "Series," "Files," "Item," and "Accession." Advanced-search options afford the ability to limit your query to material originating from either government or private sources.

In 2001, the Canadian Council of Archives began an online initiative, launching the Canadian Archival Information Network to provide access to archival holdings nationwide. The searchable ***ArchivesCanada.ca: Canadian Archival Information Network*** database offers descriptions of archival holdings, as well as links to finding aids, digital collections, and virtual exhibits. Examples of exhibits available through the gateway include the University of Saskatchewan's "Al Purdy Digital Archive," and Library and Archives Canada's "Tales from the Vault! Canadian Pulp Fiction 1940–1952." The database is an outstanding resource for identifying the holding institutions of

Library and Archives Canada Bibliothèque et Archives Canada

Canada

**Library and Archives Canada**
www.collectionscanada.gc.ca

Français | Home | Contact Us | Help | Search
canada.gc.ca

Home > Search > Archives Search

Introduction
Search All
Library Search
Archives Search
Basic
Advanced
Ancestors Search
Website Search
Search Help
Comments

Proactive Disclosure

**Search**

**Archives Search**

gabrielle roy

**Type of material:** Textual material

**Hierarchical level:** Fonds/Collections

**Online:** All

**Number of results:** 10 results per page

Submit Clear

To access archival research tools that are not included in Archives Search, please consult Databases.

**Archives Canada** is a gateway to archival resources found in over 800 repositories across Canada. Click here to search for archival holdings across Canada.

**See Also:**
On Our Website
Our Popular Resources
The Public

**Figure 8.1. A search for textual material related to author Gabrielle Roy. Source: Library and Archives Canada.**

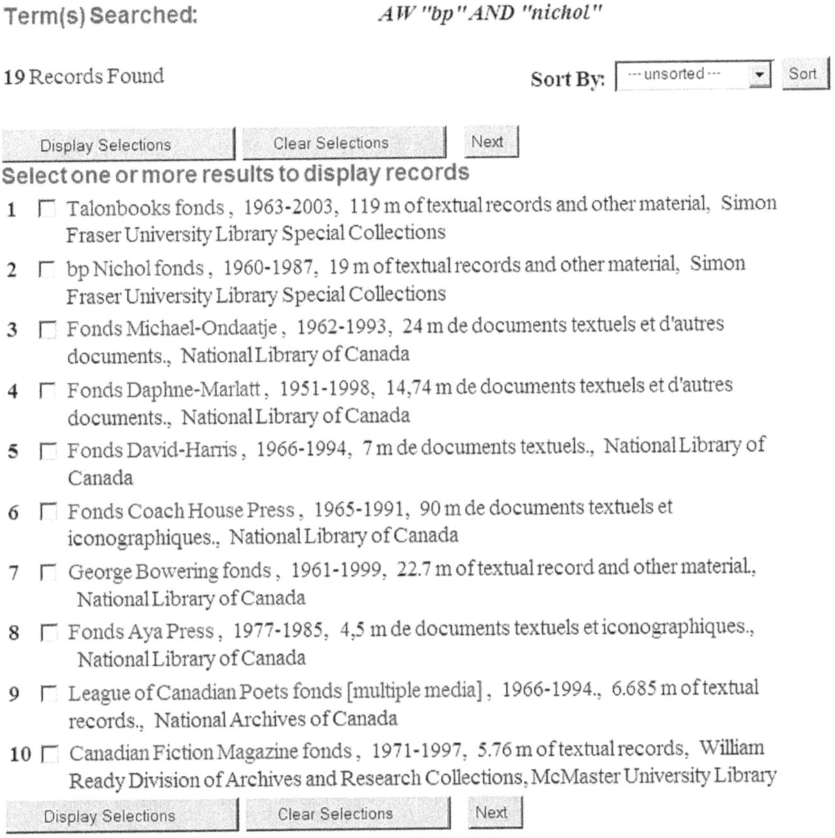

Term(s) Searched: *AW "bp" AND "nichol"*

19 Records Found Sort By: --- unsorted --- Sort

Display Selections | Clear Selections | Next

**Select one or more results to display records**

1 ☐ Talonbooks fonds, 1963-2003, 119 m of textual records and other material, Simon Fraser University Library Special Collections

2 ☐ bp Nichol fonds, 1960-1987, 19 m of textual records and other material, Simon Fraser University Library Special Collections

3 ☐ Fonds Michael-Ondaatje, 1962-1993, 24 m de documents textuels et d'autres documents., National Library of Canada

4 ☐ Fonds Daphne-Marlatt, 1951-1998, 14,74 m de documents textuels et d'autres documents., National Library of Canada

5 ☐ Fonds David-Harris, 1966-1994, 7 m de documents textuels., National Library of Canada

6 ☐ Fonds Coach House Press, 1965-1991, 90 m de documents textuels et iconographiques., National Library of Canada

7 ☐ George Bowering fonds, 1961-1999, 22.7 m of textual record and other material., National Library of Canada

8 ☐ Fonds Aya Press, 1977-1985, 4,5 m de documents textuels et iconographiques., National Library of Canada

9 ☐ League of Canadian Poets fonds [multiple media], 1966-1994., 6.685 m of textual records., National Archives of Canada

10 ☐ Canadian Fiction Magazine fonds, 1971-1997, 5.76 m of textual records, William Ready Division of Archives and Research Collections, McMaster University Library

Display Selections | Clear Selections | Next

**Figure 8.2. The results of a search for *bp Nichol* in the *ArchivesCanada.ca* database. Source: Canadian Council of Archives, *ArchivesCanada.ca*.**

materials related to a particular author, and advanced searches can be limited by province or territory. Figure 8.2 displays the results of an *ArchivesCanada .ca* search for poet *bp Nichol*.

## PREPARING FOR ARCHIVAL RESEARCH

Even in today's online environments, researchers still travel to view the unique and deep holdings of an archival collection. If your research requires you to achieve an intimate perspective on an author, a publication venture, or a specific literary event, nothing short of a one-on-one interview with an author or editor will likely compete with the level of detail and insight achievable through on-site archival inquiry.

It is a good idea to plan ahead for your research visit, as the policies governing an individual archive can be quite unique. Since many large archives have a Web presence, the home page for the institution is a good place to start. You may be able to learn a great deal about a collection simply by viewing online descriptions and finding aids. Through digitization projects, some archival material may even be accessible via the Internet, so a thorough examination of the institution's website is recommended. Since the size of an archival collection can vary significantly, from a few pages to several linear feet of material, finding aids will help you to obtain a sense of the scope of the collection.

Many archival institutions require the researcher to register prior to viewing materials, and you may be able to save time by initiating this process through the website in advance of your arrival. It is not uncommon for archival material to be subject to restrictions, and it is well advised that you contact the archive ahead of time in order to illuminate any issues of accessibility that could arise. When items are restricted, the researcher may need to request permission to consult the collection, often with additional authorization required to photocopy specific materials. Another advantage of planning ahead is that the archivist may be able to share additional knowledge of a collection with you prior to your arrival at the site. For example, living authors may still actively contribute new papers, and such recent acquisitions may not yet be described online. The archivist may therefore be able to offer information on other items in the collection that pertain to your interest.

Archival research is intense, and as such can be both exhilarating and exhausting. Be certain to give yourself sufficient time to digest the material you are viewing; to allocate a single day for investigating a large collection may be too ambitious. Remember that some archival material cannot be photocopied, or even photographed with a digital camera; in such cases, you may have to pace yourself in order to sift through the items that you have targeted. You will want to keep adequate notes during your visit, as once you leave the archive and return to your home institution, further clarification may prove difficult.

One might find it interesting to note that collections of papers are still kept in traditional filing boxes, a system which is explained in the following quote from the "Archival Introduction" to the *Alice Munro Papers First Accession*: "Experience has shown that the file or package represents the highest level of integrity for original order, whether it is a file of letters, or a file of literary manuscripts. Labelled or unidentified, a file's contents reflect most reliably a unit of organization which had intellectual meaning for the author."[4] Even though the original order of the contents of an archival folder might be maintained in the index to the collection, researchers viewing items after your use will appreciate your efforts to retain the sequence.

## CASE STUDY: A JOURNEY INTO THE ARCHIVES

The University of British Columbia (UBC) Archives hold the William Herbert (W. H.) New fonds, which includes drafts and letters related to the publication of his many works on Canadian literary research. Also found in the collection are New's papers pertaining to his editorship of the journal *Canadian Literature*. As a noted member of the literary community, New has been involved in a multitude of endeavors, and the collection naturally contains correspondence with many members of Canada's literati. A visit to the UBC Archives for an examination of the W. H. New papers affords amazing insight into the personal publishing obstacles, challenges, and accomplishments of this important Canadian literary researcher.

As with many archives, one must first register to access materials at the UBC Archives, a process which can be initiated online. Registration will allow archival staff to issue a user card granting access to the Rare Books and Special Collections Reading Room and University Archives. As an outside user, the archival staff will also need to make a copy of your photo identification. Individual belongings, such as backpacks and coats may not be brought into the archives, and lockers are therefore available upon registering with the staff at the receiving desk. While institutions have differing policies, the UBC Archives do not allow personal paper or writing utensils to enter the room, so a laptop will therefore prove useful should you anticipate note taking. Pencils are available at the study tables, and electrical outlets will allow you to maintain power to your laptop. Some researchers prefer to transcribe material using a voice recorder, noting all punctuation and orthography in order to create written transcripts at a later time.

Located in the basement of the Irving K. Barber Learning Center, a historic and aesthetically beautiful campus building, the archival environment is pleasant, and the staff helpful. Since the building is also home to UBC's School of Library, Archival, and Information Studies (SLAIS), your visit could coincide with a scheduled class or seminar, which should nonetheless not cause you any interference. Although food and drink are not permitted in the archives, a café can be found on the first floor of the Learning Center, providing some respite and sustenance during an intense day of research.

Many gems await in archival collections, and the W. H. New papers are no exception. For example, in a letter dated October 5, 1968, pertaining to

McClelland and Stewart's Canadian Writers Series, David Godfrey writes, "Dear Bill New, Good luck. You have been granted Lowry; any alcoholism picked up along the way is your own lookout."[5] A later letter, written May 14, 1971, by F. Gilbert Paci, per David Godfrey, on the publication of New's biographic *Malcolm Lowry*, reads, "I hold Lowry's work in high esteem and hope your book will generate the interest that is his due. If enough people could wring the alcohol out of his books, they might get drunk enough to appreciate him."[6] Such unpublished exchanges would not be accessible without an in-person examination of archival materials. Furthermore, on-site viewing of archival materials allows for a perspective on the day-to-day realities faced by the writer, details that might not otherwise be apparent or revealed in published sources. While subject to much speculation, a personal inspection of primary materials can be very inspiring. Footprints on manuscripts, evidence of liquid spills, timelines of publication, and the relentless comments of editors are all clues into the world of the writer. Additionally, notes written in the margins, photocopies of works accumulated during New's own archival research, and jottings on departmental scrap paper all provide evidence of the researcher's efforts to decipher Lowry's complex life and mind.

An investigation of W. H. New material from the 1970s reveals an era when telegrams were the equivalent of e-mail, and regular mail was at times copied and sent to multiple locations in order to ensure delivery to the recipient. From the various addresses on New's correspondence, including Cambridge and Bermuda, one can track his many travels and research ventures. An undated letter, circa April 1971, sent by David Godfrey from Europe while New was in Barbados, reveals the trials faced by writers and editors during the era when postal mail was the most efficient means of communication:

> Dear Bill,
>
> Yes, send us the bloody manuscript before there's another strike. This series seems to inevitably produce one. When I'm in Europe, there's one here. When I'm home, everyone's in England and there's one there.
>
> The enclosed has gone off to you in Bermuda and should have reached, but if not take whatever pearls of wisdom you find and send us stuff posthaste. Pardon corrections, haven't time to get it retyped.
>
> Dave[7]

Archival research can be extremely invigorating for the researcher; it can be comforting to witness another writer's struggles with word choice, the painstaking task of pruning a bibliography, the scrupulous readings of editors who identify facts to be checked and rechecked, meaning to be clarified and reclarified. New's genuine interest and candid fascination with his subjects is apparent in his papers. In the case of his Lowry research, New transcends speculation to reveal that the British-born author did indeed have an intimate connection to Canada. One of the more entertaining letters pertaining to Lowry appears below, in a letter dated June 2, 1960, through which we have intimate insight into New's Lowry research and his subsequent identification with the complex author:

> Dear Dave Godfrey,
> I'm beginning to feel a lot like Lowry. Coincidences abound. The world is too much with us. Or, put another way, I've been reading a half dozen of the World's Weirdest Books, including guides through the Tarot Pack, to figure out some of Life's Mysteries, including under the volcano. Nevertheless, not having yet been imprisoned unjustly in a Mexican Jail, I do not feel tempted yet to identify with him.[8]

Among the items in the collection are correspondence from Margerie Lowry in which she expresses interest in New's upcoming work. Also of note is the fact that Earle Birney was recruited by the editors of the Canadian Writers Series to make editorial suggestions to New's *Malcolm Lowry*.[9] Comments written by New in the margins of his edited drafts chronicle his reactions to Birney's reading of the manuscript.

Consisting of over sixty separate archival series donated by New, and spanning his publishing efforts between 1947 and 2009, the fonds are an excellent example of the potential richness of an archival collection. As writer, editor, literary critic, poet, children's author, and professor, W. H. New's papers reveal unexpected discoveries and fascinating exchanges between the prolific scholar and his numerous literary contacts.

## DIARIES AND LETTERS

Manuscript diaries can be difficult to locate, as copies may only be available in the holding archive, with facsimiles on microfilm, microfiche, or other even less attractive formats. Although manuscript diaries may offer an intimate portrait of the author, they might conversely contain uninteresting accounts of common day-to-day events. As John Stuart Batts cautions, "Certainly, the diary of a somebody may disappoint just as easily as that of a nobody may please."[10] Prior to making a special trip to view a particular author's diary, you may therefore first want to investigate the relevance of the item to your research aims.

On the other hand, published diaries and letters are selectively chosen from collections to illustrate or illuminate a particular interest, aspect, viewpoint, or topic related to the writer, but may also be subject to editorial changes. Printed examples include titles such as *The Selected Journals of L. M. Montgomery*; *The Bukowski/Purdy Letters: A Decade of Dialogue, 1964–1974*; and the *Letters of Bliss Carman*. One advantage of using published material is that many are comprised of items culled from private collections and disparate sources, written matter that would otherwise be difficult to access. As H. Pearson Gundy notes in his introduction to the *Letters of Bliss Carman*, archival items pertaining to the poet "are now scattered across the continent in thirty or more depositories."[11] While published diaries and letters are a time-saving device and offer an assurance of quality for some, the researcher may prefer to apply his or her own criteria in separating the wheat from the chaff. For researchers seeking an authentic approach, an in-person examination of an author's archival diaries, letters, and notebooks may still be the best solution.

Published journals and diaries often illuminate the writer's creative process and offer insight into events that shaped the authorship of a particular work. An example of this is seen in André Carpentier's *Journal de mille jours: Carnets, 1983–1986*, a published diary tracing the writer's creative and personal obstacles confronted while working on *Le rêve du diable*. The novel, as the author relates, never did materialize; however, nine short stories, in addition to several essays and articles, were seen through to completion, and the journal became the primary "witness"[12] to their development. Written, as the title suggests, over the course of one thousand days, the journal provides those familiar with the author's work an inside view of the day-to-day realities that influence the development of a creative text. Library of Congress subject headings that may be useful in locating published diaries include the following:

Montgomery, L. M.—(Lucy Maud)—1874–1942—Diaries
Novelists, Canadian—20th century—Diaries
Montgomery, L. M.—(Lucy Maud)—1874–1942—Journaux intimes
Novelists, Canadian (English)—20th century—Diaries
Romanciers canadiens-anglais—20e siècle—Journaux intimes
Poets, Canadian—19th century—Correspondence

## CONCLUSION

Although archives may have a reputation for being characteristically monastic in ambience, today's archival environments can in fact be bustling spaces, as researchers come and go, writers bask in the richness of unreplicated materials, students meet to work on group projects, and hands-on preservation classes are held. Special exhibits and rare book collections may attract a combination of local school groups, interested community members, and visitors from afar. Online environments position the researcher for a fruitful investigation of materials that were previously elusive and difficult to access. Today's archival research scenarios are quite different from those of the past, as the availability of online material, finding aids, and guides facilitate access and announce the existence of otherwise obscure items. The publication of archival guides and finding aids via the Web facilitates the researcher's ability to ascertain the usefulness of a collection prior to committing time and resources to an in-person review. Whether a manuscript is viewed online as a digitized item, or in person, the best practices discussed in this chapter serve to inform the experience of archival research.

## NOTES

1. Jean Tener and Sandra Mortensen, *The Mordecai Richler Papers*, Canadian Archival Inventories Series, no. 6 (Calgary, Alberta: University of Calgary Press, 1991), xv.

2. T. D. Regehr, review of *General Inventory: Manuscripts*, vol. 2, in *Archivaria* 3 (Winter 1976): 140.

3. For a thorough discussion of the "total archives" mission, see Laura Millar's "Discharging Our Debt: The Evolution of the Total Archives Concept in English Canada," *Archivaria* 46 (Fall 1998): 103–140.

4. *Alice Munro Papers First Accession: An Inventory of the Archive at the University of Calgary Libraries* (Calgary, Alberta: University of Calgary Press, 1986), xxv.

5. David Godfrey to W. H. New, October 5, 1968, W. H. New Papers, Malcolm Lowry Series, University of British Columbia, Vancouver, British Columbia.

6. F. Gilbert Paci per David Godfrey to W. H. New, May 14, 1971, W. H. New Papers, Malcolm Lowry Series, University of British Columbia, Vancouver, British Columbia.

7. David Godfrey to W. H. New, undated, W. H. New Papers, Malcolm Lowry Series, University of British Columbia, Vancouver, British Columbia.

8. W. H. New to David Godfrey, June 2, 1960, W. H. New Papers, Malcolm Lowry Series, University of British Columbia, Vancouver, British Columbia.

9. W. H. New, *Malcolm Lowry* (Toronto: McClelland and Stewart, 1971).

10. John Stuart Batts, "Private Chronicles in Public Places," *Canadian Literature* 121 (1989): 13.

11. H. Pearson Gundy, ed., *Letters of Bliss Carman* (Kingston, Ontario: McGill-Queen's University Press, 1981), xi.

12. André Carpentier, *Journal de mille jours: Carnets, 1983–1986* (Montreal: Guérin littérature, 1988), 11.

## *Chapter Nine*

# Web Resources

Most of our discussion thus far has centered on authoritative published materials, or formal digital collections developed by institutions such as libraries and universities. This present chapter will focus on Web resources for the study of Canadian literature. Despite the advantages and convenience of the Web, you will notice a series of drawbacks in conducting Internet research, such as unidentifiable site publishers, broken links, and content that has not been updated.

The Internet is often criticized as a publishing platform because anyone can post a website, calling into question the reliability of some online information. At the same time, electronic platforms have created a dynamic, accessible environment that fosters participation, input, and dialogue. Since websites vary dramatically in quality, usefulness, and reliability, searching for information via the Web can at times be confusing and frustrating. Although search engine performance is improving, search results are not always ranked according to an order of importance that reflects our needs. That said, search engines are continuously developing the formula used to sort results. One of the most popular and well-known Internet search engines, Google, currently uses an algorithm based on several factors to determine the order of search results. Some factors considered are the site's use of keywords, the placement of keywords, site traffic, and where the site is hosted.

Websites require sustained maintenance and a commitment from their authors. Sites placed online by academic or official institutions depend on continued development and the involvement of scholars, researchers, or subject specialists. Portal sites, if not well maintained, can be especially problematic. Since the purpose of a portal site is to provide a series of relevant links, when these are not updated, the resource decreases in its usefulness. One such portal is David Lucking's *CanLinks Directory* (http://lucking.net/canlinks).

While the site presents many useful Web-based resources for researching Canadian literature on the Net, many of the links are now broken. Lucking, thankfully, does warn site visitors by making the following statement on the front page: "Please note that as of June 2005 this directory is no longer being updated." Unfortunately, more often than not, a website is left to linger without any indication of whether the authors are still actively involved. In such cases, visitors can check to see when the site was last revised, or try contacting the site developers through a "Contact Us" link.

Web projects, including digital collections and virtual exhibitions, that began as promising ventures sometimes suffer from a series of setbacks, such as lack of financial backing, or personnel changes. Web pages that you would expect to see progress but that have not been updated in a year or more may have exhausted their potential. Such sites can have historical significance and may still be useful, but their lack of development can eventually render them obsolete. Archiving of Internet documents is an issue that institutions are struggling with, as currently a page that is removed from a server falls into immediate obscurity. Since websites can have cultural value and are reflective of our digital history, their disposability is of concern not only to historians, but also to the larger scholarly community. Sites archived using a formal system provide continued access to content while notifying users of the fact that the resource itself may no longer be actively maintained. As do many government institutions, Library and Archives Canada has a notification system in place for their archived Web pages. When you access a link to a site which is no longer being updated, you receive the following disclaimer: "You are viewing a document archived by Library and Archives Canada. Please note, information may be out of date and some functionality lost."

The *Internet Archive* (also discussed in chapter 7) is a large-scale project that has been actively archiving websites since 1996. Through the "Way Back Machine," users can view over 150 billion archived Web pages, many of which would otherwise be inaccessible. In order to search the service, you must know the exact address of the site you seek, as keyword searching is currently not supported. Many Canadian libraries contribute items to the *Internet Archive*, including the University of Toronto, Brock University, and the University of Alberta. The Library of Congress and the Smithsonian Institution are among the U.S. institutions that have collaborated with the project.

Aesthetic appeal often influences our opinion of a website and determines whether we are likely to visit it again. Although we cannot "judge a book by its cover," the appearance and usability of a site can be an indicator of its overall credibility. At the same time, we have to consider that today's Web authoring tools are quite sophisticated, and achieving a professional interface with little experience is possible for even the novice webmaster. As you conduct Internet research, you will want to remain aware of some basic principles for website evaluation, including the following:

Authority: While you can generally find who is responsible for publishing or writing a book, such information is not as obvious in Web environments. Authorial ambiguity can be problematic when using the Web for research. Who is responsible for the site, and what are their credentials? Is this a government or literary association site? If this is an institutional site, is the content provided by students or professors? Was this site the result of a class project? If this site has been developed by a literary aficionado, what other work have they done, and what other projects are they involved with? Can you determine their credentials as an authority on their subject?

Currency: Is the information on the site up to date? Are the links persistently broken? Is the contact information for the website still current? Is this a finite or ongoing project? If you are unable to determine when a site was last updated, remember that you can always attempt to contact the site developers. A reputable site should have a "Contact Us" link or feedback form available to visitors.

Accuracy: Does the site contain correct, verifiable information? Does the site provide references to authoritative sources? Can you determine where the site author found the information?

Scope and Audience: What material does the site cover and to what degree? Who is the intended audience for the site? Is it geared toward the general public, fans, literati, scholars, students, members of an association?

Objectivity: What is the motivation behind the site? Is the site commercially motivated, either blatantly or subtly? Is it designed to inform, inspire, promote, convince? Does the site have an obvious agenda, such as promoting or discrediting a particular author? Are there identifiable political motives associated with the site content? In addition to providing information, are books or other merchandise being sold on the site? If so, does this affect the overall credibility of the site?

Usability and Design: Is the site easy to navigate? Is the interface attractive? Does the author demonstrate an understanding of the basic principles of Web design?

## SCHOLARLY GATEWAYS (PORTALS)

Liu, Alan. *Voice of the Shuttle*. http://vos.ucsb.edu (accessed 29 June 2010).

Northwest Passages: Canadian Literature Online. *Canadian Literature Links*. www.nwpassages.com/links.asp (accessed 29 June 2010).

Ockerbloom, Mary Mark, ed. *A Celebration of Women Writers: Writers from Canada*, 1994–2008, 2010. http://digital.library.upenn.edu/women/_generate/CANADA.html (accessed 29 June 2010).

University of Alberta. *Canadian Literature Centre/Centre de littérature canadienne*, 2006/2010. www.arts.ualberta.ca/clc (accessed 29 June 2010).

Scholarly gateways are often maintained by motivated enthusiasts with an altruistic design on promoting and fostering interest in an author, genre, topic, or historical event. Library subject specialists likewise maintain such portals in an attempt to cull the "best of the Web" on a given topic. Basically, such gateways provide links to sites which offer some scholarly or informational value. One drawback of the scholarly gateway is that if the portal is not well maintained, links can become outdated. The best such sites are ones that selectively choose a manageable number of links that directly speak to a particular interest. In contrast, some gateways can offer a dizzying array of pages which are time consuming to review, and ultimately as a whole will have limited application to a particular researcher's interests.

A bilingual site, the ***Canadian Literature Centre/Centre de littérature canadienne*** benefits from the involvement of University of Alberta faculty, staff, and graduate students dedicated to the promotion of Canadian literary studies. While the center itself hosts readings from notable Canadian writers, the website is composed of several elements. Although not classified as a portal, the site's "Literature Online" link presents several categories of material useful to the study of Canadian literature, including resources for online texts, pertinent Library and Archives Canada sites, and a link to the Government of Canada's *Aboriginal Canada Portal.* Other areas provide resources for Canadian writers, covering various national and regional associations, networks, and guilds. Filling a much-needed hole, the site also serves as a portal to a large selection of writer's blogs, representing both well- and lesser-known names. Through a simple online form, anyone can join the *Literature Centre* to receive e-mails on center activities and events.

Mary Mark Ockerbloom's ***A Celebration of Women Writers: Writers from Canada*** is a gateway to electronic-text collections, wiki articles, author websites, award announcements, information on archival fonds, and blogs. Considering the number of links, the portal is impressively well maintained and encompasses some contemporary names, such as Michelle Sagara West and Kateri Akiwenzie-Damm. Even if you are visiting this gateway without a particular author in mind, the variety of linked pages provides great insight into the many resources for Canadian authors online. Once hosted on the Carnegie Mellon University servers, access to the site is now sponsored through the University of Pennsylvania's Digital Library Initiative.

Northwest Passages: Canadian Literature Online is an online bookseller that professes a commitment to sharing information and managing knowledge. The store's website includes ***Canadian Literature Links***, a well-known portal for Canadian literary Web research. Organized by category, the site offers access to author pages, literary organizations, literary awards, publisher sites, electronic text projects, literary periodicals, Canadian studies programs, and general Canadian literature sites. Unfortunately, as of December 31, 2009, the site announced that it would be discontinuing its bookselling operations, and the ultimate fate of *Canadian Literature Links* is therefore unknown. At the present time, the gateway remains accessible and is still helpful for alerting visitors to online material related to the study of Canadian literature.

Alan Liu's ***Voice of the Shuttle*** (***VoS***) is an often-cited portal to online literary resources. Liu maintains the site with the assistance of a development and editorial team at the University of California, Santa Barbara, English Department. Users can submit recommended links to the database for review by *VoS* editors. Items related to Canadian literature can be accessed by following the "Other Literatures in English" link from the "Literature (in English)" page. Selected resources include the L. M. Montgomery Institute and Athabasca University's Canadian Writers site. Many of the links identified are already found in the portals that we have discussed above. As a general humanities research portal, other subject areas within the gateway can be explored to inform interdisciplinary inquiry.

## ELECTRONIC TEXT ARCHIVES

*Digital Books Index*. www.digitalbookindex.org/index.cgi (accessed 29 June 2010).
*Google Books*. http://books.google.com (accessed 29 June 2010).
*Project Gutenberg*. www.gutenberg.org (accessed 29 June 2010).

In general, freely available electronic texts are limited to works that are in the public domain and are therefore no longer under copyright. As with other digital projects, electronic-text archives benefit from a series of factors, including sustained development, continued human involvement, and financial assistance. Many early projects are still viewable online but have been overshadowed by large-scale digitization initiatives and no longer appear to be updated. The University of Alberta Faculté Saint-Jean's *Bibliothèque virtuelle* (www.fsj.ualberta.ca/biblio) is an example of an electronic text project that mainly contains material now available through larger ventures, such as Canadiana.org's *Early Canadiana Online* database (discussed in chapter 7).

As one of the longest-running electronic text initiatives, ***Project Gutenberg*** provides access to a fairly impressive number of early Canadian titles. For example, several of L. M. Montgomery's works are offered in both print and audiobook format. Stephen Leacock's prose is likewise available, as are several works by Thomas Chandler Haliburton and E. Pauline Johnson. Gilbert Parker and Charles Sangster are among the Canadian poets represented in the *Project Gutenberg* catalog. It is highly likely that many of the texts available on the site can likewise be found in *Early Canadiana Online*, however the audio options available for some *Gutenberg* titles are an attractive enhancement.

***Google Books*** digitizes titles that are in the public domain, but it also has agreements with publishers to scan titles under copyright, granting access to only a percentage of the contents. Works in *Google Books* fall under one of four basic access categories, including "full view," "limited preview," "snippet view," and "no preview available." "Full view" items, essentially works in the public domain, are downloadable and readable online. "Limited preview" access is granted to titles that are still under copyright but for which *Google Books* has obtained publisher permission to display a fair amount of readable text. Very little content is visible in the "snippet view"; however, these titles are still searchable and can serve as a guide to the page numbers containing your keywords. Items designated as "no preview available" indicate that the work is under copyright and that Google was not able to attain an agreement with the publisher. Although Google's digitization projects have been marred by controversy, as a database of over ten million scanned and fully searchable titles, *Google Books* can be a very powerful research tool. Through the *Google Books* Library Project, several university partnerships have also been established, allowing users to view books from the collections of Harvard, Stanford, and Columbia universities, among a growing list of institutions.

With many electronic text services to choose from, the ***Digital Books Index*** is a convenient database for e-titles available through the Internet. *Early Canadiana Online*, *Project Gutenberg*, and the University of Toronto's *Canadian Poetry Online* (http://library.utoronto.ca/canpoetry) are among the collections indexed. Some title links will lead you to the *Internet Archive*, where works in the public domain from institutions such as the University of Victoria can be downloaded to a variety of devices. After completing a simple log-in form, you will be able to search the *Digital Books Index* by author, title, or subject. Linking to the "Literature and Texts: Canadian" subject heading will provide you with an impressive list of Canadian e-texts that can be accessed online.

## AUTHOR SITES

ABC Bookworld. *BC Author Bank.* www.abcbookworld.com (accessed 29 June 2010).

Arjatsalo, Jarkko. *Leonard Cohen Files.* www.leonardcohenfiles.com (accessed 29 June 2010).

Athabasca University. *Canadian Writers.* www.athabascau.ca/writers (accessed 29 June 2010).

Atwood, Margaret. *Margaret Atwood.* www.margaretatwood.ca (accessed 29 June 2010).

Authors Aloud. *Authors Aloud: The Voices of Canadian Literature.* www.authorsaloud.com (accessed 29 June 2010).

Library and Archives Canada. *Susanna Moodie and Catherine Parr Traill: From the Manuscript Collections of the National Library and National Archives of Canada.* www.collectionscanada.gc.ca/moodie-traill (accessed 29 June 2010).

Sony Music. *Leonard Cohen.* www.leonardcohen.com (accessed 29 June 2010).

We are living in an exciting era with regard to our ability to connect with contemporary authors. While a well-known writer may not consent to a personal interview, the Web presents opportunities for increased familiarity and acquaintance. Many current authors have their own websites to promote their publications and inform their readers of upcoming projects. Today's author sites are enhanced with Web 2.0 features, including blogs, social networking updates, and RSS feeds. You can now follow some authors on Twitter and may be able to "friend" them on Facebook. Information found on official author sites highlights upcoming book signings, speaking engagements, readings, and tours. While some authors manage their own personal Web pages, others have sites hosted by their publisher, mostly to advertise new works and as a forum for readers and fans.

For up-and-coming authors, the Web offers opportunities for self-promotion and increased exposure. Writers who may otherwise have difficulty breaking into the market through commercial venues can promote their work using blogs and social networking sites. One such new author is Ryan Arnold, who has published the entertaining but not widely distributed title *The Coward Files*. In a self-deprecating style, Arnold used a blog (http://deathtoarnie.blogspot.com) to advertise his work and announce upcoming readings, also providing links to reviews and interviews.

Academic institutions are active producers of sites to promote information, interest, and scholarship on writers both past and present. Such endeavors may consist of biographical information and bibliographies, and may serve to highlight rare and unique items from the institution's collection. The sites examined below offer a sampling of online Web pages and projects related to Canadian authors. While there are many others to explore, in general, sites that appear to be actively maintained are discussed here.

With over nine thousand authors in its database, ABC Bookworld's ***BC Author Bank*** affords access to author biographies and bibliographies. Author entries additionally consist of excerpts from relevant articles and interviews published in *BC Bookworld* (discussed in chapter 6). Content is limited to authors who have lived, written, or published in British Columbia. An advanced-search feature allows you to limit results by author tags, such as "Doukhobors," "Fishing," and "First Nations Lit." Among the many fascinating writers in the database is Muriel Wylie Blanchet (1891–1961), who authored *The Curve of Time*, a best-selling memoir of her adventures at sea in the company of her five children.

***Margaret Atwood*** has long managed her own website, which provides biographical information, a list of awards and honorary degrees, and a bibliography of works by and about the author. Atwood also announces upcoming events and incorporates social networking opportunities, as well as a link to her blog. In contrast to many such sites that are hosted by publishers, Atwood's site is self-maintained through the "O. W. Toad Office," an anagram of her last name.

Sony Music maintains ***Leonard Cohen***, a multimedia website with the purpose of promoting Cohen's music and performances. For a less-commercial approach, the ***Leonard Cohen Files*** offers information on his poetry, along with bibliographies, galleries, awards, biographical information, and links to essays. A well-developed resource, first-time visitors should consult the "Guide to the Files" link, which explains the many areas of the site and their functions. Since 1997, Cohen himself has been contributing unpublished poetry and artwork to the "Blackening Pages" section of the site.

Founded in 2006, ***Authors Aloud: The Voices of Canadian Literature*** is a database of poetry and fiction readings by over ninety Canadian writers. A noncommercial project managed by editor and journalist Trevor Cole, *Authors Aloud* is well maintained with news of upcoming public readings and writing contests. Author entries provide biographical information and links to author websites, where available. While the site features only published writers, readings by many accomplished yet little-known poets and authors are found within these pages. Visitors can also sign up to follow *Authors Aloud* on Twitter.

Athabasca University's Centre for Language and Literature has developed ***Canadian Writers***, profiles of over eighty English- and French-language authors who have been studied in courses offered by the institution. Entries provide biographical information, pertinent links, and research papers written by Athabasca University students, where available. Dôre Michelut, an Italian-born immigrant writer of Friulano origin, is among the profiled authors.

Although it is no longer updated, Library and Archives Canada's ***Susanna Moodie and Catherine Parr Traill: From the Manuscript Collections of the National Library and National Archives of Canada*** site offers background information on these two early Canadian authors. Drawing on both library and archival collections, transcripts from over two hundred letters serve to illustrate the life and times of the literary sisters. Photographs, journals, manuscripts, and artwork contribute to a rich and well-presented digital exhibit.

## CURRENT AWARENESS RESOURCES

British Association for Canadian Studies. *Literature Group*. www.canadianstudies.info (accessed 12 July 2010).
H-Net. *H-Canada Network*. www.h-net.org/~canada (accessed 12 July 2010).
*League of Canadian Poets*. www.poets.ca (accessed 12 July 2010).
*Margaret Atwood Society*. http://themargaretatwoodsociety.wordpress.com (accessed 12 July 2010).
*Writers' Union of Canada*. www.writersunion.ca (accessed 12 July 2010).

The Web facilitates the researcher's access to literary news, calls for papers, publishing opportunities, events, and academic discourse. Electronic discussion groups have become popular forums, where scholars from around the world can share information, viewpoints, reactions, and knowledge. The sites below assist the researcher in networking with scholars who may share similar interests.

H-Net, or Humanities and Social Sciences Online, is an Internet forum for the exchange of scholarly information, resources, and news. Subscriptions to H-Net, albeit free, are screened to ensure a mix of scholars, professors, researchers, graduate students, journalists, librarians, and archivists. The ***H-Canada Network*** is the Canadian studies portion of the H-Net forum, and includes access to book reviews by forum subscribers. Prior to granting access to the list, the forum requires subscribers to complete a survey, which is reviewed by moderators. To minimize irrelevant postings, all H-Net messages are screened by a moderator. Although recent book reviews and list postings can be viewed on the *H-Canada* site, undergraduate participation is not encouraged in the *H-Canada Network*.

A specialist group of the British Association for Canadian Studies (BACS), the ***Literature Group*** publishes the biannual newsletter *CanText* to advertise upcoming conferences, print calls for papers, publish reviews, and promote new websites for Canadian literary studies. Like many such entities, the *Literature Group* now operates using Facebook as a platform.

The ***League of Canadian Poets*** website is a convenient resource for learning of upcoming poetry contests, news, and events. The site also maintains a "Readings Calendar," listing events and festivals by province. As Canada's national association for professional publishing and spoken-word poets, the league produces an online members catalog and *St@nz@*, a bimonthly electronic newsletter. Noted poets George Amabile, Robert Kroetsch, and Phyllis Webb are among those listed as lifetime league members.

The website for the ***Margaret Atwood Society*** lists calls for papers, upcoming conferences, and awards. As an official affiliate of the Modern Language Association, the society meets at the annual MLA convention where it sponsors special conference sessions related to Atwood Studies. Information on previous and upcoming panels hosted by the society at various conferences is also available on the website. As discussed in chapter 5, the Margaret Atwood Society publishes a refereed journal dedicated to the author, where it prints and updates a comprehensive Atwood bibliography. Members now have access to additional content through the society's Facebook group.

There are many association sites that offer valuable information on issues of concern to Canadian writers. The website for the ***Writers' Union of Canada*** is an informative resource for maintaining awareness of news and controversies affecting Canadian authors. The front page announces "Hot Topics" and provides access to recent Writer's Union press releases. *Notices*, the union's online newsletter, announces writing contests, calls for papers, literary events, professional development opportunities, and employment postings.

## REFERENCE TOOLS AND ONLINE BIBLIOGRAPHIES

Athabasca University. *Canadian Theatre Encyclopedia*. www.canadiantheatre.com (accessed 12 July 2010).

Historica-Dominion Institute. *The Canadian Encyclopedia/L'Encyclopédie canadienne*. www.thecanadianencyclopedia.com (accessed 10 July 2010).

University of Toronto. *Canadian Poetry Online*. www.library.utoronto.ca/canpoetry (accessed 10 July 2010).

Many works that you would expect to find in print format are now also available on the Web. As you will see in the examples provided, some of the best resources are compiled through cooperative ventures that draw on contributions and input from the literary community.

Based on the print version, ***The Canadian Encyclopedia/L'Encyclopédie canadienne*** has been accessible online since 1999 through the Historica Foundation. In 2009, the Historica Foundation merged with the Dominion Institute to form the Toronto-based Historica-Dominion Institute, an organization dedicated to promoting Canadian history, identity, and citizenship. Although an interdisciplinary reference work, articles pertaining to Canadian literature are well researched and contributed by respected members of the Canadian literary community. Many topics addressing Canadian literary history, including notable figures, movements, publications, and events, are found in this resource. Article contributors, such as Geoffrey Hancock and René Dionne, are recognizable literary figures who have extensively published articles, studies, and monographs on Canadian literature.

Conceived in 1996 by Gaetan Charlebois, the ***Canadian Theatre Encyclopedia*** is currently overseen by Athabasca University, with the assistance of the Canadian Association for Theatre Research. As with many Web publications, the editorial board encourages site visitors to submit corrections, updates, and new entries, which are thoroughly reviewed prior to inclusion. Users can search the encyclopedia by browsing entry headings, or through a search feature, which offers entry title and full-text options. Linked cross-references are conveniently incorporated throughout the text of entries. This online reference work is a quality publication that benefits from the collaboration of an educational institution and the broader literary community.

Part of the University of Toronto's digital collections, ***Canadian Poetry Online*** is an excellent example of a nicely edited, well-managed, navigable online resource. Users can browse through separate lists of entries related to either contemporary or nineteenth-century Canadian poets. The main entry page for each contemporary poet consists of a brief biography (some written by the poets themselves) and links to selected representative works. A "Writing Philosophy" tab leads users to material by the poet reflecting on the craft of writing. A few of these selections are reprinted from other sources, while others represent an original contribution of the author to the project. The "Criticism" tab offers a bibliography of scholarly essays, reviews, and newspaper stories related to the writer. While there is some variation in the material found under "Other Information," many entries provide a convenient sampling of quotes illustrating the poet's reception in literary circles. Additional sections include interviews, awards, and information regarding the archival repository for the poet's papers. The value of each individual entry is largely dependent on whether the poet participated in contributing information to the site. The entry for bill bissett, for example, demonstrates the poet's active involvement in updating and supplying information to the project. A total of twenty-eight poets comprise the "Canadian Poets, 19th Century" portion of the project. These entries follow the format of entries on the University of Toronto's larger Representative Poetry Online site, with a selection of full-text poetry, notes on life and works, and brief biographical information.

## CULTURAL RESOURCES

Canadian Broadcasting Corporation. *Canada Reads*. www.cbc.ca/books/canadareads (accessed 10 July 2010).

Library and Archives Canada. *Canada: A Literary Tour/Un voyage littéraire au Canada*. www.collectionscanada.gc.ca/literary-tour (accessed 10 July 2010).

University of Calgary and Université Laval. *Our Roots/Nos racines*. www.ourroots.ca (accessed 10 July 2010).

Canadian literary research is today informed by an interdisciplinary approach, one that considers historical, cultural, and political influences. In common with the websites discussed in previous sections of this chapter, some of these are likely to develop into other projects, be discontinued, or be replaced by contemporary endeavors. Nevertheless, Canada's commitment to reflecting on its past and renewing its cultural heritage is certain to ensure a steady stream of online material to inform a greater understanding of Canadianness. Below is a sampling of Web resources that explore Canadian culture, history, and society.

Another excellent Library and Archives Canada resource, ***Canada: A Literary Tour/Un voyage littéraire au Canada*** explores Canadian literary history, authors, and themes, coast to coast, and region by region. "Literary Landscapes" examines the varied settings that have inspired and provided a backdrop for Canadian literary works. Complemented by artwork and photography from LAC collections, historians, librarians, and literary scholars contribute essays to characterize Canada's literary regions, including Acadia, Newfoundland and Labrador, and the North. Another area of the site, "Literary Cities," describes the urban locations that contribute to Canadian literary life and have come to be associated with notable authors. Several literary maps reproduced from those held in LAC collections are also available through this exhibit.

A joint project between the University of Calgary and l'Université Laval, ***Our Roots/Nos racines*** is a vast digital collection that draws on documents from Canadian history to illustrate the country's diverse heritage. With over

5,500 digitized works, visitors can avail themselves of several search options and browse features. In addition to a Boolean search interface, items can also be identified using author, title, and subject browsing. Local histories can be retrieved according to province, and users may register with the site in order to save items and apply personalized tags.

While the selections are sometimes controversial, the Canadian Broadcasting Corporation sponsors ***Canada Reads***, an annual competition which draws attention to five notable literary works of Canadian fiction from any time period. The show, which began as a radio program, involves five panelists who defend their selection over the course of five broadcast television episodes. At the end of each show, in a format familiar to viewers of reality TV, one work is voted out of the competition. While the program is commercialized for a viewing audience, the public debate the show incites offers the researcher an interesting view into the Canadian literary climate. While some in the literary press rail against the show's mainstream approach, *Canada Reads* has ignited a renewed interest in Canadian authors and their works. A French version of the program, *Le Combat des livres*, was introduced in 2004, although both versions of the program may feature works in translation from either language. For example, among the 2010 *Canada Reads* titles is the translated version of Nicolas Dickner's French-language novel *Nikolski*. Past panelists include actress Megan Follows (2002), politician Justin Trudeau (2003), and author Roch Carrier (2005). The show's website provides panelist readings, access to the *Canada Reads* blog, information on previous nominees, and related television clips.

## CONCLUSION

The variety and depth of Web material related to Canadian literary studies continues to evolve, while the fragmentary bones of earlier sites serve as evidence of previous electronic projects. In contrast to print publications, websites may be placed online as works in progress, and when these sites are left to idle without further development, their usefulness is often obscured. Due to the volatility of the Web, the resources discussed in this chapter will undoubtedly change, disappear, or even be rendered obsolete within a surprisingly short period of time. Even so, the Internet is likely to endure as a dynamic and eclectic forum for literary research and scholarly communication.

# Chapter Ten

# Researching a Thorny Problem

This chapter proposes a research scenario to model and illustrate some of the techniques, processes, resources, and stumbling blocks that may be encountered in exploring a focused literary topic. In today's information environment, a literary research question can quickly become intricate and complex. Typically, adequate material to address an in-depth study requires perseverance, flexibility, and creativity on the part of the researcher and may involve both print and online sources. As a culminating chapter, many of the resources and strategies discussed herein will now be familiar to you.

While Canadian literature offers infinite research possibilities, our present inquiry will examine posthumous critical appraisal and scholarly study of Morley Callaghan. A controversial literary figure, Callaghan's relationship with literary critics was tenuous. Despite mixed reviews, he continued to explore his craft, producing a legacy of material up until his death at eighty-seven in 1990. Literary scholars persist in debating Callaghan's merits, and a wide range of opinions regarding the writer are traceable in both scholarly and popular resources.

A researcher beginning inquiry into Callaghan's life and works may have heard of his association with the American writer Ernest Hemingway, or of his affiliation with the writers of the Lost Generation. One famous incident involves a legendary, albeit informal, boxing match between Hemingway and Callaghan which led to their eventual estrangement and to Callaghan's banishment from the graces of some contemporaries. During his lifetime, Callaghan's works received a mix of laudatory praise, condemnation, indifference, and marginalization. Often, posthumous evaluation of an author brings reevaluation and, perhaps, a more tempered consensus. Callaghan's notoriety extended beyond Canada, as his works were also reviewed in the United States and Britain. An often-cited quote from the American critic

Edmund Wilson refers to Callaghan as "the most unjustly neglected novelist of the English-speaking world."[1]

In order to establish a firmer basis for our research, we will want to explore some biographical material on Callaghan, checking first to see whether he is found within Gale's *Dictionary of Literary Biography* (*DLB*) series, discussed in chapter 2. An online search for Callaghan using Gale's freely available *Literary Index* (www.galenet.com/servlet/LitIndex) reveals that he is treated in several reference works. As directed, we will focus our energies on volume 68 of the *Dictionary of Literary Biography*, while also examining volumes 3, 14, 41, and 65 of Gale's *Contemporary Literary Criticism*. Published in 1988, two years prior to Callaghan's death, volume 68 of the *DLB* offers preliminary background information on the writer, his critics, and his admirers. On retrieval of the *Contemporary Literary Criticism* volumes, we quickly find that these are mainly comprised of reviews and essays written during Callaghan's lifetime. Published in 1991, volume 65 features a tribute to Callaghan, reprinting the text of two obituaries, one from the *New York Times* and the second from *The Times*, London. The obituaries also allow us to establish the exact date of Callaghan's death as August 25, 1990, which serves as a useful limiter in forming further searches. For comparative purposes, it may benefit our inquiry to likewise locate an obituary appearing in a Canadian publication.

Volumes in the *Contemporary Literary Criticism* series, published during Callaghan's lifetime, deliver an interesting perspective on the waxing and waning of his literary reception. A search for posthumous treatment will shed light on how the author's works have been received since his death, in addition to illuminating research questions studied during the intervening years. For that, we will first turn to online sources such as the *MLAIB* and *CPI.Q*, each discussed in chapter 4. As we know, the *MLAIB* will provide citations to scholarly material from Canadian, American, and British literary books and journals, including criticism and literary analysis. The *CPI.Q*, while containing more Canadian content, will also offer a varied list of resources, such as specialized scholarly journals, magazines, and newspaper articles, which may nonetheless reveal an interesting mix of attitudes toward Callaghan within his native country. For the purposes of our research, material printed in books and scholarly journals, as well as articles found in literary magazines and newspapers that speak to Callaghan's legacy, are all relevant. A major Callaghan bibliography is located within the *Annotated Bibliography of Canadian Authors*, volume 5; however, since this exceptional resource was published in 1984, it does not cover the desired time period. After searching online bibliographies, we will consult *WorldCat* to assist us in identifying additional items that may not have appeared within commercial databases. In the interim years since Callaghan's death, the Internet has developed into an electronic publishing platform; it will therefore serve us to extend our inquiry to Web materials.

A search of the *MLAIB* for subject *Callaghan, Morley* and *criticism*, limiting the results to material published after August 1990, returns only one article. Our apparent failure at obtaining a workable list of results is in part due to the fact that *MLAIB* item records related to Callaghan happen to contain very little descriptive information. As we will see in our second search attempt, most of the citations that interface with a search for the author will include *Canadian literature* in the "Subject Literature" field, and *Callaghan, Morley* in the "Primary Subject Author" field. For the most part, the *MLAIB* citations related to Callaghan do not present abstracts from which to derive language for a more detailed keyword search. Since Callaghan's name is rather unique, we may therefore elect to keep our search broad and use simply *Callaghan, Morley* in the "Subject" field, while maintaining our date limit. This second strategy returns twenty-two items, providing a selection of citations that suggest a sustained interest in Callaghan since his death. Thirteen of these are journal articles, four are book chapters, and five refer to book-length studies.

Turning first to the results under "Journal Articles," the twentieth-anniversary issue of *Essays in Canadian Writing* prints two articles on Callaghan, each ascertaining his quality as a writer, as well as his reception and legacy. The first, "Winner Take All," offers a rather cynical view of the value of Callaghan's literary contributions by writer and critic John Metcalf.[2] If we were looking for controversy with which to infuse our research, Metcalf delivers. Whether or not one agrees with his analysis, Metcalf's response to a piece written by David Staines in *Quill and Quire* offers a great deal of critical material to ponder.[3] Presented in the same issue, a second article, "Callaghan, Glassco, and the Canadian Lost Generation," is less reactionary, offering thoughtful analysis of the Hemingway-Callaghan fallout and its subsequent effect on the man, his work, and his reputation.

As a major Canadian literary journal, it would benefit our research to further explore the article by Gary Boire, published in the summer 1992 issue of *Canadian Literature*, "Morley Callaghan, 1903–1990." The *MLAIB* results indicate that this same issue also includes a piece by well-known author Margaret Avison: "Reading Morley Callaghan's *Such Is My Beloved*." Upon retrieval of the issue, it may interest us to note that both of these pieces were submitted to the journal's "Opinions and Notes" section and offer differing appraisals of the author. In addition to these, several *MLAIB* citations illuminate scholarly literary analysis appearing since Callaghan's death, including a Fall 1993 issue of *Canadian Literature*, which presents an article by William C. James on "The Ambiguities of Love in Morley Callaghan's *Such Is My Beloved*."

Up until this point, we have only uncovered scholarly resources from Canadian publications. Since it is often stated of Callaghan that his reach does not extend outside of Canada, we should explore citations drawn specifically from American journals. Our *MLAIB* search returns one such article, Erik Nakjavani's "On Autobiography and Multiple Personality: The Case of Morley Callaghan Remembering Ernest Hemingway," from the spring 1994/1995 issue of *North Dakota Quarterly*.

In the results appearing under "Book Articles," our search reveals that treatment of Callaghan persists in essay collections of scholarly criticism and analysis. Edited by Reingard Nischik, *The Canadian Short Story: Interpretations* (2007) features an essay by Paul Goetsch entitled "Psychological Realism, Immigration, and City Fiction: Morley Callaghan, 'Last Spring They Came Over' (1927)." Before discussing Callaghan's third published short story, Paul Goetsch, of the University of Freiburg, offers a survey of Callaghan's works, gives general biographic information, and addresses some of the issues that arise in comparing Callaghan to Hemingway. Among the three remaining citations, two constitute entries on Callaghan within reference works, such as *A Reader's Companion to the Short Story in English*. The remaining entry refers us to Gary Boire's "The Language of the Law: The Cases of Morley Callaghan," in *Dominant Impressions: Essays on the Canadian Short Story* (1999).

The *MLAIB* search also lists four book-length studies appearing since Callaghan's death, all of which are published by ECW Press. Among these is George Woodcock's *Moral Predicament: Morley Callaghan's "More Joy in Heaven"* (1993). John Orange authors *Orpheus in Winter: Morley Callaghan's "The Loved and the Lost,"* number 22 in ECW's Canadian Fiction Studies series. Two of the remaining titles, *Morley Callaghan: Literary Anarchist* (1994) and *Morley Callaghan and His Works* (1991) are both written by Gary Boire. Since, up until this point, we have uncovered two book-length studies, one book essay, and a letter pertaining to Callaghan, all written by Boire, we may ascertain that he is a rather engaged Callaghan scholar. It will be interesting to see whether his name resurfaces in additional searches.

The results thus far offer a fair amount of scholarly and critical material to inform a posthumous appraisal of Callaghan. A search of the *CPI.Q* will be valuable for investigating treatment of Callaghan in more popular sources, as well as to illuminate further scholarly titles not indexed in the *MLAIB*. We will keep our search fairly broad, using options available through the interface to limit our search to "Subject" *Callaghan, Morley*, with a date range from August 1990 forward. The *CPI.Q* automatically sorts the results by "Academic Journals," "Magazines," "Books," "News," and "Multimedia." For comparative purposes, we will examine material appearing under "Academic

Journals"; however, with some variation in coverage, most of these will replicate citations located through the *MLAIB*. One additional journal appearing within the results, *The British Journal of Canadian Studies*, is not found within the *MLAIB*. Indexed by the *CPI.Q* since 1989, the journal contains the 1999 essay by Richard Dennis, "Morley Callaghan and the Moral Geography of Toronto." A Google search for *Richard Dennis* and *Moral Geography of Toronto* indicates that the scholar is a member of the Department of Geography at University College London. This information is pertinent to our study, as it suggests evidence of Callaghan's international and interdisciplinary reach. As we proceed in our research, we will see that Callaghan's legacy as a "writer of the city" is an area that attracts a fair amount of scholarly analysis.

In further reviewing our results, we are reminded that, in contrast to the *MLAIB*, the *CPI.Q* indexes book reviews. Among the items returned, we find an additional item by Gary Boire, "Mixed Pleasures," a review of *Morley Callaghan: The Collected Stories* published in the spring 2006 issue of *Canadian Literature*. A second citation found in the *CPI.Q* that was absent from the *MLAIB* search is Stewart Donovan's "Morley Callaghan: 1903–1990," published in the East Coast journal *Antigonish Review* (Autumn 1990). From the citation, this piece appears to be another "in tribute" style essay; however, physical inspection of the item confirms that it is in fact a poem addressed to the author.

Results appearing under "Magazines" include an October 2, 1990, tribute to Callaghan by David Staines in *Quill and Quire*. This is likely the piece that Metcalf reacts to in his essay "Winner Take All" and would therefore be worth pursuing. Several such "in memoriam" style pieces appear in Canadian publications during the months following the author's death. In this case, *Quill and Quire* features Callaghan on the cover of the publication, and David Staines pens a heartfelt tribute, referring to the writer as "a disciple of international literature."[4] Other pieces that may catch our eye are "Morley Callaghan and the Test of Time," published in *Books in Canada* (September 2005), and Adele Freedman's "Banishing Morley," in *Elm Street* (April 2002). A noteworthy item is the appearance of Callaghan's *Such Is My Beloved* (1934) at entry 17 of "A 450-Year-Long List, in Which We Present the Hundred Most Important Canadian Books Ever Written," printed in the *Literary Review of Canada*'s January/February 2006 issue.

*CPI.Q* "News" items include an article from the December 1996 issue of *Toronto Life* surrounding the theft of letters from Callaghan's estate, encompassing valuable pieces related to his friendship with Hemingway.[5] While this article centers on a specific event, it does also testify to the continued legend of the Hemingway-Callaghan relationship. Another curious piece is an article from the March 29, 2003, edition of the *Globe and Mail*, "Clash of the

Literary Titans," which reports that the Canadian Broadcasting Corporation produced a miniseries that same year entitled *Hemingway vs. Callaghan*. We should later explore the *CBC Digital Archives* (discussed in chapter 9) for more information regarding the posthumous portrayal of Callaghan in media and film. Since his death, quite a few articles have appeared in the *Globe and Mail* to confirm that Callaghan is still a beloved figure in his hometown of Toronto. A book review entitled "Why Morley Callaghan Still Matters," printed in the October 25, 2008, edition, discusses *A Literary Life: Reflections and Reminiscences, 1928–1990*. Published in 2008, *A Literary Life* represents a collection of original essays, newspaper and magazine articles, book reviews, columns, and transcripts from the CBC program *Anthology*, all lovingly accumulated by Callaghan's son Barry. This title bringing to fruition a project that his father had been working toward up until the year of his death. With full-text coverage of Canadian journals, newspapers, and magazines, the *CPI.Q* affords a unique perspective on Callaghan's impact.

As stated in chapter 4, when aiming for comprehensiveness, literary scholars recommend searching both the *MLAIB* and *ABELL*. Since we have already examined the *MLAIB* and *CPI.Q*, it will benefit our study to see what additional material, if any, is found within this third database. A "Subject" field search for *Callaghan, Morley*, limited to items published between 1990 and 2010, retrieves twenty-eight hits. While many of these are familiar to us by now, the first item listed is strikingly new: "Polemics of Realism: A Subversive, Anti-Colonial Strategy in Morley Callaghan's *The Loved and the Lost*," by Shobha, published in *Transplanted Imaginaries: Literatures of New Climes* (2008). Because this article appears within a collection of essays related to a common theme, it would be interesting to review the other selections within this volume. A *Google Books* search might offer a preview of the table of contents; however, in this case, the title only affords a "snippet view," with little legible text. A search in *Book Review Digest* does not locate a published review; nor do *WorldCat* or *ABELL* searches. Another option is to investigate the title through *Amazon.com*, where, although the information is not scholarly, we find a "Product Description" indicating that this title investigates multicultural texts. Although we should still pursue an in-hand examination, this essay contributes to evidence of Callaghan's continued impact as a writer of the immigrant experience. A second item that stands out among the results in *ABELL* is Barbara Helen Pell's *Faith and Fiction: A Theological Critique of the Narrative Strategies of Hugh MacLennan and Morley Callaghan*. Published in 1998, this full-length study comparing the author and his contemporary Hugh MacLennan will be useful for ascertaining the sustained fascination of literary scholars with Callaghan's religious themes and influences.

As we have now completed our search of online commercial indexes for Callaghan treatment, we should further consult *WorldCat*. A *WorldCat* search will also afford a broad overview of posthumous activity related to Callaghan, whether published as monographs, journal articles, audiovisual material, or Web resources. In order to focus our investigation on materials appearing after Callaghan's death, we will use the "Advanced Search" option. A keyword search for *Morley Callaghan*, limited to works published after 1990, reveals some of the items already discussed and illuminates new directions. This search also finds titles by Morley Callaghan published as reprints or short story collections after 1990; we could eliminate these by performing the above search as a subject search; however, this strategy unfortunately also removes most of the journal articles from our results. Another strategy for eliminating reprints of Callaghan's fiction would be to use *WorldCat*'s "Content" field to limit the search to nonfiction material.

Once our results are displayed, we can use *WorldCat*'s "Refine Your Search" links to review these by format. Among the articles not found within the *MLAIB*, *ABELL*, or *CPI.Q* is Natalia Vid's 2008 essay, "The Symbol of the City in Morley Callaghan's Strange Fugitive: Adaptation of American Urban Discourse or Reinforcements of Canadian Multicultural Identity." *WorldCat* lists this as an article appearing in the publication *Inventing Canada*; however, the record does not give us any further details. A Google search for *Natalia Vid* and *Inventing Canada* reveals that this essay was printed in volume 6 of Peter Lang Publishing's Canadiana series. A nice feature of the "Refine Your Search" links is the ability to filter the results by author and year of publication. These filters are useful for identifying writers who frequently study Callaghan, as well as Callaghan scholarship for a given publishing year.

In addition to critical and scholarly investigation, in ascertaining Callaghan's posthumous reach, we may also examine whether his works continue to be reprinted or anthologized within larger collections. One such item found through *WorldCat*, *All I Thought about Was Baseball: Writings on a Canadian Pastime* (1996), reprints Callaghan's "Fast and Loose," an article on the 1940 Toronto Maple Leafs. The editors also supply an amusing quote regarding the author, describing him as "a Canadian novelist and broadcaster who once kayoed Ernest Hemingway."[6]

Now that we have fully researched commercial databases and catalogs, we will now turn our attention to *Google Books*. It should be noted that *WorldCat* continues to incorporate Web 2.0 enhancements, and your library may now offer a direct link from catalog records to *Google Books* previews. In contrast to the resources examined up until this point, *Google Books* sets itself apart from commercial databases and library catalogs through the ability to conduct full-text searching of monographic material. A *Google Books* search for *Morley Callaghan*, restricted to material published between 1990 and 2010, locates reprints of several Callaghan titles, many of which have been recently produced by both Exile Editions, Canada, and McClelland and Stewart, Canada. While McClelland and Stewart is an established firm, a simple Google search finds that Exile is a successful publishing house founded by Callaghan's son, Barry. Flexing its full-text muscles, *Google Books* also shows that Callaghan continues to be mentioned anecdotally in a variety of works, such as Mordecai Richler's *On Snooker: The Game and the Characters Who Play It* (2001). A *Google Books* search for *Winner Take All* and *Metcalf*, for example, uncovers Aritha Van Herk's "Boxing the Critics: Sucker Punches, Shooting Niagara and Other Boys' Games of Criticism" from the December 1994 issue of *Canadian Forum*.

Although much of the material retrieved through Google Scholar replicates the published monographs and scholarly articles discovered thus far, since content is not restricted by discipline, a search also reveals a few new items. One such example is F. Hale's "The Postfigurative Christ in Morley Callghan's *Such Is My Beloved*," printed in the South African journal *Acta Theologica* (2005, issue 1) and available as an open-access article. It should be mentioned that this item also appears under the format "Internet Resource" in the *WorldCat* search described above.

A review of websites will reveal how interest in Callaghan translates to the online universe. Athabasca University's *Canadian Writers* site, discussed in chapter 9, is likely to highlight the author. As a writer who is studied through the institution's language and literature courses, the site offers a brief biography of Callaghan and presents several additional items of interest. One of the links takes us to the website for the CBC biography program *Life and Times*, with video excerpts from a 2003 documentary and a link to additional material from the *CBC Digital Archives*.

The results obtained in our searches offer an intriguing mix of Callaghan material to inform our study. In reviewing scholarly sources, we are pulled into the undertow of competing and contradictory critical appraisal of the author. Popular sources offer insight into print and media tributes that appeared in the years following his death. Our challenge here will be to select the items that we feel best reveal interesting evidence, or lack thereof, regarding Callaghan's permanence as a notable Canadian author.

## CONCLUSION

As this volume illustrates, Canadian literary research is an increasingly fascinating and complex field of study. In a rapidly changing research environment, additional resources, websites, and methods will develop and further enrich the exploration of literary topics. We can expect that in the years to come, consortial initiatives and government-funded projects will continue to augment the online accessibility of previously elusive materials. Despite the inevitability of change, the strategies and techniques discussed in this volume should continue to inform a solid approach to researching Canadian authors and their works. As you navigate print, online, and Web resources, keep in mind that reference librarians may offer specialized expertise related to your research and can assist in addressing issues of online searching, accessibility, and current awareness.

As this title goes to print, a *WorldCat* search reveals that a steady influx of fascinating research related to specific areas of Canadian literary studies is soon to be published, a trend that we can expect for the foreseeable future. Strategies discussed throughout this book will serve to inform catalog and database searches in identifying further monographs, reference works, essays, and articles to guide a rich and genuine literary investigation.

## NOTES

1. Edmund Wilson, "Morley Callaghan of Toronto," *New Yorker*, November 26, 1960, 224.

2. For more information on Metcalf's career, we can conveniently consult the online *Canadian Encyclopedia*, www.thecanadianencyclopedia.com, discussed in chapter 9.

3. "Winner Take All" is a curiously impassioned, almost abrasive response to a *Quill and Quire* obituary which was written by David Staines as a tribute to the deceased author. Due to the essay's polemical tone, the researcher may wish to explore whether Staines himself ever responded to the piece. In his conclusion to the essay, Metcalf explains that he "was depressed that Professor Staines's Callaghan obituary didn't provoke even one letter of derisive protest," a puzzling statement considering that we would not typically expect an obituary to incite such a reaction. A *Google Books* search for *Winner Take All* and *Metcalf* locates writer Aritha van Herk's "Boxing the Critics: Sucker Punches, Shooting Niagara and Other Boys' Games of Criticism" from the December 1994 issue of *The Canadian Forum* (32–35), where, in keeping with the themes of her essay, she refers to Metcalf's "pugilistic attack on Callaghan" (34).

4. David Staines, "Morley Callaghan: 1903–1990," *Quill and Quire*, October 1990, 8.

5. See Stephen Smith, "Purloined Letters," *Toronto Life* 30, no. 18 (December 1996): 61–62, 64. The papers in question were not held at an archival institution, but rather were kept inside the safe of an antiquarian bookstore. Information on the location of Morley Callaghan's personal papers can be found by consulting the *Annotated Bibliography of Canada's Major Authors* (*ABCMA*), discussed in chapter 2. In

consulting the *ABCMA*, we learn that Callaghan material may be found in several archival collections. The *Dictionary of Literary Biography* likewise offers information on the location of Callaghan's papers, citing archival collections at the York University Library, the University of Toronto, Concordia University, McMaster University, the Metropolitan Toronto Library, the Public Archives of Canada, and among the Lorne Pierce collection at Queen's University. Annotations for each of the collections housing Callaghan material can be found in the *ABCMA*.

6. William Humber and John St. James, eds., *All I Thought about Was Baseball: Writings on a Canadian Pastime* (Toronto: University of Toronto Press, 1996), 347.

*Appendix*

# Resources in Related Disciplines

Literary research is a process which is not generally charted in a set, systematic fashion. As we begin a project or inquiry, we cannot always predict where our quest will take us. Researchers must remain flexible, responsive, open to additional avenues, appreciative of serendipity, and ready to recognize unusual discovery. In today's interdisciplinary academic environments, it is not uncommon to find that other areas of study can edify and enrich your work. The selected resources that follow represent a sampling of titles, both general and specific, by which your research may be further informed. Canadian literary research may naturally lead you into additional unanticipated disciplines. This appendix identifies reference works and online indexes that serve as a point of departure for interdisciplinary inquiry. This list is certainly not exhaustive, but rather illustrative of the variety and range of material available to today's researcher.

## GENERAL

### Reference Guides

Blazek, Ron, and Elizabeth Aversa. *The Humanities: A Selective Guide to Information Resources*. 5th ed. Englewood, CO: Libraries Unlimited, 2000.

In its fifth edition, this title has advised and informed students, librarians, and scholars for over thirty years. While the currency of such print resources is precarious in the electronic age, the authors also identify online resources and databases for a balanced and contemporaneous perspective on modern humanities research.

Kieft, Robert H., ed. *Guide to Reference.* 12th ed. Chicago: American Library Association, 2008. www.guidetoreference.org.
First published in 1902 as *Guide to the Study and Use of Reference Books*, this is a standard resource used by the library profession to identify and qualify appropriate resources. Published under the editorship of Robert H. Kieft, the Web version incorporates links to digital collections, databases, and Internet resources and is available via subscription.

## Research Guides

Booth, Wayne C., Gregory G. Colomb, and Joseph M. Williams. *The Craft of Research.* 3rd ed. Chicago: University of Chicago Press, 2008.
Booth, Colomb, and Williams collaborate to produce another edition of their thoughtful guide. Written in an unaffected style, chapter subheadings include topics such as "Guard against Inadvertent Plagiarism" and "Work through Procrastination and Writer's Block." Useful for focusing one's research, this title's strengths lie in the inspiration, encouragement, and gentle correction it offers.

## Indexes and Bibliographies

*Academic Search Complete.* Ipswich, MA: EBSCO. http://search.epnet.com.
As a general database, *Academic Search Complete* facilitates interdisciplinary research, with full-text access to over 1,800 publications. Indexed titles such as the *Canadian Historical Review*, *Canadian Journal of Behavioral Science*, *Canadian Literature*, *Canadian Social Trends*, *Canadian Ethnic Studies*, *Canadian Folk Music*, *Canadian Journal of Political Science*, *Essays on Canadian Writing*, and *Theatre Research in Canada* are indicative of the multidisciplinary reach of this premier resource. Since coverage varies from title to title, check EBSCO for clarification of indexing and full-text access.

*ProQuest Dissertations and Theses.* Ann Arbor, MI: University Microfilms International. www.proquest.com/products_pq/descriptions/pqdt.shtml.
While scholars will have access to many Canadian theses through the *Theses Canada Portal*, (discussed in chapter 3), *Dissertations and Theses* offers U.S. content and additional retrospective coverage, from 1861 forward. As an index, most items are not available in full text without additional fees; consult your institution's interlibrary loan services prior to committing personal funds toward the items you identify.

## ARCHIVES

Kirsch, Gesa E., and Liz Rohan, eds. *Beyond the Archives: Research as a Lived Process*. Carbondale: Southern Illinois University Press, 2008.
This title presents an excellent collection of case studies and research narratives to illustrate the process of inquiry and the joy of discovery. The theme of serendipity resurfaces in many of the contributions, as scholars lead the reader through a research scenario. Many of the essays are intensely personal, showing the creativity, persistence, and passion of the scholar in pursuit of knowledge. Although the contributions center on American themes, illustrative accounts, expressed enthusiastically by the authors, transcend geographic boundaries.

Lacasse, Daniel, and Antonio Lechasseur. *The National Archives of Canada: 1872–1997*. Ottawa: The Canadian Historical Association, 1997.
Lacasse and Lechasseur offer a thoughtful and enlightening discussion of the development of the National Archives. Published as a booklet by the Canadian Historical Association, this title describes the unique history of Canada's public archives, and the country's commitment to its historiography. The annotated bibliography, found at the conclusion of the work, refers the researcher to additional sources of information on Canadian archival history, from journal articles to unpublished theses and reference books.

Public Archives of Canada. *Archives: Mirror of Canada Past/Miroir du passé du Canada*. Toronto: University of Toronto Press, 1972.
Published as a bilingual edition in commemoration of the centennial of the Public Archives of Canada, this catalog showcases the fascinating range of materials housed at the National Archives. Divided into four sections, literature is explored under the "Society and Culture" heading; other areas examined include "Land," "People," "Government," and "Economics." Reproductions of documents, photographs, maps, letters, newspapers, and paintings enliven the text.

## ART

*Art Index*. New York: H. W. Wilson, 1984–. www.hwwilson.com/databases/artindex.htm.
H. W. Wilson Company has developed several arts databases, each offering a slightly different version of the base product. *Art Index Retrospective*

(1929–1984) examines journals, yearbooks, and book reviews for both English-language publications and international titles. The same journals are covered in *Art Index* (1984–), *Art Abstracts* (1984–), and *Art Full Text* (1984–), each with variations in features, such as access to abstracts or full-text articles.

Dombowsky, Philip. *Index to National Gallery of Canada Exhibition Catalogues and Checklists, 1880–1930/Index des catalogues et des listes d'exposition du Musée des beaux-art du Canada, 1880–1930*. Occasional Paper no.7. National Gallery of Canada Library and Archives, 2007.

Exquisitely published, this volume follows the award-winning *Index to Nineteenth-Century Canadian Catalogues of Art* (2004) in the National Gallery of Canada Library and Archives Occasional Paper series. The title begins with the dual-language essay "The National Gallery of Canada: The First Fifty Years," detailing the gallery's exhibition loan program, the special exhibition program, and the exhibition of Canadian art abroad through 1930. Indexing 10,209 entries from forty-nine catalogs and sixty-five published checklists for National Gallery exhibitions of the period, entries are conveniently organized by artist. An online version is published as *Index to Art in Canada to 1930* at www.gallery.ca/indexartcanada.

Hill, Charles C. *The Group of Seven: Art for a Nation*. Ottawa: National Gallery of Canada, 1995.

It is difficult to imagine a discussion of Canadian art history without at some point referencing the Group of Seven and their influence. Published to accompany a cross-country exhibition, Hill traces the genesis of the movement as well as its players, critics, patrons, influences, and legacies. Reproductions of all of the 179 paintings exhibited during the National Gallery tour are incorporated, along with photos of past exhibitions and of the artists themselves.

MacDonald, Colin S. *A Dictionary of Canadian Artists*. 8 vols. Ottawa: Canadian Paperbacks, 1967–2006.

As the compiler of the first eight volumes, the *Dictionary* undoubtedly represents a labor of love for Colin S. MacDonald, who has clearly contributed endless hours to this project. Detailed entries often present information that MacDonald could only have gained through personal interviews and in-depth research. This unique reference work is touted as being "the most extensive bibliography ever published on this subject." Critical pieces from periodicals, such as *The Gazette* and the *Ottawa Citizen*, are incorporated, and entries conclude with a list of references. Where applicable, the location and dates of solo shows, prizes, awards, and collections are listed. Even if the reader is unfamiliar with the artist in question, McDonald's intimate portraits engage and delight. Between 2007 and 2009, the National Gallery of Canada acquired copyright to various volumes of the *Dictionary*, with plans for electronic publication. Volume 9, edited by Anne Newlands and Judith Parker, is available in online format only. Hosted by the Canadian Heritage Information Network, all volumes are now freely searchable through the *Artists in Canada* database (www.pro.rcip-chin.gc.ca/bd-dl/aac-aic-eng.jsp).

Newlands, Anne. *Canadian Art: From Its Beginnings to 2000*. Willowdale, Ontario: Firefly Books, 2005.

Newlands offers a selection of works by three hundred Canadian artists who exemplify a range of backgrounds, notoriety, periods, media, and styles. Alphabetically arranged by artist, included are images of drawings, photographs, paintings, public memorials, structures, and multimedia pieces. Generally selecting one work representative of each artist, accompanying notes clarify additional context and background.

*Oxford Art Online*. New York: Oxford University Press, 2007–. www.oxfordartonline.com.

Providing access to *Grove Art Online*, *The Oxford Companion to Western Art*, the *Encyclopedia of Aesthetics*, and *The Concise Oxford Dictionary of Art Terms*, *Oxford Art Online* is a convenient resource for art research from any period or place. Image searching is available, and queries may also be limited to one of the aforementioned titles. A search for Canadian architect Étienne-Joseph Gaboury, for example, finds both a biographical and a subject entry in *Grove Art Online*.

## CANADIAN HISTORY

*America: History and Life*. Santa Barbara, CA: ABC-CLIO, 1964–. See www.abc-clio.com/products/serials_ahl.aspx.

A standard database for the study of Canadian and U.S. history, *America: History and Life* contains abstracts for articles appearing in 1,700 journals from 1964 forward. Content is not limited to English-language titles, and book reviews are also indexed. *Beaver*, *Ethnologies*, and the *Canadian Historical Review* are among the Canadian titles covered. This resource is also available as *America: History and Life with Full Text*.

Bumsted, J. M. *The Peoples of Canada: A Pre-Confederation History*. 2nd ed. Don Mills, Ontario: Oxford University Press, 2009.

In its second edition, Bumsted's *History* serves as a standard postsecondary text. Chapters are complemented by numerous timelines and sidebars which include translated legends and myths of the First Nations peoples. Images, maps, and biographical sketches of Canada's earliest settlers bring history to life, and researchers will appreciate the bibliographies that follow each chapter. Interesting and little-known facts are scattered throughout, such as the insert on "Playing Card Money," a phenomenon which developed during a shortage of coined currency.

Bumsted, J. M. *The Peoples of Canada: A Post-Confederation History*. Don Mills, Ontario: Oxford University Press, 1992.

Picking up where *Pre-Confederation History* left off, Bumsted continues his discussion of the events immediately following confederation. Bumsted's concluding chapter in the 1993 edition, "Towards the 21st Century," offers an interesting assessment of the issues and players that will affect the future, as he asks, "What kind of country will Canada then become?" a question which, almost two decades after publication, we can now at least in part answer.

Hallowell, Gerald. *Oxford Companion to Canadian History*. Don Mills, Ontario: Oxford University Press, 2006. Also available through *Oxford Reference Online*, www.oxfordreference.com.

With 1,700 entries, the *Oxford Companion to Canadian History* addresses events, notable figures, institutions, associations, and places, also clarifying significant terms that may be unknown to those with little knowledge of Canadian history, such as "garrison mentality," "filles du roi," and "charivari." A compact title encompassing a vast range of topics, cross-referencing, and an index are useful for identifying additional content relevant to your research.

Hayes, Derek. *A Historical Atlas of Canada*. Seattle: University of Washington Press, 2002.

Supported by an entertaining text, Hayes presents the history of Canada exclusively using historical maps versus "modern redrawn" versions. Every variety of map imaginable is found within this stunning work, and the reader soon feels that Canada's history is perhaps best conveyed through its geography. The atlas begins with some early depictions of the country, including misrepresentations by explorers who were yet unfamiliar with the vast land. This resource is an engaging read, for the history buff, the scholar, the general reader, and even, perhaps, the disinterested.

Taylor, Brook M. *Canadian History: A Reader's Guide*. 2 vols. Toronto: University of Toronto Press, 1994.

With individually authored essays examining various historical periods, this reference work surveys resources for Canadian historical research. Contributors highlight notable reference titles to inform each period, also identifying specialized periodicals, bibliographic studies, and general works. The application of a particular source to a given period of study is also addressed. The chapters convey the expertise of the authors within their fields, as history professors, scholars, and archivists are among the contributors. J. M. Bumsted, for example, pens the essay "British North America and Its Imperial and International Context."

## CANADIAN STUDIES

James, Patrick, and Mark Kasoff, eds. *Canadian Studies in the New Millennium*. Toronto: University of Toronto Press, 2008.

Ten individually authored chapters consider current issues in Canadian studies from an interdisciplinary perspective. Chapters include "Literary and Popular Culture," "Native Peoples," and "Trends and Prospects." Students and scholars alike will appreciate the list of Web resources and further readings offered at the conclusion of each chapter.

Wright, Donald, ed. *Canadian Studies: An Introductory Reader*. Dubuque, IA: Kendall/Hunt Publishing Company, 2004.

This title provides initial discussion and a basic understanding of Canadian history, culture, politics, literature, and sociology. Individual sections are comprised of two or more essays by notable authors, scholars, and political figures. The *Reader* considers an interesting mix of topics, exploring icons such as Laura Secord, Louis Riel, and Group of Seven artist Tom Thompson. Additional sections examining hockey and the figure of Anne of Green Gables in Canadian popular culture inspire reflection.

## CULTURE

*Anthropology Plus*. Dublin, OH: OCLC. www.oclc.org/support/documentation/firstsearch/databases.

Offered through OCLC, this title combines Harvard University's *Anthropological Literature* and the Royal Anthropological Institute's *Anthropological Index*. Indexing over six thousand sources from the late nineteenth century to present times, this is a standard database for anthropology, archaeology, and related studies. *Canadian Native Studies*, *Anthropologie et sociétés*, the *Journal of Northwest Anthropology*, and *SAIL: Studies in American Indian Literatures* are among the indexed titles.

Cooke, Nathalie, ed. *What's to Eat: Entrées in Canadian Food History*. Montreal: McGill-Queen's University Press, 2009.

A series of contributed essays illuminate the plurality of Canada's food traditions. Part 1, "Eating Canadian: What Do and Did We Eat?" is a collection of six essays, including Margery Fee's "Stories of Traditional Aboriginal Food, Territory, and Health." Other essays consider the cuisine of New France and the early history of chocolate in Canada. Part 2, "What Do Our Food Stories Tell Us about Who We Are or Were?" approaches Canadian food history through published cookbooks. Essays on global Chinese cuisine, and the phenomenon of metaphorical recipes in community cookbooks, enrich the discussion. This work is informed by contributors from a variety of disciplines, such as Andrew Smith, editor in chief of *The Oxford Encyclopedia of Food and Drink in America*, who coauthors "Talking Turkey: Thanksgiving in Canada and the United States."

Magosci, Paul Robert, ed. *Encyclopedia of Canada's Peoples*. Toronto: Multicultural History Society of Ontario, 1999. www.multiculturalcanada.ca/ecp.

Based on the print publication, the online version presents articles on Canada's ethnic groups, as well as immigrant communities and aboriginal cultures. Subheadings explore all aspects of a community's origin, history, and identity, considering, for example, "Arrival and Settlement," "Family and Kinship," as well as "Group Maintenance and Ethnic Commitment." Additional entries consider "Canadian Culture and Ethnic Diversity," "Canadian Identity," "Immigration Policy," "Resources and Research Methods," and "Themes in Immigration History." This publicly available online resource is an excellent contribution by the Multicultural History Society of Ontario toward a richer understanding of Canadian ethnicities.

## FILM AND MEDIA STUDIES

Cook, Pam, ed. *The Cinema Book*. 3rd ed. London: British Film Institute, 2009.

With coverage of national cinemas and film theory, each section is accompanied by a case study, highlighting a specific film within a national cinema, era, or genre.

Druick, Zoe, and Aspa Kotsopoulos, eds. *Programming Reality: Perspectives on English-Canadian Television*. Waterloo, Ontario: Wilfrid Laurier University Press, 2008.
A series of individually contributed essays enlighten both Canada's television past and current directions. From the history and influence of the CBC to contemporary programs such as *Canadian Idol* and *Trailer Park Boys*, this title offers a vivid immersion in Canadian programming.

*Film and Television Literature Index with Full Text*. Ipswich, MA: EBSCO. www.ebscohost.com.
Valuable as a resource for all areas of film and television scholarship, this database examines film and television theory, screenwriting, film production, preservation, cinematography, technical studies, and reviews. Full-text access to over one hundred journals and indexing for over 670 publications facilitates comparison and discovery of media-related research. An attractive feature is the full-text coverage of *Variety* movie reviews, from 1914 to present. The *Canadian Journal of Film Studies* and *Canadian Screenwriter* are among the titles indexed.

Lerner, Loren Ruth. *Canadian Film and Video: A Bibliography and Guide to the Literature*. 2 vols. Toronto: University of Toronto Press, 1997.
An essential resource for researching Canadian film, this title offers 24,800 entries from both English- and French-language sources, many of which are impressively annotated. Volume 2 facilitates discovery through author, film and video title, and subject indexes. Using the "Film and Video Title" index to search for Farley Mowat's *Never Cry Wolf*, we are directed to entries 13577–13583 for Carroll Ballard's 1983 adaptation of the novel.

Melnyk, George. *One Hundred Years of Canadian Cinema*. Toronto: University of Toronto Press, 2004.
Melnyk delivers a well-researched history of Canadian film, its relationship to the United States, and its various genres. With adequate attention given to Quebec film, aboriginal filmmakers, and the role of the National Film Board, this engaging read incorporates documentaries, feature films, and experimental works for a well-rounded discussion of Canada's national film history.

## LANGUAGE AND LINGUISTICS

Bouchard, Chantal. *Obsessed with Language: A Sociolinguistic History of Quebec*. Toronto: Guernica Editions, 2008.
Language policy and language rights are central to the history of Quebec and indeed the history of Canada. Bouchard's study considers the development of Quebec French and attitudes toward Quebecois language communities.

Fee, Margery, and Janice McAlpine. *Guide to Canadian English Usage*. Don Mills, Ontario: Oxford University Press, 1997.
Informed and supported by examples from written texts, this volume explores the intricacies and subtleties of Canadian English. Incorporated in the entries are examples of usage taken from Queen's University's *Strathy Corpus of Canadian English* (http://post.queensu.ca/~strathy/index.html), an online database of canonical, scholarly, and popular Canadian texts.

*Linguistics and Language Behaviour Abstracts* (*LLBA*). Ann Arbor, MI: ProQuest-CSA, 1973–. www.csa.com/factsheets/llba-set-c.php.
Indexes dissertations, journals, monographs, book chapters, and book reviews related to all aspects of linguistics and language sciences. Coverage includes the *Canadian Journal of Linguistics*, *Algonquian and Iroquoian Linguistics*, and *Language in Society*.

## MUSIC

Edwardson, Ryan. *Canuck Rock: A History of Canadian Popular Music*. Toronto: University of Toronto Press, 2009.
This is a carefully crafted work, extensively researched to illuminate the personalities and events that shaped contemporary Canadian music history. Edwardson explains the controversies surrounding Canadian content regulations, the influence of multinational record labels, and the impact of MuchMusic, Canada's first music video channel.

Koskoff, Ellen, ed. *The Garland Encyclopedia of World Music*. 10 vols. New York: Garland Publishing, 2001.
An impressive reference work with an international focus, this title treats Canada extensively in volume 3. First Nations music is also well covered, as are the musical traditions of the individual regions of Canada. References inform additional research, and electronic access is available through Alexander Street Press's *Music Online*.

Mersereau, Bob. *The Top 100 Canadian Albums*. Fredericton, New Brunswick: Goose Lane Productions, 2007.
Mersereau solicited input from a jury of deejays, musicians, and reviewers to develop a list which includes albums by Neil Young, The Tragically Hip, Leonard Cohen, Alanis Morissette, Bryan Adams, Blue Rodeo, Harmonium, and many others. Although francophone artists are underrepresented, this title offers a revealing view of Canadian popular music from the 1960s forward.

Morey, Carl. *Music in Canada: A Research and Information Guide*. New York: Garland Publishing, 1997.
Morey's selective guide covers general works, such as reference sources, catalogs, and bibliographies, but also engages special areas of research, such as "Native Music," "Folk and Ethnic Music," "Media," "Commerce," "Periodicals," and "Archives and Collections." This title represents an unprecedented resource for informing an in-depth study of Canadian music history and genres.

*RILM Abstracts of Music Literature*. New York: RILM, 1967–. For subscription information, see www.rilm.org.
Providing citations and abstracts for journals, conference proceedings, monographs, reference works, and book chapters, *RILM Abstracts* is a standard database for scholarly music research. Indexed journals include the *International Journal of Canadian Studies*, the *Canadian University Music Review*, and the *Canadian Journal for Traditional Music*.

Sadie, Stanley, ed. *New Grove Dictionary of Music and Musicians*. 2nd ed. 29 vols. New York: Grove, 2001. Part of *Oxford Music Online*. www.oxfordmusiconline.com.
A comprehensive resource offering over twenty-nine thousand entries of varying length on all aspects of musicology, with accompanying illustrations and bibliographies. A section on Canada appears in volume 4, offering an overview of the country's music traditions.

## PHILOSOPHY

Borchert, Donald M., ed. *Encyclopedia of Philosophy*. 2nd ed. 10 vols. Detroit: Macmillan Reference, 2006. Also available in e-book format through Thomson Gale. www.gale.com/gvrl.
Signed articles contributed by scholars explore a range of philosophical topics. This edition adds two volumes to the previous 1967 project, with 450

new entries for topics representing new developments in the field. Three bibliographic lists found in volume 10 identify an international selection of "Philosophy Dictionaries and Encyclopedias," "Philosophy Journals," and "Philosophy Bibliographies."

Bynagle, Hans E. *Philosophy: A Guide to the Reference Literature*. 3rd ed. Westport, CT: Libraries Unlimited, 2006.

Analyzing general works, research guides, indexes, bibliographies, directories, and other reference sources, Bynagle delivers a well-arranged guide to philosophical resources. Thoughtful annotations offer adequate detail for selecting the most relevant items.

Honderich, Ted. *Oxford Companion to Philosophy*. New York: Oxford University Press, 2005. Also available electronically through *Oxford Reference Online*. www.oxfordreference.com.

A handy, one-volume resource with over two thousand entries written by over three hundred authorities in the field. A succinct essay on "Canadian philosophy" highlights the origins, developments, and complexities of the discipline.

Irvine, Andrew D., and John S. Russell, eds. *In the Agora: The Public Face of Canadian Philosophy*. Toronto: University of Toronto Press, 2006.

With contributions from notable Canadian philosophers, this volume explores Canadian perspectives on national unity, 9/11, higher education, culture, the environment, and a host of other topics.

*Philosopher's Index*. Bowling Green, OH: Philosopher's Information Center, 1967–. Available online through multiple vendors. www.philinfo.org.

With international coverage of scholarly research, the *Philosopher's Index* provides access to over 680 philosophy journals. Additional content includes books, anthologies, contributed essays, and book reviews. The *Canadian Journal of Philosophy*, the *Canadian Journal of Law and Jurisprudence*, and *Symposium: Canadian Journal of Continental Philosophy* are among the indexed titles.

## POLITICS

Booker, M. Keith, ed. *Encyclopedia of Literature and Politics: Censorship, Evolution, and Writing*. 3 vols. Westport, CT: Greenwood Press, 2005.

A three-volume reference work that explores the intersections of literature and politics, with separate articles treating English and French Canadian literature. Additional essays address authors F. R. Scott, Margaret Atwood, Marshall McLuhan, and Michael Ondaatje. Entries conclude with a selected bibliography of sources for further research.

Delury, George E. *World Encyclopedia of Political Systems and Parties*. New York: Facts on File, 2006.
Organized by country, this source offers a good introduction to the political history and organization of countries around the world. A discussion of major political parties examines their organization, membership, leadership, financing, and future prospects. A selection of additional resources is found under "Further Reading."

*PAIS International*. San Diego, CA: ProQuest-CSA Social Sciences, 1972–. www.csa.com/factsheets/pais-set-c.php.
Covering publications from over 120 countries, *PAIS International* not only offers scholarly content, but also government information, "gray literature," publications of international agencies, microfiche, the Internet, research and conference reports, and more.

*Worldwide Political Science Abstracts*. San Diego, CA: ProQuest-CSA Social Sciences, 1975–. www.csa.com/factsheets/polsci-set-c.php.
Indexes literature related to political science, international relations, law, and public administration for coverage of over 1,700 titles. Canadian titles include the *Canadian Journal of Political Science*, *Canadian Public Policy*, and the *Journal of Canadian Studies*, among others.

## RELIGION

*ATLA Religion Database*. Chicago: American Theological Library Association. www.atla.com/products/catalogs/catalogs_rdb.html.
Indexing such titles as the *Canadian Journal of Orthodox Christianity*, *Ecumenism*, the *Journal of the Canadian Church Historical Society*, and the *Journal of Religion*, *ATLA Religion* is a premier database for identifying religious studies scholarship.

Choquette, Robert. *Canada's Religions: A Historical Introduction*. Ottawa: University of Ottawa Press, 2004.

Choquette authors a thoughtful study of the history and diversity of Canada's religious groups, from the sixteenth century forward. Although much of the work focuses on Catholicism and Protestantism, other significant religions are revealed throughout. Essentially an overview of Canada's religious history, further research is informed by a list of suggested readings at the conclusion of each chapter.

Jones, Lindsay, ed. *Encyclopedia of Religion*. 2nd ed. 15 vols. Detroit: Macmillan, 2005. Also sold through Gale in e-book format. www.gale.com/gvrl.

Revising Mircea Eliade's 1987 edition, an impressive range of entries fill fifteen volumes for a comprehensive resource serving researchers through concise discussion and helpful bibliographies.

Keller, Rosemary Skinner, and Rosemary Radford Ruether. *Encyclopedia of Women and Religion in North America*. 3 vols. Bloomington: Indiana University Press, 2006.

Approaching a range of topics and religious traditions, Canadian essays include Carolyn Sharp's "Determined Builders, Powerful Voices: Women and Catholicism in Nineteenth and Twentieth Century Quebec and Canada." Also of interest are Marilyn Fardig Whiteley's "Protestantism in British North America (Canada)," Phyllis D. Airhart's "Women in the United Church of Canada," and Lori M. Wilson's "Turning off the Taps: Public Policy in Canada."

## SCIENCES

Bynum, W. F., and Roy Porter. *Companion Encyclopedia of the History of Medicine*. New York: Routledge, 1993.

The editors identify seventy-two topics related to the history of medicine, with attention also given to non-Western interpretations of the field. Complemented by extensive lists of further reading, essays are accessible to the uninitiated.

Heilbron, J. L., ed. *The Oxford Companion to the History of Modern Science*. New York: Oxford University Press, 2003. Also available through Oxford Reference Online. www.oxfordreference.com.

Concise entries contributed by an international roster of over two hundred authorities explore the history of science and the lives of noteworthy scientific figures. Covering the period from 1550 forward, topics are discussed in an engaging manner, while bibliographies provide additional reading.

Krige, John, and Dominique Pestre, eds. *Companion to Science in the Twentieth Century*. New York: Routledge, 2003.
Through over forty essays, the *Companion* offers an introduction to both general and specialized topics in the field of science. Relationships between scientific disciplines and society, politics, the academy, and individual countries are explored, as are the research methods, achievements, and controversies of specific areas, such as computer science and immunology. A rare read to engage both the amateur and scientific scholar, contributors ensure that the essays are informative and palatable.

*Web of Science*. New York: Thompson Reuters. http://thompsonreuters.com/products_services/scientific/Web_of_Science.
The *Web of Science* encompasses the *Arts and Humanities Citation Index*, *Social Science Citation Index*, and the *Science Citation Index Expanded*. Searches may be limited to one of these indexes, or performed using all three services. Scientific Web research is facilitated through the Scientific Web Plus search engine, accessible via the *Web of Science* interface.

## SOCIAL SCIENCES

Cormier, Jeffrey. *The Canadianization Movement: Emergence, Survival, and Success*. Toronto: University of Toronto Press, 2004.
Cormier writes an interesting history of the efforts to reinforce Canadian identity amidst American and British influences.

*PsycINFO*. Washington, DC: American Psychological Association, 1806–. Available through several vendors. www.apa.org/pubs/databases/psycinfo.
A department of the American Psychological Association, *PsycINFO* affords access to over 1,800 sources, including journals, books, book chapters, theses, and reports published in the field of psychology. International coverage of topics such as educational psychology, communication studies, and treatment and prevention guarantees the addition of over sixty thousand new records each year.

Ritzer, George, ed. *The Blackwell Encyclopedia of Sociology*. 11 vols. Malden, MA: Blackwell Publishing, 2007.
A standard reference work for the field, this extensive encyclopedia offers over 1,700 entries on important figures, concepts, and developments.

*Sociological Abstracts*. San Diego, CA: ProQuest-CSA Social Sciences, 1952–. www.csa.com/factsheets/socioabs-set-c.php.

This title indexes journals, books, book chapters, reviews, dissertations, and conference papers for the field of sociology and related disciplines. Abstracts offer convenient clarification on the relevance of a given source to your present inquiry.

## THEATER

*International Bibliography of Theatre and Dance with Full Text.* Ipswich, MA: EBSCO. www.ebscohost.com.

With full-text access to over 170 journals and 330 monographs, this online database supports convenient searching of articles, books, book chapters, and dissertation abstracts. *Canadian Theatre Review*, *Jeu: Cahiers de théâtre*, and *Modern International Drama* are among the indexed titles.

*International Index to Performing Arts* (*IIPA*). Ann Arbor, MI: ProQuest, 1864–. iipa.chadwyck.com.

Examining all aspects of the performing arts, this database provides citations to more than 240 journal titles published worldwide. It is also available as *IIPA Full Text.*

Kennedy, Dennis, ed. *Oxford Encyclopedia of Theatre and Performance.* Oxford University Press, 2003. Available online through *Oxford Digital Reference.* www.oxfordreference.com.

Covering all time periods, this resource offers over 4,300 entries written by more than three hundred contributors. Several entries, such as "Manitoba Theatre Centre," "Len Cariou," and "John Hirsch," address Canadian topics.

# Bibliography

Bell, Suzanne S. *Librarian's Guide to Online Searching*. Westport, CT: Libraries Unlimited, 2006.

Bissell, Claude T. "Literary Taste in Central Canada during the Late Nineteenth Century." *Canadian Historical Review* 31, no. 3 (September 1950): 242.

Caldwell, Rebecca. "Brick Celebrates 25th in Its Eclectic Tradition: First and Foremost a Literary Journal, the Magazine Never Had Designs on Becoming a Scholarly Publication." *Globe and Mail*, 31 May 2003, R13.

Chamberlain, John Edgar. "The Listener." *Boston Evening Transcript*, 12 August 1891.

Davey, Frank, ed. *Tish: 1–19*. Vancouver, British Columbia: Talonbooks, 1975.

Distad, Merrill. "Newspapers, Magazines, and Commercial Journals." In *Encyclopedia of Literature in Canada*, ed. William H. New, 807–813. Toronto: University of Toronto Press, 2002.

Fetherling, Doug. Review of *Canadian Literary Landmarks*, by John Robert Colombo. *Quill and Quire* 51 (January 1985): 22.

Fraser, D. M. "Margaret Atwood's *Surfacing*." *3 Cent Pulp* 2, no.1 (May 1, 1974): 1–4.

Fraser, John. "Big Ideas, Slick Packages: It's the . . . Academag? Scholazine?" *Globe and Mail*, 4 December 2004, F9.

Humber, William, and John St. James, eds. *All I Thought about Was Baseball: Writings on a Canadian Pastime*. Toronto: University of Toronto Press, 1996.

Kennedy, Leo. "Canadian Writers of the Past: Archibald Lampman." *Canadian Forum* 14 (May 1933): 301–303.

Leacock, Stephen. "A Children's Corner." *The University Magazine* 1, no. 1 (December 1901): 81.

McBride, Jason. "The Plight of Small Magazines." *Quill and Quire*, September 2009, 18.

Metcalf, John. "Winner Take All." *Essays on Canadian Writing* 51/52 (Winter 1993/Spring 1994): 113–145.

New, William H. *Malcolm Lowry: A Reference Guide*. Boston: G. K. Hall, 1978.

Robertson, Anthony. Review of *Malcolm Lowry*, by William H. New. *West Coast Review* 7, no. 1 (June 1972): 57.

Smith, Stephen. “Purloined Letters.” *Toronto Life* 30, no. 18 (December 1996): 61–62, 64.

Southron, J. S. “Canadian Generation.” Review of *Trente Arpents*, by Ringuet. *New York Times*, 13 October 1940, 90.

Staines, David. “Morley Callaghan: 1903–1990.” *Quill and Quire*, October 1990, 8.

Van Herk, Aritha. “Boxing the Critics: Sucker Punches, Shooting Niagara and Other Boys’ Games of Criticism.” *Canadian Forum* 9 (December 1994): 32–35.

Villani, Sergio. “Fin d’une revue littéraire.” *LittéRéalité* 20, no. 2 (Winter 2008): 5.

Wilson, Edmund. “Morley Callaghan of Toronto.” *New Yorker*, 26 November 1960, 224.

# Index

# About the Author

**Gabriella Reznowski** is the librarian for languages and cultures at Washington State University Libraries. She earned a B.A. in English from the University of Manitoba and an M.L.I.S. from the University of Alberta. As a daughter of the prairies, she grew up in the multicultural milieu of Winnipeg where she was exposed to Ukrainian classes on Saturdays, Flamenco lessons on Wednesdays, and the Interlake Riviera all summer long.

www.ingramcontent.com/pod-product-compliance
Lightning Source LLC
Chambersburg PA
CBHW071359100726
47908CB00004B/1039
* 9 7 8 0 8 1 0 8 7 7 6 8 9 *